The New Early Years Professional

The New Early Years Professional

Dilemmas and Debates

Edited by Angela D. Nurse

Routledge
Taylor & Francis Group

LONDON AND NEW YORK

First published by Routledge
2 Park Square, Milton Park, Abingdon, Oxon OX14 4RN

Simultaneously published in the USA and Canada
by Routledge
270 Madison Ave, New York, NY 10016

Routledge is an imprint of the Taylor & Francis Group, an informa business

British Library Cataloguing in Publication Data
A catalogue record for this book is available from the British Library

Library of Congress Cataloging in Publication Data
A catalog record has been requested

ISBN-10: 1 84312 423 8

ISBN-13: 9781843124238

Typeset by RefineCatch Limited, Bungay, Suffolk
Printed and bound in Great Britain

Contents

Preface

I would like to thank all of the contributors to this book and to acknowledge their support in working with me to produce it. Essentially, it is the work of a number of people from a variety of professional backgrounds who have striven together to develop programmes at Canterbury Christ Church University, which we hope are interdisciplinary in nature and value the child in his or her social context. We have welcomed into our writing team Dr John Powell from Manchester Metropolitan University, who has also, with his institution, been at the forefront of developing early childhood studies programmes since the early 1990s. Dr Gill Bottle worked with us at Canterbury for a long period and I am delighted that she has found the time to write with us while she settles into her new university and home.

The broad brief the team was given was to reflect upon their experiences as children; members and creators of families; practitioners; and now lecturers in higher education, and to identify the major dilemmas and debates in the field. These are both personal and also in the minds of the students with whom they have worked. It is not a 'what' and 'how to' book, of which there are many excellent publications now in this field; rather, we hope it is one which asks 'Why?' and 'What for?' I estimate that there are more than one hundred years of professional experience within the team. This embraces backgrounds in health, teaching, psychology, social work and research, but added to this is our wealth of experience in dealing with children and families, our own or other people's. The team also brings another dimension to the book; all the writers are passionate about their work and reflect deeply upon it. They recognise that the lives of children are complex, just as are the situations in which they live. In a world of fast communications it is easy to minimise differences when we should be alert to the richness and variety of human experiences, especially as children. The authors revel in this richness and strive to instil their passion into those they work with, whether students at all levels, or practitioners and colleagues, locally, nationally and globally. I hope that this book demonstrates this passion and communicates it to all who read it.

As well as acknowledging my gratitude to Tracey Alcock of David Fulton Publishers, and my colleagues, I would also like to thank all those who have supported me throughout my career in the Early Years field. They are many, but I would like to single out a few who have been especially encouraging: Audrey Curtis, who was my MA tutor at the beginning of all this; Tricia David, who entrusted me with our Early Childhood Studies degree; and Pam Calder, whose enthusiasm, passion and energy as Chair of the Early Childhood Studies Degrees Network has encouraged us all when the pace of change has seemed overwhelming.

Finally, this book is also a tribute to my family, without whom it would never have come to fruition. Rebecca and Eleanor initiated my interest in young people and Callum has continued it. Some of their stories appear in the book. They have all confronted my book-learnt theories and made me think.

Thanks go also to my husband, Phil, who is often my researcher and critical friend and who has suffered alongside me.

Angela D. Nurse
June 2006

About the contributors

Jane Arnott is a senior lecturer in Community Nursing at Canterbury Christ Church University and the Continuing Professional Development Lead for Primary Care. She has a background in health visiting and workforce development. She teaches a range of topics across the pre- and post-registration Interprofessional Programmes which include public health, person-centred care and community specialist practice.

Alan Bainbridge is a senior Lecturer in the Department of Childhood Studies at Canterbury Christ Church University. Before this he taught for 18 years, both in this country and abroad, and has a general interest in the psychological basis of teaching and learning. He places particular significance on using psychodynamic principles in research and is presently working on the motivational experiences of adult learners and how new professionals develop their workplace identity. He is a principal A-level examiner for Psychology and Education and is a school improvement consultant.

Gill Bottle is a senior lecturer in the Department of Education at the University of Gloucester. She teaches on a range of QTS courses and is responsible for those courses based on the Foundation Stage. She has worked in primary education for over twenty years. She is particularly interested in Early Years, and her doctoral studies interrogated the links between early mathematical experiences in the home and those at school. She has written about early mathematics for several academic and practitioner journals and is the author of *Teaching Mathematics in the Primary School* (2005, Continuum). She is co-editor of *Sound Beginnings: Learning and Development in the Early Years* (2006, David Fulton Publishers).

Jane Greaves is Senior Lecturer in Community Nursing and the Programme Director for the Community Specialist Programme, leading the Health Visiting pathway at Canterbury Christ Church University. She has practised as a health visitor in Kent for many years and as an educator in a variety of organisations.

Pamela May is a senior lecturer in Early Years at Canterbury Christ Church University. She teaches on foundation degrees and Early Childhood Studies programmes. She has been a nursery teacher, head teacher and co-ordinator of a specialist early years PGCE. She is co-editor of *Sound Beginnings: Learning & Development in the Early Years* (2006, David Fulton Publishers).

Angela D. Nurse is Principal Lecturer in Early Years at Canterbury Christ Church University. Formerly she was head of the Department of Childhood Studies and during her long career at the University has been responsible for the Early Childhood Studies degrees, the Foundation Degree in Early Years and number of other programmes grounded in a multi-disciplinary approach to working with very young children and their families. She is also Deputy Chair of the Early Childhood Studies Degrees Network. Much of her teaching career has been with very young children with a variety of special needs, mainly in inner London and in Kent. As well as running a specialised nursery for children with speech and language difficulties, she has worked in an advisory capacity with teachers and colleagues in the other statutory services and within the private and voluntary sectors. She has worked extensively with parents, often in their own homes. She has been a registered nursery inspector and chair of the governing body of her local school, which includes children with physical impairments. She has contributed to a number of publications, both in the UK and in France, including *Teaching Young Children* (1999, Paul Chapman Publishing), *Young Children Learning* (1999, Paul Chapman Publishing) and *Experiencing Reggio Emilia* (2001, Open University Press).

John Powell is a senior lecturer in the Institute of Education at Manchester Metropolitan University with particular interests in early childhood studies, equal opportunities, children's rights, multi-professional issues, and professional development and research. He has been engaged in several areas of research including the evaluation of Early Years Excellence Centres (1999–2002), projects concerning teenage parents and education (2001–4), children's centres and service provision evaluation (2004–5), and the problematics of touch in Early Years and with children with complex disabilities (2004–5). He is currently involved in researching the issues relating to the Five Outcomes in fostering as a set of practices and experiences for parents/carers and practitioners. His doctoral thesis (completed July 2002), entitled 'Teaching across the social divisions', explored the construction of identities in a range of educational contexts. His previous research includes developing the Shankill Project in Belfast (1996) and managing the Kirklees Early Childhood Project (1997–2000).

Sally Robinson is Principal Lecturer and Professional Lead for Health Studies at Canterbury Christ Church University. She has a background in nutrition and nursing, and teaches health education, health promotion and public health to a wide range of undergraduate and postgraduate students.

Sue Soan is a senior lecturer for the Centre for Enabling Learning at Canterbury Christ Church University. Prior to this she worked in a variety of educational settings, first as a classroom teacher, then as a subject co-ordinator and, for over a decade, as a SENCo. She has worked with young people throughout the key stages, including in a number of Early Years environments. She is particularly interested in the areas of motor control development; speech, language and communication needs; Early Years; and social, emotional and behavioural needs. She is also the Lead Academic at Canterbury Christ Church University for Gifted and Talented programmes, working closely with the National Academy for Gifted and Talented Youth (NAGTY). She is the author of several books on special educational needs and inclusion and is the editor of a primary special needs co-ordinator's file.

Introduction: dilemmas and debates

THIS BOOK EXPLORES the dilemmas and debates that are, or should be, present for everyone who studies childhood in depth. Its intention is not to tell practitioners *how* to execute their professional roles, rather to raise questions about the nature of what we are doing and why. It is structured in such a way that general changes in the nature of our society are explored at the beginning to set the whole publication in context. Following that, specific aspects will be highlighted and explored in individual chapters. Each of the chapters is written by someone who is not only a practitioner and a teacher in a university, but who is also passionate about the lives of children and their families. We hope that the issues raised, which form the background to a study of early childhood, can be used as starting points for a deeper exploration of the aspects and issues, and others which interest or perturb readers.

At the end of each contribution there will be a number of questions for reflection, which each author considers to be crucial to the aspect he or she is exploring. Additionally, each chapter will include a relevant bibliography. Hopefully this will ensure that the seminal texts that Early Years practitioners and students, at a variety of points in their careers and studies, should be familiar with are all included. We add the proviso that the number of relevant texts, in both traditional written and electronic forms, increases substantially year by year. At the end of this introduction is a section that considers the use of different sources of information, with some advice about their use.

The DfES (2002a:25) has estimated that in recent years, the 'childcare and related occupations group is the second fastest growing sector of the UK labour market', next to telecommunications. This has been echoed in more recent publications such as the Cumbrian paper *News & Star* (31 January 2006). Unlike many of our European neighbours, however, the UK has never developed a co-ordinated approach to childcare and preschool experience, although there have been moves in the past decade to attempt to do so. Responsibility has been split between the statutory agencies (health, social services and education) and shared with the private (for profit) and voluntary (non-profit) sectors. Consequently, the education and training of those working with very young children have varied according to the origins of the service in which they are employed. This has ranged from virtually none, to postgraduate level.

Statutory school age begins the term after a child has his or her fifth birthday, a fact often overlooked due to children being admitted into school, and often to a formal curriculum, much earlier than this. This also contrasts with the age children in other societies start formal schooling. In other European societies school starts at age 6 or even 7. Although the case for education or, I would suggest, 'schooling', seems fairly well established, the nature of the curriculum and its form are not yet agreed, particularly for very young children. As we write this, the government has published *Early Years Foundation Stage: Direction of Travel* (DfES 2005), setting out its intention to merge '*Birth to Three Matters*' (DfES 2002b) with the *Curriculum Guidance for the Foundation Stage* (DfEE 2000) to produce a new phase in the English education system. *Every Child Matters* (DfES 2003) will form an important basis for this, and also included will be elements of the National Standards for under-eights daycare and childminding. It also, however, refers to Jim Rose's *Review of Reading* (2005) with its emphasis on 'good teaching' and synthetic phonics. This has caused great anxieties among those whose professional philosophy is far more child-centred and based on the value of child-initiated activities supported by adults as the way of ensuring the child comes to love learning and understand the world. We wait to see how this affects practice and whether there are radical changes in the way training and preparation for practice are developed in the future.

The key to improving practice and the quality of what we can offer to young children (both 'high on the government's agenda', to utilise current phraseology) is to understand the issues. As practitioners, as well as authors, we became aware early on in our careers that there are no easy or 'correct' answers, or any answers at all, to the major questions about childhood. The questions and responses also alter over time as we gain more personal and professional experience and as the expectations of our society and cultures are revised. If we are currently practitioners, we add the dimension of professional role and practice. If we are aiming to work with young children, we may have already selected our pathway into the profession we have chosen, perhaps based on knowledge gained from those who are already part of that particular group. We may have decided to learn more about children and families before finally making our choice, perhaps studying psychology, social science or childhood as discrete disciplines.

The nature of professionalism

This leads to a debate on the significance of the word 'professional', included in the title. Defining the word 'profession', and how it applies to the array of people who work with young children and their families, is a complex task. 'Profession' in our society has been associated with a group of people who work in a defined way for an explicit purpose. People who belong to traditional professions, like law or medicine, are usually highly educated in a specific way. They are admitted to the profession, accept its philosophies and boundaries and abide by its guidelines and strictures. They learn their professional knowledge before they practise, or at least alongside practising, rather than building their professional knowledge (i.e. theory) after substantial experience, as happens with many who work with young children. The use of a distinctive language, 'jargon', ensures that those who have not been admitted to the profession, or the public its members deal with, are disadvantaged, made powerless and excluded from understanding fully how the system works (and how to work it for themselves). This safeguards particular professions, ensuring that the power, status and rewards remain with those lucky enough to be admitted to the select group. For a long time the term 'profession' was reserved for traditional enclaves – medicine, law, the Church, to name a few – but in the second half of the twentieth century, as some of the old class structures and power bases started to break down, the meaning of the term 'professional' started to be questioned. These questions arose early on, for example, with regard to teachers, because they came from a much wider educational and social background than did most members of the 'professions' earlier in the last century. Some teachers had received very little training, or no training at all, and had learnt 'on the job'. There was a debate some thirty years ago as to whether secondary school teachers could be deemed 'professional', while primary school teachers were certainly not. The widening of access, first to secondary education then to higher education, allowed children from state schools and poorer families to enter universities and polytechnics in greater numbers than ever before. These graduates confronted the old professions and eventually many were allowed entry, though this is not to say that there are not still issues to do with social class, gender and ethnic background. It is interesting to note that many graduates, often women, who were the first in their families to enter university in the 1960s or early 1970s, still feel marginalised within their professions, awaiting the 'tap on the shoulder' and an indication that they should not be there, even when they are respected and hold important senior positions within their organisations. The term 'glass ceiling' has also been coined, meaning that people who are not traditionally awarded the top posts can theoretically get them but that there is still a barrier in place. This feeling is echoed by groups of mature students, given opportunities to return to degree-level study via foundation degrees, for example, who lack confidence and are nervous not only about their academic ability but also about their right to a place at university. These feelings of alienation can, however, be turned to good use as a starting point in working with people who do not feel naturally at ease within an educational setting.

This context, then, allows us to begin to explore the meaning of the term 'professional' in our title. Here it takes on the meaning of all those who work with young children and their families, who have some training and expertise, but with differing qualifications and experience. This is an 'inclusive' model of a 'profession', rather than the 'exclusive' view held traditionally. Whereas traditional professionals work within a very hierarchical structure to a set of agreed aims, so far there have been few specific guidelines or priorities applied to all those who work in this field. Some practitioners may come from other professional backgrounds where, although we all work with the same groups of children (often concurrently), there are different expectations and guidelines. For example, one family could use a number of different forms of childcare during the week, have a child attending school and a child with additional needs, involving a variety of medical personnel and sometimes social services. Many of the practitioners these parents meet would regard themselves as members of their own professional group, but they are also Early Years practitioners – an Early Years teacher, for example.

Issues in training

This raises questions about initial education and training for those who work in the field, where issues to do with level, content and outcomes are fiercely debated. Currently, early years practitioners follow a number of pathways into work. It is possible to start to work with young children with no qualifications at all, other than a liking for children or experience as a parent. From here it is possible to ascend the 'climbing frame' (an idea suggested by Tricia David, adopted by the Qualifications and Curriculum Authority (QCA) and developed by Lesley Abbott and Gillian Pugh (1998)) to first-degree level and beyond, via the NVQ system, as well as other more college-based programmes. Others may enter at different levels with a variety of pre-existing qualifications. Well over a decade ago, Early Childhood Studies degrees were created to provide not only a progression route for those who wanted to find out more (and had attained the entry qualifications to do so), but also to improve the quality of what we offered very young children in the UK. These programmes are intended to be multi-disciplinary, not necessarily as a prerequisite for entry into specific careers. Those of us who initiated and led such programmes understood the complexities of working with young children and their families and had a vision of a new kind of graduate Early Years practitioner, who, even if joining one of the existing traditional professions, understood and was prepared to share his or her knowledge of young children. These programmes are sited in different university faculties and schools and can lead to a variety of career pathways in educational administration, social work, work with charities and paramedical posts (speech and language therapy, for example), as well as to work in early years provision. Some do lead into postgraduate teaching programmes, but not all.

The nature of future practitioners in the field is currently being debated as more and more of the responsibility for the care and education of very young children moves to the education service. Do we wish all to become 'teachers' or should we create a new professional title, such as the suggested 'pedagogue', following the example of our European neighbours; such as Sweden, where half the staff in each childcare centre is university-trained? As this book nears completion, draft standards for the Early Years Professional Status (EYPS) are being compiled. Interested parties were invited to take part in a consultation in early summer 2006. This was supported by four national conferences. The consultation report was published in August (CWDC 2006a), highlighting the significant points raised by the respondents. This was followed quickly by a revised, but still 'draft', set of standards (CWDC 2006b). Before this, however, a number of universities and other training bodies had been selected to provide 'Phase 1' of the EYPS training, based on the first set of draft standards, so that the first group of graduates with EYPS status would appear at the end of 2006. Feedback from this programme would be incorporated, along with responses from the consultation, into the final set of standards. The government wishes to have EYPs in all children's centres by 2010 and in all full daycare settings by 2015 (CWDCb: 4). EYPs are seen as 'agents of change dedicated to improving practice in the early years sector' (CDWC 2006a: 2). This is an enormous undertaking, considering the point from which we are starting and has been put in place hastily. There are a number of questions that this immediately raises, not least the relationship between EYPS and Qualified Teacher Status (QTS), as well as for other professions. This is a serious debate, not only because it cuts across many current employees' allegiances to particular professions, but also because it affects the lives of children and families as well as of those who will work in the field in the future. When the ECS degree programmes commenced, we wanted our graduates to be passionate and reflective practitioners, who were advocates for young children. This is still our aim.

The issues raised above have implications for managing and developing provision and defining the role of the 'new early years professional'. Most of us working in the field are finding it increasingly difficult to keep track of alterations in policy, new initiatives and changes in roles and responsibilities relevant to our work. This is the case whether we work for the government, in nationally provided services, in local provision, private or voluntary, or in places, like universities, where we try to understand and interpret government policy and explain it to others. Those of us who have worked passionately over many years with and for young children, frequently find the current situation confusing and contradictory, although we welcome open-heartedly the government's current focus. The impetus for mothers to return to work within the government's ten-year strategy seems to contradict support for parents' childrearing roles found in other documents such as the *Curriculum Guidance for the Foundation Stage*. Other contradictions arise because very few seem to hold a complete picture of what is happening in all corners of the field, with a consequence that work is duplicated or potential resources are ignored. This impacts particularly on training. In 2001/2, as the foundation degree framework was developed, the DfEE proposed a foundation degree in early years to raise the level of qualification in the sector, introducing the Senior Practitioner status, and thus aimed to improve the quality of practice in early years provision. What this actually meant in reality was never defined, and now the EYPS has superseded this, applying to full graduates (level 6) rather than foundation degree graduates (level 5). The DfEE also seemed unaware that Early Childhood Studies degrees had been developed over the preceding decade, aimed precisely at increasing knowledge and understanding and improving practice. More recently, the Higher Level Teaching Assistant (HLTA) status has been introduced which, although not a qualification, has cut across the progress universities have been making in establishing these foundation degrees. We wait to see how the EYPS is implemented.

Conclusion

As we move into reading the following contributions and contemplate how we learn about 'childhood', we need to consider where our knowledge comes from and how it relates to and shapes our view of ourselves as 'professionals'. Our study of what is deemed 'essential knowledge' has, in the past, depended not only on experience and practice but also on our close familiarity with what has been written down in an academically acceptable way. This is what has been given 'status' in any academic study of a specific area. Understanding what we are reading, and being tested on it, learning the language of profession-specific seminal texts, has given us entry through a gateway jealously guarded by those who are already members of that professional community. We are not now asked to read great works in Latin or Greek, but some of the authors' work we are expected to read at degree level certainly seems, at first glance, as difficult as that! Examples here include Piaget's work, even in translation, or research reports that contain a good deal of statistical evidence.

The ways in which we now gather information, building into a comprehensive picture of early childhood, are varied. In the last few decades we have been able to access knowledge from increasingly rich sources. The internet has opened the door to so much, not only directly, like photos and film, but also in seeking out further resources. Ancient documents, policy documents, acts of parliament, legislation from other countries and books that have long been out of print are now readily available to us. There are translation devices that ensure that we have access to materials produced in different languages. Authors and producers can often be contacted directly. Autobiographical accounts offer interesting starting points, along with newspaper and magazine articles, radio programmes, documentaries and films. A number of these have been quoted throughout the book as *indications* of starting points, as these can capture our interest and raise our awareness of significant issues. Then more traditional sources of academic and professional knowledge can be investigated to ensure that we have analysed the issue thoroughly and understand its relevance to a wider context. Seeing *Angela's Ashes*, for example, may lead to reading Frank McCourt's book, then to Malachy's (1998) (his brother) autobiography, before investigating the social, cultural and historical context of the Republic of Ireland and the cause of the troubles with the UK. In a wider context, it raises the issue of children growing up in severe poverty. With this wealth of information, we need, however, to be critical in recognising where the material we are using originated, checking its content and understanding the reasons for publication. Professionally, we have to be sure that we are basing our judgements and decisions on a sound foundation.

In raising contentious issues, we should not ignore them, even if the complexities of the questions sometimes seem overwhelming. By avoiding them and failing to work towards a conclusion, or at least partial consensus, we are often not working in the interests of the children. Where there are dichotomies between parents' and children's needs, we should remember, in the words of the Children Act 1989, that 'the child's welfare is paramount'. This has become my mantra. Sometimes this will require an adult to take responsibility, seemingly in contrast to the child's wishes, but not always. If we asked the children, they could often provide us with a very clear solution, as long as we listen to what they are saying. Changes in our lives mean that we cannot foretell what our children will face in 20, 30, 40 or 100 years' time, just as our parents did not know what would confront us. The speed of these changes, however, has increased. Therefore we are even less able to predict how people will lead their lives and what they will need to know and be able to do by the end of the twenty-first century. As new early years professionals, that is our challenge.

Questions for reflection

1. What is the nature of 'professionalism' in the early years?
2. What level of qualification is necessary to work with young children and their families?
3. Should we create a new 'profession' for early years practitioners or do existing professions provide a sufficient depth of understanding and expertise?
4. What is 'quality' in early childhood education and care?

References

Abbott, L. and Pugh, G. (1998) *Training to Work in the Early Years: Developing the Climbing Frame.* Buckingham: Open University Press.

Children Act 1989. London: The Stationery Office.

Children's Workforce Development Council (CWDC) (2006a) *Early Years Report* (based on the consultation on the responses to the draft standards on the Early Years Professional Status). Leeds: CWDC. (http://www.cwdcouncil.org.uk/projects/eypsconsultation.htm)

Children's Workforce Development Council (CWDC) (2006b) *Early Years Professional National Standards*. Leeds: CWDC. (http://www.cwdcouncil.org.uk/projects/eypsconsultation.htm)

DfEE (2000) *Curriculum Guidance for the Foundation Stage* (0500/QCA/00/587). London: Department for Education and Employment.

DfES (2002a) *Guidance: Care Standards Act 2000 – Part IV*. London: Department for Education and Skills.

DfES (2002b) *Birth to Three Matters*. London: Department for Education and Skills, Sure Start Unit.

DfES (2003) *Every Child Matters*. London: Department for Education and Skills.

DfES (2005) *Early Years Foundation Stage: Direction of Travel Paper*. London: Department for Education and Skills.

McCourt, F. (1996) *Angela's Ashes*. London: Flamingo.

McCourt, M. (1998) *A Monk Swimming: A Memoir*. London: HarperCollins.

Websites

Children's Workforce Development Council – www.cwdcouncil.org.uk/projects

News & Star (Cumbria) (31.01.2006) – www.newsandstar.co.uk

Rose Review of Reading – www.standards.dfes.gov.uk/rosereview

1

Putting the Early Years into context

Angela D. Nurse

Intro

THE WORLD OF early childhood is a complex one. This chapter attempts to raise issues that will encourage reflection and initiate debate. A number of the issues raised are not intended to be 'comfortable'. The 'squirm factor' is better faced, however, in reading a book and arguing about it with friends and colleagues than being faced, unprepared, with a similar dilemma in one's professional role.

The study of early childhood at undergraduate level and beyond is relatively new. In setting the scene, we need to recognise the speed of change both within society and also in higher education as we develop programmes that are appropriately challenging for our students. Part of the rationale for this book was to help students look at issues critically and analyse what they actually meant. Within an academic study of this field, many disciplines play a part. I was once asked to define its place in the hierarchy of university degree subjects and that was very difficult. No one discipline predominates in a study of early childhood, nor should it, or we run the risk of dividing children up into segments, claiming bits for each and ignoring the 'whole child'. At the beginning of our degree programme, the students were always asked to suggest areas of study that they were likely to meet. Psychology and sociology came high on the list, followed by politics, history, religion, law, economics and health. Towards the bottom, and with a little bit of mercilessness, we arrived at archaeology and a discussion of the aspects of childhood that this could bring to light. This chapter also intends to initiate reflection on the ways we find out about other childhoods and how we use this knowledge to build a better understanding of the place of children in our society and elsewhere.

The opening sentence to the introduction raised a debate immediately; the existence of a distinct phase of our lives that we call 'childhood' is, in itself, problematic. We see the existence of a 'childhood' through our own eyes, coloured by our own experiences and expectations as children growing towards adulthood or already grown into adults, maybe with children of our own. Our interpretation of childhood varies over time and according to place, and this interpretation depends not only on the nature of the evidence we have but also on our ability to assess it as fairly as we can. We all hold different views of the nature of childhood because of the experience of growing up in families or circumstances that can vary enormously because of the views and expectations of our parents, community and society as a whole at the time we grew up. Our philosophies are affected by this and it is sometimes very challenging to move away from the comfort of steadfast opinions when we are faced with new experiences and knowledge.

History: changes in UK society

In establishing a context for this publication, we need to consider general changes in society in the UK, touching on aspects like the Industrial Revolution and the development of the British Empire, which resulted in emigration and immigration, the results of which are still apparent today. Other events during the nineteenth and twentieth centuries, especially the impact of the two world wars, affected the lives of our families and those around us, often quite dramatically. Interest in history has exploded in recent years, though tensions exist between those who study history as an academic subject and the popularised version enjoyed through television, the internet and books. Yet according to a Department for Education and Skills survey published in 2003 and reported in the *Times Educational Supplement* (25.04.03), two-thirds of British students (66%) have ceased to study history at school by the age of 14. The popularisation of history leads us to know sometimes a great deal about specific episodes in history (Troy, the Romans, Henry VIII and his wives, and so on) but does not provide a framework against which we can set changes in society, helping us to recognise the impact of these changes and to understand how we react, at individual, family and societal levels. Much of the history studied at universities has centred on the deeds of great men, in politics, in the Church and at war. It has been harder to find out about the lives of ordinary people and families, and especially about children.

Events in our past still rebound today. Without knowledge of the background to, for instance, the struggles between the Irish and the English or the history of the slave trade, we can make judgements about populations which are based on prejudice rather than knowledge and understanding. Arnold (2000: 13) suggests that the study of history is 'about making sense of that mess, finding or creating patterns and meanings and stories from the maelstrom'. There are a number of sayings now that lead us to reflect on the meaning of history or knowing about past experience. Arnold (ibid.: 6) quotes L. P. Hartley, from *The Go-Between*: 'the past is a different country; they do things differently there'; though in many ways things are much the same, particularly in the area of feelings, and we cannot always dismiss things in the past because it is 'a foreign country'. The question has often been posed, 'How do you know where you are going if you don't know where you are coming from?'. How can we understand the forces which govern and motivate us if we do not know their origins? Soren Kierkegaard (1813–55), a Danish philosopher, postulated: 'Life can only be understood backwards; but it must be lived forwards'.

Studying history also helps us to look at 'evidence' and 'analyse' and 'criticise' fully what is presented to us. These academic skills exercise the students and practitioners we meet, as well as ourselves. There have been, however, few books published that focus purely on a study of history of children. This may be because the sources have been limited; but, as Hendrick (1997: 3–4) points out in his consideration of the neglect of children as historical subjects worthy of study:

> Children, however, lack political significance: they do not have the vote nor do they have a political movement like feminism or socialism to represent their interests. Children are usually viewed from the perspective of *becoming* (growing to adult maturity), rather than *being* (children as their own persons) . . . As children do not have overt political identities, historians tend not to be very interested in them as historical subjects, and certainly not as people in their own right.

From a sociological perspective, however, much has been written recently about the nature of childhood and the place of children within society. It is interesting to reflect on the different approaches and methodologies of the two disciplines (history and sociology) in the interpretation of childhood.

The world of early childhood is multi-faceted, subject to an ever-increasing number of pressures as scientific knowledge expands and global and national government priorities change and confront some of our most cherished philosophies. For example, those of us who have worked with young children and the people who work with them now can hold very strong beliefs about children's autonomy and the value and necessity of play. At the time of writing, however, it appears that the autonomy that practitioners have had in constructing environments and devising programmes for very young children is under threat. Issues to do with 'raising standards' have resulted in the disappearance of time for children 'to be'. With the pressure to acquire ever more complex skills at an earlier age, we risk demotivating children. My grandson, just starting key stage 2, is expected to understand things that I did not tackle until I was well into secondary school. At age 7 he was asked to rewrite *Jack and the Beanstalk* from the giant's perspective. This is quite a sophisticated task for a little boy only just comfortable with reading. The difficulties in raising expectations to this level are that many face failure and lose the motivation to try.

The UK system

The origins of the system we have in the UK are diverse. Families in the upper strata of society employed staff to help in the rearing of their children. Wet nurses were used to feed babies, and nurses and governesses cared for and educated children, at least until they went to boarding school. At the other end of the economic and social spectrum, particularly before the Industrial Revolution when work was centred on the home and community, care for the youngest child was provided by the immediate or wider family until he or she could join the family workforce. Childcare became a problem as work moved away from the home and community into factories and city centres, and children, on grounds of safety, were removed from the parents' places of employment.

Pioneers

As a reaction to this, there were a number of well-known pioneers in the nineteenth and early twentieth centuries who worked to protect and support young children and their families. These were often factory or mill owners who were philanthropic but also recognised that caring for your workforce led to increased productivity. A visit to one of the industrial sites, such as Styall in Cheshire offers an opportunity to experience the reality of some children's lives in the nineteenth century. The most renowned of this group of pioneers is probably Robert Owen, a mill owner in New Lanark in Scotland. He created a community where families were well housed in comparison with many of their contemporaries, food was provided at reasonable cost and healthcare was available. The origins of the Co-operative Movement are to be found in his New Lanark site. Additionally, care and education were provided for young children. Owen provided a school, opened in 1816, which had an enlightened curriculum including first-hand experience, music and dance as well as more traditional subjects like reading, writing and geography. Later, the McMillan sisters developed nursery education in Deptford, where the health needs of the children were central to the educational philosophy they developed and expanded in their training college. From their work comes the tradition of nursery education in the UK, one adopted by many other nations. The McMillan Legacy Group (1999: 5) in the introduction to its publication wrote:

> Margaret and Rachel McMillan swept away old ideas to create a revolution in the care, health and education of young children. Their vision and perseverance changed the way children were treated on every level, from the most practical nurture to a new educational curriculum.

The growth in the nineteenth century of philanthropic societies (charities) took away the onus from national governments to provide for the needs of their citizens. Support was centred securely with the voluntary sector until the twentieth century when national systems of support were established (health, social security, access to the legal system and so on). It was not until 1871 that primary education was available for all children, not only for the privileged, though schools had existed long before that. Many had been provided by the Church, which had a much greater impact on people's lives in earlier centuries. This split in responsibility between the state and the voluntary sector has never been fully explored and debated openly. As a nation, we have never really asked ourselves where the responsibility ultimately lies for very young children. How far can, or should, the state intervene in the private relationship between a child and its parents? What are the parents' responsibilities *vis-à-vis* the state's?

Population: concerns about the future

The focus on very young children's early development has intensified as the UK has recognised that its continuing prosperity depends upon the ability of coming generations to be well educated and creative in developing new ways of making wealth. Other countries in the world have taken over traditional industries, like engineering and textiles, and produce goods at much reduced prices. At the same time it has been recognised, especially by the states of the European Union, that there are serious declines in birth rates, and also an ageing population which will need to be cared for and pensions will have to be paid. The demographic trends in Europe are being researched by the Joint Council of Europe and the first results were published by Eurostat (2005). The report indicated that no state within the EU had a fertility rate which 'came close to the replacement level of about 2.1 children per woman'. Additional statistics give estimates of further reductions in the EU birth rate, resulting in a net loss of population by 2050 of 20 million people. This takes immigration into account. Germany, for example, where the birth rate is currently running at 1.3 children per woman (Connelly 2006), is particularly under stress, losing a third of its population per generation. This is reflected in the trends of other developed nations such as Japan. A cynic could protest that the focus on young children could be much more a result of economic factors than the result of a holistic interest in the child. Yet, despite being one of the members of the G7 group, an elite association of the world's seven richest nations, the UK continues to insist that we cannot afford to introduce universal, state-funded, early years provision which is available free or at minimal cost to all who want or need it.

Poverty

Many who read this book will have grown up and lived in an affluent society that has generally supported their basic needs well. In the UK, for example, we have had access to free healthcare and free education, with the option to choose to pay if we so wanted, and to social services and the law if our lives are in crisis. Even if the pattern of delivery is different, this provision is found across most of Europe, in Australia, New Zealand, other more affluent states across the world, and in much of north America, though there are considerable concerns in the USA about the inequalities in access to healthcare and other services for those who are poor. This is not to say that everyone in our society has been given these opportunities; the divide between the richest and poorest has increased, and the End Child Poverty Campaign reported in its newsletter (p.8), in the summer of 2002, that:

Not one child in the UK lives in poverty – 3.9 million do. The UK has the fourth largest economy in the world and yet we have one of the highest levels of child poverty of all industrialised countries. In fact we have the highest level of child poverty in the EU.

(Graeme Brown, ECP Development Director)

A central tenet of the present government's policy is to put an end to child poverty. Poverty in the UK is relative, rather than absolute. That is to say, most families have food to eat, clothing and shelter, even if this is limited in comparison with the quantity and quality of what other families have. 'Poverty' also includes 'poverty of experience' so that limited financial means prevent children from joining in with many of the activities that are deemed 'essential' for today's children, such as sports, arts, music and foreign travel. We must recognise, however, that many financially poor families lead very rich lives, often providing their children with many opportunities to discover their world and to be creative. In many places in the world children live in absolute poverty, have little shelter and security, die from hunger and suffer from illnesses for which there are no remedies and few medical staff to treat them. A visit from a group of education staff from Beijing put these issues into perspective very clearly a little while ago. I had shown them a programme which was produced by a major TV channel at the time when the government's policy on ending childhood poverty was introduced. This presented a family living in, to our eyes, dire poverty with all the consequences that went with it. Children rarely went to school, had parents who were substance abusers and routines within the home were almost non-existent. The family was marginalised by others in the community and confronted all our expectations of 'good parenting'. I had shown this earlier to European colleagues to gauge their reaction (they saw the UK as a very affluent country with few problems such as these) and had met with an expected response. To the Chinese, however, these children were living far better lives than many children in their own country. They had shelter, good clothing, food, heating and access to free healthcare and education. This illustrates clearly how different circumstances can result in different interpretations. Nevertheless, for the children in the film to be successful in our society they need the basic requirements of a healthy and happy life, which protect their futures.

The policy document *Choice for Parents: The Best Start for Children* reiterated, 'In 1999 the government set an ambitious long-term goal to halve child poverty by 2010 and eradicate it by 2020' (HM Treasury 2004, section 2.23). One of the intentions to enable the strategy to work is to encourage more mothers, particularly those who are single parents, to return to work. One of the issues that needs to be debated here is the effects on young children. Families may be cash-poor but may be very rich in other ways, and perhaps it is identifying and supporting these strengths that can lead to a more balanced society. Meeting this challenge, in whatever way, however, does not just depend on government will to provide more funding; it depends on changing the public's attitudes towards the loss of personal, life-long achievement for these children. In a more selfish vein, their loss is also ours as a society.

Childhood: rights and ethics

More is being written about children's rights and the ethical considerations we should have in working, researching and writing about children, but how we pay regard to this in our daily working lives can be suspect. At this point in any deliberations about ethics, I am minded to tell the story of a video about child development that I was involved in making some twenty years ago. This was one of a series of films made in nurseries at that time and focused on two children who were thought to have special needs as they entered nursery. The children's progress was monitored and details of this were included with the video as well. Permission was gained from the parents and other adults involved and the final version of the video was shown to them before it was published. It was well-produced and received and has been much used over the years in our child development programmes at all levels. The point is that no-one ever asked the children whether it was acceptable to them that part of their lives has been shared with hundreds of students over the years. The children will now be in their mid-twenties and may well be parents themselves. Not only do the videos exist but also written accounts of their backgrounds, which are used to inform observational work. As a mother, I know that video recordings were made by a speech therapist of my elder daughter, Rebecca, when she was 3 or 4. Her reaction now is that she would not mind them being used for training purposes, though she would like to see the recordings. She has, however, grown up knowing that her drawings, writing, photos and sayings have been constantly and openly used to illustrate my teaching, along with examples provided by her sister and her son!

To illustrate the complexities of the questions about the nature of childhood, some of which are based firmly in ethical arguments, and to explore our own values and assumptions, we can take examples from real situations where there has been considerable angst and debate. One illustration, widely reported in the media in 2000, involved conjoined twins born in the UK to deeply religious parents from Malta. The dilemma arose because without separation the twins would both die. By attempting to separate them, one was sure to die but the other was likely to survive. The ethical and religious issues in this case took many weeks to resolve and eventually the decision was taken to separate the twins against the parents' wishes. This raised an intense debate at the time and illustrated the way modern medical advances have added a further dimension to the decisions that we have to make within our society. This is because our *capability* in doing something outruns our *ability* to decide whether we should do it, or not. These ethical dilemmas can disquiet our working lives and the everyday decisions we have to make. A pertinent illustration from everyday early years practice emerged from a conference session where practitioners were discussing multicultural issues:

> A situation had arisen where a young boy, just four years old, enjoyed playing in the home corner, revisiting events at home where he had watched his mother preparing food. The family was from a religious and cultural background where gender roles were clearly separated and defined. Although the child's mother accepted her son's role-play, his father, who was considerably older than his mother, did not. On one of the infrequent occasions when he arrived to collect his son from nursery and found him playing in the home corner, he was very upset and demanded that staff prevent his son from playing there in the future.
>
> (Professor Tricia David, personal communication)

The participants in the conference debated this episode at the time and it has been considered further by generations of students and practitioners since. There has been some consensus but never an absolute answer to the difficulties this raises for those who have grown up in a different place and time. It involves us facing our own prejudices and expectations, particularly with respect to gender roles, accepting that our knowledge may be very limited (for example, was the father's response typical of *all* males in his community?), understanding the structure of the family and power relationships within and between communities, and so on. Then we need to consider the father's own response to living in a society that may be radically different from the one in which he grew up and one that he may have had little choice in adopting. These are questions which early years practitioners are required to consider whatever the professional context in which they are working. This incident occurred in a nursery class, but could easily have occurred on a children's ward or during a social worker's home visit.

The United Nations Convention on the Rights of the Child (UNCRC) laid out in 1989 a set of guiding principles for the protection and support of all the world's children. The states that signed this promised to write the principles of the Convention into their own national legislation to give it the force of law in their own countries. At the time of writing all but two (USA and Somalia) have done so. It is a debate in itself to consider the reasons why these two nations have not yet ratified it, although Somalia has been war-torn and has had no central government since 1991. Part of the difficulty in the USA has been the continuing opposition to it from more fundamentalist religious groups who fear the diminution of family authority and growth of state intervention, particularly with respect to physical punishment.

In the UK the response was the Children Act 1989 which applied to 'all services provided by the local authority', a fact that many local education authorities chose, at least at first, to ignore. It stated that 'the welfare of the child is paramount' and that parents have responsibilities as well as rights. This was in clear contrast to other legislation at the time, particularly in education, where parental and governmental 'rights' were dominant. At the time it was introduced the UNCRC was generally very well received. Historically, it was a time when many states that had been dominated by extremist governments, in eastern Europe or South Africa for instance, they had started to develop democracies and were perhaps feeling more secure in their futures. Criticisms that have arisen more recently, however, have centred on a vision of childhood that is very much anchored to the affluent 'first world', not taking into account the particular social, cultural and geographical circumstances in which children across the world find themselves. Under the UNCRC we can perceive these as detrimental to their development, which in many ways they are, but by doing so we ignore the reality of many children's lives. For example, the number of families in southern Africa affected by the HIV virus is increasing, often resulting in elderly relatives or very young children being solely responsible for the family, economically as well as emotionally. Equally, while never condoning what goes on in Romanian orphanages, we need to explore and understand more fully the factors in that society which led to the neglect of so many young children.

The UNCRC has also been criticised more recently for seeing children as vulnerable and in need of protection. Brian Corby (2006: 246) recognises that it is difficult to put all the principles of the UNCRC into practice across a world where there are extremes of poverty and wealth, as well as a range of cultures, but concludes that 'the principles espoused in the Convention do form a yardstick by which countries can measure themselves and others and be measured'. Advocates of children's rights, however, have advanced ideas that emphasise the strengths of children instead of their supposed weaknesses. In 2000 (in an interview with Will Hutton), Claire Short, then Secretary of State for International Development, caused uproar when she did not openly oppose child labour, recognising that, 'it is only a reflection of extreme poverty and if we stop it we only condemn children to worse – beggary and prostitution'. The response of many groups of street children has been to create 'families' of their own where sets of rules apply that protect and support their own members, particularly the younger ones, in reaction to suppression by adults who do not honour the children's 'rights'. Adults who have worked successfully with these groups have recognised the strengths of these relationships and worked with them, instead of imposing adult expectations. Children elsewhere have been recruited as soldiers at very young ages and been expected to carry out the same duties as adults. This is in contrast to children from much more privileged societies where we condemn a parent who leaves a child of a similar age alone at home, even for an very short period, in an environment that is altogether much safer. Even in our own society, where there are serious concerns about adults being far too protective towards children (and thus seriously hampering their ability to protect themselves), many thousands of children are responsible for adults who have needs of their own – perhaps who are dependent on drugs or who have a disability. Chapter 10 explores this more fully.

Conclusion

This chapter has attempted to raise questions about issues that do not appear in detail elsewhere in the book but which are important to our understanding of the complexities of the early childhood field and crucial to the decisions we have to make on a daily basis in our work as early years professionals. The key to success in working with children and families often lies in being honest about our own lack of knowledge, or attitudes that have never been questioned.

Questions for reflection

1. What are the aspects of early childhood circumstances and practice that concern you most, and why?

2. What do you think should be done about your concerns, and by whom?

3. What does history have to tell us about the status and conditions of children in the past? How does this knowledge help us in our daily work with children and families?

4. Outline, and then debate, your views on the rights of children and their value and status in our society.

References

Arnold, J. (2000) *History: A Very Short Introduction*. Oxford: Oxford Paperbacks.

Brown, G. (2002) 'End child poverty once and for all'. Newsletter, Summer.

Connelly, K. (2006) 'German women told: "We need more babies" '. *Daily Telegraph*, 28 January.

Corby, B. (2006) *Child Abuse: Towards a Knowledge Base* (3rd edn). Maidenhead: Open University.

Eurostat (2005) *Population in Europe 2004: First Results* (15/2005). Luxembourg: Office for Official Publications of the European Communities.

Hendrick, H. (1997) *Children, Childhood and English Society, 1880–1990*. Cambridge: Cambridge University Press.

HM Treasury (2004) *Choice for Parents: The Best Start for Children*. London: The Stationery Office.

Hutton, W. (2000) 'A third way for the Third World?'. Interview with Claire Short. *The Guardian*, 12 December.

McMillan Legacy Group (1999) *The Children Can't Wait: The McMillan Sisters and the Birth of Nursery Education*. Deptford: Deptford Forum Publishing Ltd.

Mansell, W. (2003) 'A bleak future for history'. *Times Educational Supplement*, 25 April.

Websites

Eurostat – http://epp.eurostat.cec.eu.int

Soren Kierkegaard – www.sorenkierkegaard.org

United Nations Convention on the Rights of the Child – www.ohchr.org/english/law/crc.htm

2

Multi-agency development and issues of communication

John Powell

Introduction

THIS CHAPTER EXPLORES historical, legislative, political and practice issues that have impacted upon and helped to fashion the current situation in providing a more diverse range of services and practitioners for early years children and their families. The chapter discusses professional values and their influence on children's needs and participation rights, and considers some of the challenges to effective inter-professional practices and how these may impact on children's involvement and inclusion in matters that affect them.

Setting the scene

Every Child Matters (DfES 2003) followed Lord Laming's Inquiry into the death of Victoria Climbié which dramatically raised the profile of children and their families as well as the importance of tighter inter-agency working. As Laming emphasised in his report's conclusions:

> Sadly the report is a vivid demonstration of poor practice within and between social services, the police and the health agencies. It is also a stark reminder of the consequences of ineffective and inept management.
>
> (Laming 2003:15)

In 2004 the Children Act was enacted and provided the legal basis for policy changes that emphasised the need for the development of more effective service working for children. The Act established:

- a Children's Commissioner to champion the views and interests of children and young people;

- a duty on Local Authorities to make arrangements to promote co-operation between agencies and other appropriate bodies . . . in order to improve children's well-being.

(DfES 2004c: 5)

These commitments symbolise radical changes to practitioner relationships in children's services so that they can be seen to be much more a part of a coherent strategy representing closer multi-agency work practices. Under *Every Child Matters*, working practices should be co-ordinated more frequently and coherently and communication that crosses agency boundaries should become custom and practice. In order to achieve this the policy and practice modifications promoted by *Every Child Matters* are extensive. However, the government believes that the gains of implementation of its policies will lead to a reliable national system that promotes effective and accessible communication between practitioners, children and their carers. In other words dealing effectively with the 'gross failure of the system and the widespread organisational malaise' highlighted in the Laming Report that led to the death of Victoria Climbié. (Laming 2003: 4).

Apart from the move to closer multi-professional working arrangements, *Every Child Matters* (HM Treasury 2003) and the Children Act (2004) emphasised the importance of effective communication with both children and their carers.

Every Child Matters

Every Child Matters (2003) takes the government's concerns about the shortfalls in the child protection system identified by Lord Laming and develops it in line with other issues that it had already identified concerning deprivation, and it attempts to tackle this long-term problem through a policy of inclusion. The Children Act 2004, through the new appointment of the Children's Commissioner, has prioritised the right of children to have their views represented across a wide range of situations that affect their lives. The government has also identified children's well-being as an area that practitioners should aim to improve by working together co-operatively. While the development of services outlined in *Every Child Matters* can be shown to have clear links to the Laming Report into the death of Victoria Climbié, there are also links to wider political objectives such as a commitment to eradicating poverty. *Every Child Matters* recognises that there are socio-environmental factors, such as poverty and deprivation, that can lead to many children becoming vulnerable and over which neither they nor their families have any control. As Holland points out:

It is known that living in poverty provokes stress, due to factors such as overcrowding, lack of play facilities, fewer leisure opportunities and the lack of means to purchase respite from caring responsibilities.

(Holland 2004 : 90)

The above reference serves to highlight the additional difficulties likely to be experienced by children and their families, and therefore highly likely to impact on children's well-being.

The eradication of child poverty is seen by the government as more likely to be achievable by concentrating resources in local communities through developing support for struggling families and vulnerable children. At the heart of each community *Every Child Matters* identifies an increased number of Sure Start children's centres which will 'play a key role in communities alongside schools and general practitioners as a focus for parents and children to access services' (DfES 2003 : 26). The Sure Start initiative is accompanied by other developments such as Full Service Extended Schools, which are also discussed in *Every Child Matters*:

The Government wants to integrate Education, Health and Social Care Services around the needs of children. To achieve this, we want all schools to become extended schools – acting as the hub for services for children, families and other members of the community. Extended schools offer a range of services (such as childcare, adult learning, health and community facilities) that go beyond their core educational function.

(ibid.: 29)

There is, consequently, the development of social policy that contains clear strands that relate to both protecting children from ill-treatment and preventing the development of child poverty by supporting parents into employment. These policy areas mean that Sure Start children's centres and extended schools develop wider and more complex roles than has previously been the case, and while their core provision will be childcare and educational provision, they will also offer the opportunity for a range of different professional practitioners to work together, sometimes in multi-agency teams. Schools, in particular, will, in future, no longer be the sole domain of teachers or of education but will also be home to social workers and health workers. The range of educational provision will also vary from being child-focused to providing life-long learning opportunities for carers. The intention behind this is to provide ways back into education for people, many of whom may have been receiving benefits.

The availability of a range of practitioners located either on a regular or ad hoc basis, in children's centres or extended schools meets the recommendations of the Laming Report, which are taken forward by *Every Child Matters*, to provide a coherent inter-disciplinary, multi-agency service that is able to respond quickly and effectively to the issues and concerns in the community. Prevention also takes place by identifying and supporting vulnerable families in their communities through services available in the children's centre or extended school, such as feeding groups, which aim to meet the needs of inexperienced parents and their babies or toddling children, who may be causing concern through their problematic eating habits. Children's centres and extended schools also provide a meeting-place where parents and carers can share their concerns and, where appropriate, seek advice from the multi-agency staff located there.

The services that are developing may be seen as more integrated and interrelated in the ways in which they operate in the community. However, it may be questioned whether the development of integrated service provision with a strong community presence alone will be able to achieve a greater degree of inclusiveness for children and their families, and allay their concerns, or whether communication, which is vital for the process to be effective, is likely to remain an issue. This particular aspect of working together within the context of *Every Child Matters* will be considered later in the chapter.

Partnerships with children and their carers

One particular message from the government emphasises the importance of partnerships as potentially effective ways of developing new joint working practices which, it claims, may be constructed along recognisable and clear lines that include pooling budgets, delegating responsibilities to a 'lead' organisation and integrating front-line health and social services staff into a single organisation (Hudson *et al.* 2001, cited in Glendinning *et al.* 2001). This practice is repeated across a number of key areas of provision, including childcare, through the Sure Start strategy, which is pledged to offer children's centres where they are needed most – in the most disadvantaged areas – to provide families with childcare, health and family support, and advice on employment opportunities. These children's centres will, in turn, link up with Sure Start local programmes, neighbourhood nurseries and Early Excellence Centres (Sure Start 2004).

The outcomes framework cited in *Every Child Matters – Change for Children* (DfES 2004b) provides the focus for professional concerns and a means for understanding the components that constitute well-being. Well-being is a concept that suggests a means of understanding if children and their families are in need of additional support, or not. Well-being is constructed through a framework based on five outcomes. The five outcomes aim to offer a focus that will lead to improvement in the lives of children by clarifying what constituent parts make up well-being. This approach should also incorporate the views of children, and should, according to the Children Act (2004), take account of their wishes and feelings. There is, therefore, a sense of not simply gearing up services that practitioners view as necessary for children, but also a process that takes into account children's views of the services being offered.

This approach aims to overcome stereotypical barriers that often exist between professional practitioners and members of the community by not simply making practitioners more accessible for service users but also by including children and their parents in the decision-making process.

The government has identified three distinct areas where participation should take place:

- where individual decisions are being taken about children's own lives;

- where services for, or used by, children are being developed or provided locally;

- where national policies and services are being developed or evaluated.

(DfES CYPU March 2001 : 6)

Issues regarding interprofessional professional communication with children and their carers

The discussion has so far been concerned with identifying the aims of social policy arising from the Laming Report and carried forward by *Every Child Matters* and the Children Act 2004. We will now consider some of the issues that are likely to be experienced by parents, carers and children, as well as the professional practitioners working with them. Although *Every Child Matters* places a great deal of significance on developing a common language as a means of developing relationships between parents, carers, children and practitioners, there are several hurdles that will need to be overcome, if indeed that is possible.

First, the problem of language between parents, carers and professional practitioners may centre on the way that communication takes place and who appears to initiate the exchange in terms of ideas present within the language. For example, in the case of child protection investigations, Thoburn *et al.* (1995) identified a number of issues that caused parents problems and which led to them sometimes feeling excluded. These included being uncertain about the relevance of the roles of different agencies, uncertainty about their rights and uncertainty about whether they were being listened to. It may be equally difficult for parents to listen to practitioners who appear to be accusatory or sitting in judgement on their ability to care for their children. In other words, the purpose behind the discussion can be perceived by both parents and practitioners as one that is critical and judgemental of each of them.

These issues concerning the style of engagement immediately reveal a further set of issues regarding the status of professional practitioners in relation to parents and carers and the possibility of meaningful communication developing in situations where imbalances of power are present but remain unaddressed. While the involvement of professional practitioners can appear difficult for parents, it may be even more difficult for a child to participate in a way that *Every Child Matters* would wish for, and the more practitioners who are involved the more likely it is that communication will seem unequal and weighted to represent professional perspectives. This is, of course, of pivotal concern for the development of more equal interactive relationships and fundamental to the success of *Every Child Matters*. In relation to children becoming more involved in decision-making, Alderson (2000) points out, by citing an example of children being excluded from school, that they do not have rights in English law to 'speak to the adults who exclude them, or to appeal' (p.39). However, this is an omission that was found to be disturbing to the UN Convention on the Rights of the Child. There are attempts to introduce advocates who will be able to facilitate children's involvement; the Children's Commissioner is a strong example of someone who has the responsibility to champion the views and interests of children and young people (see the Children Act 2004). In this regard, Al Ainsley-Green, the Children's Commissioner for England, has recently raised concerns about bullying, perceptions of young people in society and the importance of facilitating participation as a means of actively representing children's views in decision-making.

Communication between practitioners

The discussion now moves on to consider the difficulties experienced by practitioners in developing inter-agency communication. Failures of communication can occur partly because of a lack of a desire to let go of the specific involvement and accept the need for other professional contributions, which suggests that different practitioners will tend to have a different understanding of the nature of their involvement and the needs of parents and carers. To be able to do this effectively requires a close examination of personal practices, rituals and routines, and an acceptance of their lack of appropriateness (White and Featherstone 2005).

Morrow and Malin (2004:169) discuss the issues arising from working in partnership with parents and have noted the impact on professional roles in a variety of contexts including the staffroom:

> Within Sure Start, parents and professionals had more direct, more informal, contact with each other than previously. The extent to which this relationship had changed varied according to professionals' previous background and experience together with the demands of their current role.

This raises questions about the impact of direct and close working with children and carers, including confidentiality and the sense that with close professional contact the barriers and distance between professionals can often be reduced. There are clearly concerns surrounding those moments when practitioners make contact in the staffroom and ad hoc conversations relating to service users ensue. Can such ease of communication sacrifice the clearly defined ethical understandings of what it is acceptable to talk about, and when? However, this may result in a child being viewed by a group of practitioners, representing different disciplines and professional perspectives, as having multiple social constructions connected through combined perceptions of 'concern'. The health visitor might primarily view a child as a medical construction living within a social context, while a teacher might view the same child mainly as an educational construction operating within a different social context. It is not that either of these views is incorrect but that each will tend to perceive the child through the filter of their own professional discipline.

The hierarchies of communication and participation are emphasised with children and their carers who, despite the discourse of participatory rights, are subject to 'what is essentially an adult-driven framework' (Craig 2003: 49). The degree to which children are able, and invited, to participate in decision-making is difficult because, as James *et al.* (1998) suggest, childhood is demarcated and 'Erected by a gerontocratic hegemony and policed by discipline, the boundaries are legitimised through ideologies of care, protection and privacy' (p.38).

This argument connects to suspicions of Foucault who might describe the increasing presence of a large group of practitioners as providing a further opportunity of applying a 'disciplinary' and 'normative' gaze from the disciplines of diverse childcare institutions so that parents and children can be 'trained correctly' (Foucault 1977: 179). The practitioner's position, Foucault might have argued, is to place parents and children under a system of surveillance, examination and discipline that reinforces a code of normative values approved by the institution(s). The term 'institution' in this instance refers to contexts such as Sure Start children's centres and inclusive and extended schools. However, it is also important to consider that the practitioners who have contact with a child and her family/carers may also be deemed to be an institutional manifestation representing a normative discourse that is government-driven and therefore connected to the five outcomes (discussed earlier), which in this light may be viewed as reinforcing a set of normative perspectives leading to economic activity for parents, now and in the future. This reading interprets policies and practices driven by *Every Child Matters* as actively managing child protection and prevention systems through a system of routine surveillance, apparently concerned with responding to perceived needs of vulnerable children but which is ultimately concerned with regulating parental and carer practices.

> Disaffection and non-participation are an important concern of governments in much of the world, given more generalized worries about the behaviour of young people and the desire to promote social cohesion. There are also more specific concerns about educational achievement and its connection to the future prospects of young people and the labour force needs of the economy.
>
> (Hayden and Blaya 2005: 1)

These conditions can subsequently lead to a system that identifies those who are outside the 'norm' as 'others' and failing to reach their full potential. This may not be problematic in itself, and may mean that much needed support is made available. Conversely, however, it might also lead to a situation whereby children and their families are subjected to negative stereotyping, which would tend to undermine their part in any interactive participatory system or shared language.

A Common Assessment Framework (CAF) described in *Every Child Matters: Change for Children* (DfES 2004b) is seen as important to the integrated strategy for targeting resources to the most deprived and vulnerable families. In addition, it argues (p. 6) for the integration of services as a way of safeguarding children and supporting them in reaching their potential, through improved information, and then targeting support effectively. The CAF will be used by all practitioners for identifying concerns and developing a plan of action to meet them. There are, however, risks that as the number of practitioners involved increases, the voices and concerns of children and their carers will become less audible and certainly less visible. It is also likely that the children will be viewed by professionals as necessary and symbolic of their professional focus rather than as participating partners.

The idea of paying attention to the voice of children and their carers will be a major challenge, one that most child abuse inquiries since 1974 have identified as a key concern but which has so far been unresolved.

Stevenson (1989), in the same year as the Cleveland Inquiry, argued that there were several potential barriers to inter-agency co-operation, which included the different structures and organisational systems that practitioners came from. She added that practitioners from different professional organisations would tend to be working to different standards and have different historical backgrounds and cultures that informed their practice. Training, she pointed out, had been conducted in unitary agency contexts that tended to reinforce individual agency's values and belief systems, while, conversely, she believed inter-agency training should allow for a cross-fertilisation of agency constructs. These were points that were similarly made by Laming in 2003. Reder *et al.* (1999: 65) argue that:

> inter-professional communications are embedded within multiple relationship contexts and that during every professional interchange personal, professional, institutional and inter-agency factors colour how the messages are relayed and received.

The attempt to show that inter-professional communication is likely to operate with ease between practitioners can be shown to be unconvincing when considered in more detail. What at first appears as rather uncomplicated, at a closer examination reveals a sense of complexity. The factors that determine that interdisciplinary inter-action is anything but straightforward focus on individual agency identity and the way that this connects to practitioners' understanding of their professional identity and what makes them different from professionals from other disciplines. This is not solely due to the way that professionals are educated and trained, as identified by Stevenson and Laming (see above), but more to the ways that professional work and identities are characterised and constructed, and how individuals perceive themselves in their professional roles.

An example of the difficulties that may be experienced is seen in a recent piece of research that examined the integration of Connexions staff into the life of a school. A number of issues were identified by the research. Primarily, staff in partner agencies were confused about the variety of different roles played by Connexions Personal Advisers (PAs) and unclear about PAs' legitimate roles, responsibilities and authority. There was lack of clarity resulting in a continuing suspicion that Connexions had not brought the radical changes some had hoped it would. However, PAs found some providers difficult to work with because of conflicting priorities and working practices. Despite some progress, there was little systematic or effective information sharing. This was most likely to occur within multi-disciplinary teams working from the same base. Failure to share information sometimes resulted in an incomplete assessment of needs and inappropriate patterns of support (Coles *et al.* 2004).

This suggests several difficulties likely to be experienced by many multi-disciplinary teams and includes the following areas that need to be clarified and monitored:

- confusion about the legitimate role;
- lack of clarity about responsibilities and authority;
- disappointment that change was not fulfilling;
- conflicting priorities and working practices; and
- little systematic or effective sharing.

Legitimacy arises not only from the ways that organisational structures may define it, but also from inter-professional compatibility and the belief that different professionals actually will contribute to the work. This means that for services to be able to develop effectively in inter-professional teams there should be opportunities for 'its practitioners to use interpersonal skills. Payne (1995) describes these interpersonal skills as "enabling, negotiating, mobilising, resources, networking and advocacy" ' (in Skerrett 2000:66).

Skerrett points out that, in the case of social work, one of the central professional paradigms in individual work with service users is concerned with casework, where the concern is to refine the central focus and actively seek contact from other practitioners who are also involved in responding to the same service user's needs. However, social workers have begun to resemble care managers, which means that 'the role is that of an outsider, a broker, who links those with needs to those who have resources to meet them' (Skerrett 2000:68).

Skerrett makes the point that social agencies – and she particularly identifies social work – are in a process of dynamic change that has seen the practitioner role change substantially over the years. It can be argued that education and health practitioners are similarly likely to have gone through changes of role over the years to meet the changing demands on their services.

Inter-agency dynamics

The scenario suggested by *Every Child Matters*, as discussed earlier, is one where all the relevant participants would be involved in open mutual sharing through an interactive language framework that welcomes all views as equally valid. However, this state of affairs raises further questions concerning power arising from what is perceived in any group of professionals as the valid interpretation of events. Different professionals may also appear to be more knowledgeable in certain situations than others, enabling their views to appear more knowledgeable and therefore more important. In addition, particular 'experts' may find it difficult to be flexible in their thinking, asserting that only they have the expertise and professional knowledge to make judgements about particular issues of concern. Of course, it would be an appropriate expectation that a group of practitioners bring their own areas of expertise to any discussion, but it could also be potentially unhealthy and even dangerous for any one voice to dominate the decision-making process. Carers and their children may also find it difficult to penetrate the meaning of technical terms or the agenda that may lie behind it. Indeed, it is possible for jargon to be intuited by parents as confirming a hierarchical structure that places them at the lower end of it, leaving them feeling that little has changed. In this scenario it is hardly likely that trust, identified in *Every Child Matters*, will be developed or the belief that co-operation in the decision-making process will be beneficial. A partial explanation may be that practitioners are more likely to be seen by children and their carers as representatives of institutional structures that are often viewed as hierarchical and impersonal. On the other hand, a set of inclusive strategies that encourage sharing, and give the impression of there being a 'level playing field', may lead to carers and children sharing their innermost concerns and risk being condemned by their own trusting nature, as any information shared may confirm professional stereotypes. The process of assessing any inter-professional situation is highly dependent, however, on the quality of professional interactions and therefore the multiple perspectives brought by professionals to the context in which they are involved.

It may also be problematic for the development of an inter-professional group perspective(s) if each practitioner perceives her or his status and relevance as relative to the views of other colleagues from other professional disciplines. The positions that individuals assume in groups may reflect their sense of status and importance and may result in a group dynamic characterised by a sense of fracturing of any shared inter-professional perspective. The fracturing and reforming of a group's professional perspectives can be a healthy dynamic but one that may not be entirely effective if agreement cannot be reached about which views count, before deciding how to act in 'the best interests' of a child.

It is therefore likely that practitioners will allocate themselves a place in a hierarchy of 'expertise' where some feel powerful while others feel marginalised. This, in turn, might reinforce a group hierarchy based on perceptions of 'competence' and 'expertness', determined by strong professional characters, that may undermine any attempt at a more egalitarian system. This is an important concern as it can undermine the ability of some practitioners to be able to feel fully committed, which in turn can lead to marginalisation, reinforcing existing barriers to communication and possibly leading to divergent and ineffective practices, with the risk that little may change and children remain at risk of not receiving adequate support (similar to the situation referred to by Stevenson earlier).

Conclusion

The development of inter-agency, inter-professional teams and their associated practices are still in their early stages and this chapter has revealed that there are major tensions to consider. It is still difficult to appreciate the extent of the changes that are impacting on so many agencies, practitioners, children and their carers at the same time. The systems that are being set up are clearly strongly influenced by government and professional agendas rather than those of parents or children. There are also fractures among the practitioner communities based on power dynamics that are bound to impact on the ability to develop a common language. This issue is central to the development of effective inter-agency working.

The sense of a 'united' inter-professional perspective perhaps requires access to a 'loose' form of common discourse as the basis for a shared language with less surveillance and more risk-taking as the basis for a shared developing professional and community perspective. In this respect Wenger (1998: 9) suggests that: 'A perspective is not a recipe; it does not tell you just what to do. Rather, it acts as a guide about what to pay attention to, what difficulties to expect, and how to approach problems'.

It is probably the case that any attempt at producing a common language or a recipe for a shared perspective will still be open to misinterpretation due to the domination of more powerful groups with more powerful voices. For communication to be effective it needs to be the outcome of joint consultations between parents, carers, children and practitioners. The act of participation must be seen to be 'joint' if it is to be seen as a serious and central feature of inter-professional practices that have any real chance of overcoming the issues that have been discussed in this chapter.

Questions for reflection

1. Should we aim for a multi-disciplinary approach to working with children and their families? What would be the advantages and disadvantages of working towards this? Are there systems and practices in any other countries of which you are aware that could form the basis for discussions about our own practices and beliefs?

2. What do you perceive may be the barriers in the UK to creating a truly multi-disciplinary 'early years' profession? Can you suggest ways in which these barriers could be overcome?

3. As an early years professional, where do you think your allegiances lie? Do you consider yourself a 'professional' in your own right, or do you align yourself with a more traditional professional body such as teaching or social work? What comments would you like to make about the status of early years professionals?

References and further reading

Abel-Smith, B. and Townsend, P. (1965): *The Poor and the Poorest*. London: Bell.

Alderson, P. (2000) *Young Children's Rights: Exploring Beliefs, Principles and Practices*. London: Jessica Kingsley.

Carvel, J. (2004) 'Children's services shake-up biggest in 30 years'. *The Guardian*, 5 March.

Coles, R., Britton, E. and Hicks, L. (2004) *Building Better Connections: Interagency Work and the Connexions Service*. London: Policy Press.

Collins English Dictionary (2000) (5th edn). Glasgow: HarperCollins.

Craig, G. (2003) 'Children's participation in community development', in Hallet, C. and Prout, A. *Hearing the Voices of Children: Social Policy for a New Century*. London and New York: RoutledgeFalmer.

Department of Health (1997) *The New NHS: Modern, Dependable* (Cm 3807). London: HMSO.

DfES/CYPU (2001) *Tomorrow's Future – Building a Strategy for Children and Young People*. London: Children and Young People's Unit.

DfES (2003) *Every Child Matters* DfES/(CM 5860). London: The Stationery Office.

DfES (2004a) *Every Child Matters: Next Steps*. Nottingham: TSO.

DfES (2004b) *Every Child Matters: Change for Children*. Nottingham: TSO.

DfES (2004c) Children Act 2004. London: The Stationery Office.

DHSS (1974) *Report of the Committee of Inquiry into the Care and Supervision Provided in Relation to Maria Colwell*. London: HMSO.

Egan, G. (1994) *The Skilled Helper* (5th edn). Monterey, CA: Brookes/Cole, cited in Horwath, J. (2005) *The Child's World: Assessing Children in Need*. London: Jessica Kingsley.

Foucault, M. (1977) *Discipline and Punish: The Birth of the Prison*. London: Penguin.

Gergen, K. J. (1999) *An Invitation to Social Construction*. London, Thousand Oaks, CA and New Delhi: Sage Publications.

Glendinning, C., Abbott, S. and Coleman, A. (2001) ' "Bridging the gap": new relationships between primary care groups and local authorities'. *Social Policy and Administration*, 35(4), 411–25.

Glennerster, H. (2000) *British Social Policy since 1945* (2nd edn). Oxford: Blackwell.

Hayden, C. and Blaya, C. (2005) 'Children on the Margins: comparing the role of school in England and France'. *Policy Studies*, **26**(1).

Hill, M. (2004) *Understanding Social Policy* (7th edn). Oxford: Blackwell.

HM Treasury (2004) *Choice for Parents: The Best Start for Children: A Ten Year Strategy for Childcare.* Norwich: HMSO.

Holland, S. (2004) *Child and Family Assessment in Social Work Practice.* London: Sage.

Hudson, B., Young, R., Hardy, B. and Glendinning, C. (2001) *National Evaluation of Notifications for Use of the Section 31 Partnership Flexibilities of the Health Act 1999: Interim Report.* Leeds: Nuffield Institute for Health and Manchester: National Primary Care Research and Development Centre, cited in Glendinning, C., Abbott, S. and Coleman, A. (2001) ' "*Bridging the gap*": new relationships between primary care groups and local authorities'. *Social Policy and Administration*, **35**(4), September, 411–25.

Laming (2003) *The Victoria Climbié Inquiry: Summary and Recommendations.* London: HMSO.

James, A., Jenks, C. and Prout, A. (1998) *Theorizing Childhood.* Oxford: Blackwell.

Lianos, M. (2005) '*Social control after Foucault*' (trans. D. Wood and M. Lianos). *Surveillance & Society*, **1**(3), 412–30 (http://www.surveillance-and-society.org).

Morrow, G. and Malin, N. (2004) 'Parents and professionals working together: turning rhetoric into reality'. *Early Years*, **24**(2).

Payne, M. (1995) *Social Work and Community Care.* London: Macmillan.

Prout, A. (2003) *Hearing the Voices of Children: Social Policy for a New Century.* London and New York: RoutledgeFalmer.

Prout, A. and Prout, A. (1997) *Constructing and Reconstructing Childhood: Contemporary Issues in the Sociological Study of Childhood.* London and Washington DC: Falmer Press.

Reder, P., Duncan, S. and Gray, M. (1999) *Beyond Blame: Child Abuse Tragedies Revisited.* London and New York: RoutledgeFalmer.

Shotter, J. (1993) *Cultural Politics of Everyday Life: Social Constructivism, Rhetoric and Knowing of the Third Kind.* Buckingham: Open University Press.

Skerrett, D. (2000) 'Social work – a shifting paradigm'. *Journal of Social Work Practice*, **14**(1), 63–74.

Stainton Rogers, R. and Stainton Rogers, W. (1992) *Stories of Childhood: Shifting Agendas of Child* Concern. New York and London: Harvester Wheatsheaf.

Stevenson, D. (1989) *Child Abuse: Professional Practice and Public Policy.* Hemel Hempstead: Harvester Wheatsheaf.

Sure Start (2004) (http://surestart.gov.uk/).

Thoburn, J., Lewis, A. and Shemmings, D. (1995) *Paternalism or Partnership? Family Involvement in the Child Protection Process.* London: HMSO.

Wenger, E. (1998) *Communities of Practice: Learning, Meaning and Identity.* Cambridge: Cambridge University Press.

White, S. and Featherstone, B. (2005) 'Communicating misunderstandings: multi-agency work as social practice'. *Child and Family Social Work*, **10**(3), 207–16.

The family in context

Angela D. Nurse

THIS CHAPTER AIMS to make us aware of what it is like to grow up in a family in the UK today and to face some of the assumptions we make when we work with children who do not come from families 'just like ours'. Other chapters in this book will refer to families and parents but this one will focus on some of the issues we will need to consider in working successfully, and often intimately, with families. As early years professionals, we need to think about the children we meet in our daily lives and to take into consideration the families they come from, which, hopefully, support them but sometimes do not. My reflections on the family do not derive specifically from the studies I have undertaken nor the qualifications I have. I am not a trained psychologist nor have I studied sociology in depth, but I come from a family, have created a family of my own and have worked, over many years, with parents and families, often in their own homes. Not all of these families have been like mine; many have made me reflect on my own and made me wish that we could absorb some of their qualities. Others have made me despair, but that has been in comparison with the picture I carry in my head of what a family should be, because of my individual experience. As long as children thrive, 'families' have a right to live their lives in the way they choose, in most circumstances. Families also change and this can happen very quickly.

Statistics

It seems so easy to talk about the 'family'. The first pictures that come into the mind of someone my age are of a mother, father and two children. The romantic, western ideal has been that parents fall in love, marry, have children and stay happy forever. This is far from the reality of many families in the UK today. We have one of the highest divorce rates in Europe, with 2.7 people per thousand divorcing in 2002. This was exceeded only by Belgium and Lithuania. An increasing percentage of children are born outside marriage, though many into stable relationships. We have one of the highest rates of teenage pregnancy, although the average age at which a mother has her first baby has also risen from 27.72 years to 28.70 in 2002. All European countries show such rises and the number of children in each family is falling. More and more people are choosing to live alone. Mothers are encouraged to work, and in some areas of the UK more women work than men. The employment rate for women rose from 60 per cent in 1993 to 65 per cent in 2003, though some will be working part-time. The UK has the highest percentage of young people under 18 living in jobless households (nearly 18 per cent) despite the fact that full-time working hours in the UK are exceeded only by Poland and Greece and stand at an average of 43 hours per week. These statistics are collated periodically by Eurostat and make fascinating reading, much of which confronts our perceptions of the social and economic place of the UK in comparison with its neighbours.

A figure of 2.4 children used to be stated as the norm for families. In more recent years, the birth rate has fallen quite dramatically and we now no longer produce enough babies to replace us all. The replacement figure is given as 2.1 children per family. If I look at the two families to which I am closely related – my own and my husband's – I can see that the last three generations illustrate clearly that we are in a crisis.

My mother was an only child and my father had one brother. I have two brothers, neither of whom have children. I have two children. My husband is one of six. Two of his siblings do not have children. The other four have produced eight. Across my generation, within the two families, there are fifteen adults, taking into account partners. We have therefore produced only two-thirds of a child for each family member rather than just over one, which statisticians consider 'healthy'. Why is this important? It is not only to do with who will be available to work and produce wealth to provide for us in our old age; it is also to do with how we view the nature of childhood and the kinds of experiences we offer our children as they become a rare and valued product, kept safe from all possible, often imaged, harm. It is also interesting to look at the gender distribution in our extended family. Of the ten children, only three are girls. This has happened naturally, but in many societies, particularly China and India, where strict population controls have been in force, there are similar, unnatural, discrepancies in gender distribution. This is not to say that we in the UK are averse to considering selecting the gender of the children we have. The media have opened up this debate, both in factual reporting of cases where there are medical implications in producing a child of a specific sex and also in creating dramas that explore the whole issue of assisted fertility and a woman's right to a child. The BBC created a three-episode drama, *The Family Man*, shown in 2006, which explored a number of issues to do with fertility treatment.

What is a 'family'?

The debate over the 'family' has been raised numerous times in the past few years. For most of us this has meant thinking about families as groups of people who are genetically related. Others have thought of 'families' as groups of people who come together by choice because they connect well with each other, share certain views and support each other in their daily lives. There have also been discussions on such concepts as the 'extended' and 'nuclear' family. These sociological terms apply to the rather romanticised ideal of a time when different generations of the family lived together and supported each other, rather than living in isolation in the seclusion of their own homes. Both these are generalisations which cannot wholly account for the reality. Not all families enjoy being in close proximity to their relations. Younger members of an extended family can resent the power and influence of an ageing matriarch or being expected to enter into the family business. Yet those who have little family support and do not easily develop friendship networks can succumb to depression, with sometimes considerable impact on their children. Judy Dunn (2002) reported her longitudinal study of 492 children growing up in a variety of families at a Marriage, Divorce and Family Workshop (MDFW) in March 2002. In her report she notes that:

> The drawings and maps of their families given to us by children as young as five and six paralleled the interview accounts of older children, with sensitivity to biological and step-relations, and significant links between closeness to grandparents and adjustment. Children's accounts of what their parents (resident and non-resident) know about them and how much they influence them were linked to their adjustment, as were their accounts of shared family activities.
>
> (Dunn 2000)

In considering the variety of forms families take, the importance to children of contact with grandparents and other family members has to be considered. Grandparents have traditionally played a significant part in socialising children in many parts of the world, especially if families have moved from different areas of the world, but not necessarily so. My mother looked after my daughters when they were very small as I returned to teaching, but many young mothers now have mothers who work and are not available to share childcare. Grandparents can often relate the stories that have been passed down through the generations and ensure that children maintain their family languages and cultural and religious practices, which form part of their identity. They are a bulwark against the all-powerful parent, defusing conflicts in opinion by remembering (and reporting) when parents had been small and difficult themselves. They can get away with sharing things with small children that parents cannot easily do – forbidden visits to McDonald's and watching the *Teletubbies* come to mind. I had no surviving grandmothers as I grew up, but watching my mother-in-law with her brood of ten made me realise what I and my brothers had missed. The closeness of a relationship between child and grandparent offers a different kind of secure relationship as children mature. Grandparents, however, have very few legal rights in maintaining a relationship with their grandchildren, particularly when partnerships break up and there is bitterness between parents which overrides the needs of the child. There are now websites that support grandparents, especially those who find themselves in distressing situations.

In considering the British family we must be aware that there are a variety of families that live in our society and which do not conform to the standard pattern described above. Some families will be created where the partners are of the same sex; others will derive from assisted fertilisation or surrogacy where one parent is not biologically related to his or her child; some will be 'reconstituted' from couples, who have divorced, bringing children from previous relationships into the new partnership; in others, the father may take on the role of 'househusband' while his partner works full-time. Others will have come to the UK from other parts of the world. We can make no generalisations about these communities, especially as, if originally immigrants, they move into the second, third or even fourth generation. Not all families of Asian origin expect their children to conform to arranged marriages nor do all families from certain religious backgrounds have very large families. Dwivedi (1996) writes about varying communication styles between different ethnic groups, giving examples of differences in responding, for example, by shaking hands, rather than bowing, as a greeting. Many of the children we work with will be bilingual – the majority of the world's children speak at least two languages and it is we who are out of step in speaking only one fluently. This is often perceived by early years professionals as a 'problem' but should be viewed far more positively. We need to be aware, however, as English is a major world language (carrying with it power and prestige), that children and families for whom English may not be the first language may sense difficulties. Dwivedi warns:

> When bilinguals speak in their second language their lack of proficiency affects their perceptions of themselves in relation to others; they may feel that they themselves are less intelligent, happy or confident and this can block and disrupt their affective communication. (p.154)

We need to approach these situations with empathy, care and professionalism. Dwivedi states that, 'it is impossible for any professional to be fully knowledgeable of the cultural contexts of all children' (p.158). Yet we need to support children and their families and encourage them to take a full part in our society. It is also very interesting to learn their stories and so unpick any misconceptions. One of our mature students was from Iraq. The events happening there were seen by the whole group through her eyes and we all learned so much more, particularly when her parents visited and then had to return. The decisions she had to make about her family's future – whether to stay here in relative safety or try to return to re-establish their lives there – brought home to us very quickly the realities that many people have to face. It was part of our 'hidden curriculum' which was so much more powerful in its impact because of her presence than all the lectures I could have constructed from using textbooks. Dwivedi goes on to explore professional practice (p.158):

> It should, however, be possible to develop and maintain a curious and respectful frame of mind in listening to children and their families which implies a respect for the differences which will inevitably exist in cultural attitudes and values. It should be possible for all professionals to be open to learning from children and their families about those differences. Such a process may at times be clumsy both on the part of the professional and of the family members, but an atmosphere where the inevitableness of clumsiness is openly acknowledged can be conducive to mutual education.

Families in distress

As practitioners we often know very quickly when there has been a change in family circumstances. A child who was happy and secure within the setting becomes sad and withdrawn or, conversely, angry and suddenly difficult to manage. In most instances parents are quick to tell us the reasons why, but sometimes there needs to be a little probing. There may have been a breakdown in the parents' relationship or a death in the family. A new baby can result in a change in behaviour, however well the older child has been prepared.

Sometimes parents keep from sharing things that are going to happen to the family from small children because they think knowing will upset them more or because they feel they will not understand. Working in London many years ago I was asked to visit a nursery school to talk with a father who was very distressed about his sons biting any child or adult who came near him. The child was nearly four years old. The team in the nursery were very experienced and had tried hard to stop this, but biting is a very powerful tool for young children. The nursery had a mixed intake of children from a number of different cultural and social groups. The father was a professional journalist working on a respected newspaper and felt his inability to cope with and change his son's behaviour very deeply. He was open and honest with me and we worked together over several weeks to alter what was happening. So difficult was the situation that I even succumbed to using a 'star chart', where the boy was rewarded for every period that he managed to desist from using his teeth. This was partially successful; we shifted him from biting to pulling hair, but we felt at least we were moving in the right direction. On the final occasion I met the father, he thanked me (for my limited success) and told me this would have to be the last meeting. When I asked why he replied that the family was moving to a new house outside London. We had talked about family events, but this had not been mentioned. Had he told his son? No, he thought he was too young to understand the implications and timescale. I asked him to talk it through with his son because I was sure the little boy would understand. The father did so. The nursery reported that the biting (and hair-pulling) stopped immediately.

In this case the family dynamics had temporarily gone askew and it took careful work by the nursery team not to damage the relationship with the child and his family for the future. In some families the dynamics are so disrupted that even if the professionals working with the child and family are aware of what is happening there is little they can do to change matters other than support the child and ensure that the setting becomes a haven where the child can relax and be a child, leaving behind the responsibilities he may be carrying. I discuss 'young carers' elsewhere in the book (see Chapter 10), but children find themselves sometimes in situations where it is not easy to define exactly what is happening and we find it hard to know how we should proceed. Children can learn to take responsibility very early in their lives if parents do not retain it for themselves. Children look after parents who are ill or who have problems with addiction. They can also, very early on in their lives, take on the role of 'parent', particularly if they are the first-born. A parent with a young, but mature, child can sometimes find it easy to rely on that child emotionally as well as practically, expecting him or her to look after younger siblings but also to provide comfort and companionship to parents who have lost the will to establish their own relationships with other adults because of depression and lack of self-worth. Once a child is socialised into this role it is very difficult to avoid playing it out in adulthood. They often join the caring professions and rarely put their own needs first.

Families with children with special needs

Another scenario occurs when a family is suddenly and unexpectedly presented with a child with a disability or medical need. The dynamics of a family in this situation are such that there is often a great deal of heartache and adjustment to be made before the baby is fully integrated into the family. The sense of loss some parents feel can live on for decades, along with a mother's guilt that something she did during pregnancy caused it. Barry Carpenter has for many years worked in the field of special needs, particularly with families, and in 1997 edited a book whose contributors looked at the different effects on the members of having a child with a special need, but also on the networks and strategies each develops as he or she adjusts to new priorities. The relationship between parents and professionals and the idea of 'partnership' are explored in this book. He looks towards 'informed supporters' (p. 29) now, rather than professionals as experts who do not always understand the uniqueness of every family. Elaine Herbert's contribution, which resulted from her research into the fathers' responses, highlights how little support they had received in comparison with their wives. Their role was to maintain 'normality' in a difficult situation. I have known fathers who have taken a leading role, but it is usually mothers to whom the professionals turn.

We may be responsible as professionals not only for children who have special needs but also for their siblings. I once worked with a very special family; there were three children, two of whom had a rare, inherited form of cerebral palsy that affected movement and speech especially, but they were bright, confident children who soon learned to use alternative means of communication. Later, the mother developed multiple sclerosis, but this was a close-knit family who received a lot of support from the father's employers and their church. The third child had not inherited the disability. The middle child (I will call her Kay) was used to taking a caring role and accepted her mother's illness (diagnosed when she was 5) apparently quite well. After my responsibility for the family ended, I visited a mainstream school where a child with special needs had just been placed. I was greeted by the teacher who was also the SENCO, who replied that everything was fine. The little girl was settling down well and it was very nice to see that she was being helped by another child who spent all her playtimes looking after her, as well as supporting her in class. Of course, this child was Kay, just six years old. There were issues to do with confidentiality here, but Kay needed her time in school to be carefree so that she could, in part, experience a childhood with her friends, and this was critical to her ability to keep on top of the situation at home. A quiet word with the head teacher, who knew the circumstances at home, led to a resolution and some space for Kay.

These illustrations are included, not only to show different family structures but also to ensure that early years professionals understand the impact of family life on the children's individual lives and develop empathy, as well as strategies shared with parents, to support them.

The role of fathers

In the battle for women's rights, fathers have often been sorely neglected in our discussions of the family. In the UK varying circumstances have led to different impacts upon men because of changing economic circumstances and also because of women's ability to control their own fertility by using contraception and, increasingly, opting to have children by artificial insemination. Under our law, fathers have few rights in comparison with women unless they are married at the time their baby was born or both parents register the child (Baxter 2005). Some men choose to stay at home and become 'house husbands', perhaps because their partners have greater earning potential or are more committed to a career. Other men have no choice. Changes to the heavy industrial base to the British economy have dramatically reduced opportunities for work in certain areas of the country and what is often available is part-time, poorly paid or very specialised. Consequently, women have filled many of these jobs. At the other end of the spectrum, men in the professions and other more secure, adequately paid jobs find themselves working longer hours in more stressful circumstances. This does not only affect men, but is also part of the difficulties of maintaining a satisfying family life that enables children to grow securely, but can be compromised when two parents work.

One of the arguments that has been posited centres on men's emotions and their suitability to rear children. The anecdote below illustrates how deeply men can feel about their children and how, often in a profession that is dominated by females, we can hold views that are stereotyped and negative.

Tim, a member of the security staff at work, recently became the father of twins. As is often the case, the twins were tiny and had to spend some time in the special care unit. His little girl reached a good weight earlier than his son and was allowed to go home. We had already seen the photos he had taken of them just after they were born and he brought his daughter to meet us as soon as he could. There was sadness mixed with his delight, however, because his son was still in hospital on his own. He felt the separation keenly and spent as much time as he could with him, taking his sister back so that they were near each other, as he recognised the importance of the 'twin' relationship. I talked about research in New Zealand where staff looking after pre-term twins had placed the stronger twin in the same incubator as her brother (against normal practice) who was in distress. She had placed her arm around his shoulders. This had caused the little boy's heart rate to steady and he had calmed significantly. 'Yes, yes,' replied Tim, 'that happens, I've seen it!'.

It is not exceptional that in many families the young child bonds more strongly with the father rather than the mother. The reasons for this can be varied, perhaps to do with the mother's feelings and health at the time the baby was born, prior experience, gender issues or personality traits. Although it always seems to shock, some women do leave their families when the situation becomes unbearable for them. Many fathers stay at home, 'for the sake of the children', when the adult relationship is long over. We have to accept, however, that more fathers abandon their families in our society than do mothers. Divorced fathers' wishes to stay involved with their children are often hampered by the angry feelings of ex-partners and other adults within the family. The UK has one of the highest divorce rates in Europe (Eurostat 2005 (see website)). One in three marriages is dissolved, though many divorcees go on to marry again. It is too simplistic to say that divorce always has a negative impact on the children – it depends on the circumstances and how they are handled – but we need to be aware that children's circumstances are changing and they need understanding and support through the change.

A project organised by the University of Edinburgh (Milligan and Dowie) in 1998 asked 'What do children need from their fathers?. The children's responses fell into these five categories of need:

■ for a role model;

■ for quality time with their fathers;

■ for supportive behaviour;

- for love; and

- for physical contact.

How far can we go to reinforce these?

Cared-for children and adoption

The time when childless families were able to select a baby for adoption is long gone as the stigma attached to young single mothers has receded and abortion has been legalised. The Adoption and Fostering Information Line advises that waiting for a baby usually takes from three to ten years. Children now available have often suffered trauma or may have a special need. They are generally older and may have siblings. There are always attempts to keep families together and to place children within families who share the same cultural background, though this is not always possible and this policy has caused anxiety when placements are refused by social services departments because the general public's feelings are that a family is better than long-term institutional care. As a result of adoption difficulties in the UK, and sometimes for altruistic reasons, a number of prospective parents have adopted from other countries, such as the Far East and Romania. Adoption within the UK and from elsewhere is not an easy process, demanding long reports on the family's suitability before it has been agreed. There have been relaxations, however, on upper age limits and on single-parent adoptions, especially for those children with very special needs. There is much more openness now in the adoption process as professionals realise the importance of children retaining details of, and perhaps maintaining contact with, families of origin. The necessity for children to know their origins is described vividly in Kate Adie's (2005) book where she gives a historical and global account of children who have been abandoned ('foundlings'). This had been her start in life. A research study for the Nuffield Foundation, led by Dr Elsbeth Neil (2002) of the University of East Anglia, found that 'in a sample of 168 children aged under 4, only 11 per cent had no contact with adult birth relatives at all. Eighty-one per cent had 'letterbox contact', involving regular letters and reports, while 17 per cent saw their birth families face-to-face. Arrangements varied hugely, with some meetings frequent and friendly, and others only taking place once a year – but both adoptive and birth parents agreed that some sort of contact was enormously valuable.' The research concluded that 'ongoing contact helped alleviate some of the birth parents' anguish, bringing a range of benefits including:

- reassurance that their child is all right;

- making the loss of their child easier to accept;

- helping them to feel more positively about the adoptive parents; and

- seeing a positive role for themselves in their child's future.'

It is quite likely that early years professionals will work with parents and carers of fostered or adopted children and those in long-term group care. Some of the same issues, as outlined by Dwivedi above, may arise concerning our lack of knowledge and how much the systems have changed in the past few years. There will be a need to ask for information, particularly if this situation is stressful to those involved in it.

Whose responsibility: state or private?

At the time of writing, there is considerable debate, and probably a number of battles, taking place in the higher echelons of government about the nature of what we should provide, as a nation, for our children and what should remain within the private domain of the family. A return to 'Victorian values' was promoted by the Conservative government in the 1980s. It was felt by many that few of the politicians recognised what these values meant for women and children in the nineteenth century. This debate over the years, though never very open, has centred on the nature of the relationship between children and families and the state, whether this means the state as a whole or certain institutions within it. For example, several authors have argued for a triangulated relationship between children, parents and schools (Nurse and Headington 1999). At the moment, the balance seems to be moving towards the state with a range of 'family-friendly' papers and legislation designed to support children and families, though, in reality, impinging on nearly every aspect of family life. Two papers on the state of the family written from two different perspectives illustrate how difficult it is to view the family objectively. The first, by O'Neill (2002), reviews the state of the family concluding that the 'fatherless' family results in dire outcomes for the 'social fabric', with increased crime and violence, decreased community ties, growing 'divorce culture' and dependence on state welfare. She interprets the evidence in her concluding paragraph (p.20): 'to indicate the traditional family based upon a married father and mother is still the best environment for raising children and it forms the soundest basis for wider society'.

Bristow (2004) reviews the 'evidence' in a different way, stating that in her interpretation of the statistics 'even this brief overview indicates that there has been no major transformation of the family'. Her view is presented as:

> The thrust of New Labour's family policy is simple. Parents should be responsible for raising children – there is no wider vision of any alternative way of doing things. But they should not be trusted to get on with it themselves . . . But for all the apparent choices people have now about how to organise their personal family situation, the real, political choice, to do with how society could best organise its relationship with the family as a social and economic institution, is conspicuously absent. There are individual men and women, there are families, and there is the therapeutic state. Bristow (2004: online)

There is a difficulty in describing the primary relationship between child and parent without using words such as 'belongs' or 'owns', which do not reflect the responsibilities nor the subtleties which we embrace when we become parents or carers. Lee (2005) has also had difficulties with the terms we use in describing adult relationships with children. He explores the term 'owned' and 'possession' and how the interpretation of these terms varies according to time and place. The relationship is more that of 'guardianship' or 'safekeeping', where we understand that it is not only temporary but also ever-changing, as the child becomes independent and able to make choices for him- or herself. The relationship between parent and child should be a reciprocal one, but we have seen above that there are families where this is not so. Yet we are beginning to recognise how capable even newborn babies are of initiating communication between infant and adult. The work of Colwyn Trevarthen and his research team shows very clearly how often a very young baby initiates interaction. Parents imitate babies' facial expressions, as well as being able to affect babies' engagement by their own actions, such as showing a sad face.

Conclusion

Many of the anxieties my parents had about the future of society have not come to pass. Men still create and care about children; there are few 'test-tube babies', and creating human beings artificially has not taken the route that science fiction led us to believe it would. We are not cloned from our parents. More and more value is being placed on children's emotional development, as well as the acquisition of formal skills. The family is still with us, even if its nature has changed.

Questions for reflection

1. Reflect on your family of origin. What impact has its structure had on you as an adult? What is your 'ideal' family and how does this meet with any other models you may have met?

2. What do you think should be the relationship between the family and the state?

3. What should be the role of fathers in the twenty-first century? How can we ensure, as early years professionals, that we support their involvement with their children?

4. How can we ensure that we understand and develop reciprocal relationships with families that have had experiences different from ours?

References

Adie, K. (2005) *Nobody's Child*. London: Hodder & Stoughton.

Baxter, C. (2005) 'Legal issues', in Jones, L., Holmes, R. and Powell, J. *Early Childhood Studies: A Multiprofessional Perspective*. Maidenhead: Open University Press.

BBC (2006) *The Family Man*, 23 March, 30 March, 3 April.

Bristow, J. (2004) *What Future for the Family*? (www.spiked-online.com).

Carpenter, B. (1997) *Families in Context: Emerging Trends in Family Support and Early Intervention*. London: David Fulton Publishers.

Davie, R. Upton, G. and Varma, V. (eds) (1995) *The Voice of the Child: A Handbook for Professionals*. London: RoutledgeFalmer.

Dunn, J. (2002) *Children's Views of Parents and Changing Families* (www.opo.org.uk/mdfw).

Dwivedi, K. N. (1996) 'Race and the child's perspective', in Davie *et al.*

Lee, N. (2005) *Childhood and Human Value*. Maidenhead: Open University Press.

Milligan, C. and Dowie, A. (1998) *What Do Children Need from their Fathers?* University of Edinburgh, Centre for Theology and Public Issues, Occasional Paper no.42.

Neil, E. (2002) *Contact after Adoption: The Contribution of Adoptive Parents' Empathy for Children and Birth Relatives* (www.uea.ac.uk/swk/research/summaries/contact_adoption2).

Nurse, A. D. and Headington, R. (1999) 'Balancing the needs of children, parents and teachers', in David, T. (ed.) *Young Children Learning*. London: Paul Chapman Publishing.

O'Neill, R. (2002) *Experiments in Living: The Fatherless Family*. London: The Institute for the Study of Civil Society (CIVITAS).

Trevarthen, C. in Gregory, R. L. (2004) *Oxford Companion to the Mind* (2nd edn). Oxford: OUP.

Websites

Europe in Figures: Eurostat Yearbook 2005 (http://epp.eurostat.cec.eu.int)

Adoption and Fostering Information Line (www.adoption.org.uk)

The Grandparents' Association (www.grandparents-association.org.uk)

Child development and psychology

Alan Bainbridge

CHILDREN HAVE BEEN ever-present within human society yet the study of their development is a fairly recent one. This chapter seeks to consider why this may be the case and, in doing so, introduces and debates some of the difficult issues that surround this subject. The understanding provided by psychology will be of particular interest as this dominates the theoretical debate of child development and will be shown to have historically similar origins. It could be argued that as psychology is a discipline dedicated to understanding the human condition, then the investigation of child development is fundamental to this greater goal; for a study of children may lead to a clearer understanding of what it is to be an adult. What is clear, though, is that the study of the area of child development is very influential and widespread and impacts on many of the helping and caring professions including nursing, teaching, early years provision, childcare and social work; therefore a clearer understanding of child development will contribution greatly to the health and well-being of young people.

It is ironic that, despite the fact that adults and children have been present, side-by-side, in human societies from the beginning of time, there is still a need to learn more; surely by now the mature, experienced and rational adults will have gained enough insight to enable them to understand childhood experiences. It is, potentially, here that the first difficult issue in studying child development arises, as it seems logical that if we have all experienced this process we should all appreciate what it involves. Yet the search for meaning continues. The essential problem is how to investigate the experience of children in such a way that their voice, thoughts and feelings are made clear. If we were to rely on adult memories and reflection then no doubt a whole array of different experiences would be presented, interpretations given, fantasies conjured up and difficult memories 'erased'. If we next consider some historical insight, then the road to the influence of psychological thinking within child development will be made clearer.

During the seventeenth and eighteenth centuries two influential philosophers provided very differing views on the nature of childhood. John Locke famously regarded children as a blank slate, or *tabula rasa*. Their minds were initially empty but by experiencing the world under the supervision of adults, their minds were formed. Adults could therefore influence a child's development by providing the correct sort of instruction at the right time. The French philosopher Rousseau agreed with Locke's assumption that instruction of children by adults was necessary but his rationale was entirely different. Rousseau saw the child as being born pure, only to be corrupted by civilisation. Here the role of the adult was to provide a nurturing environment linked to the child's staged developmental needs. So Locke sees the need to guide the child whereas Rousseau allows the child to be in control. The next century provided an opportunity for these philosophies to be 'tested'.

The story of the Wild Boy of Aveyron can be regarded as a seminal moment in the understanding of the study of child development as it provided in a unique way an insight into what factors may be responsible for becoming an adult. The 'Wild Boy' was a young child found existing by himself near a village in France in 1800; he was thought to be about twelve years old and locals had observed him for some time eating berries and roots. If they attempted to give him clothes he rejected them. As the boy did not speak, and made only a few noises, he became known as the 'Wild Boy'. Rather than see the boy placed in an asylum a local doctor agreed to take care of him. It was his view that the boy's lack of social contact had prevented a normal development, and therefore if he was to provide such contact, the boy would become 'civilised'. Unfortunately, despite considerable effort, the boy only made limited progress; he was able to recognise a few words, use a chamber pot and show affection to his carers but was never able to interact normally in society. This experience poses questions about both the role of social influence and discrete maturational periods that Rousseau would support, as well as the selection of the appropriate instructional techniques that Locke would regard as necessary to bring about development of the mind.

The nineteenth century provided further momentum in the study of children and particularly what they could and could not do at certain ages, as this was the time of the industrial revolution when children as young as 4 could be found working in factories and mines. The studies carried out attempted to discover what children could cope with before they began to suffer! It was generally agreed that a 12-hour day was suitable, with others suggesting ten hours, to allow the other two to be used for religious and moral education. What is interesting is the greater concern for religious and moral education rather than physical, cognitive or emotional development; it seems here as though the child's moral development, whatever that entailed, had more value than other areas. Maybe 'being good' and not questioning religious teachings provided a compliant workforce. What this situation did provide was a climate of research and scientific activity to 'find out' about children, and this climate was about to undergo rapid change.

In the mid-nineteenth century Darwin published *The Origin of Species* and from this point children began to be viewed as more than little and slightly imperfect adults. Their behaviour became interesting in its own right and could be compared with other species to provide insight into the process of human evolution. Observations were made that compared physical development and physiology with other species and also, significantly, what it was that separated humans from the other animals. This was to fuel interest in the development of the mind and eventually to the influence of psychology in the study of child development. The study of child development is now a complex and multi-disciplinary one, so to talk of psychology as providing the only insight into children's development would be false and disrespectful of other important disciplines, such as sociology, anthropology and neuroscience. The influence of psychology is our focus here, but even this contracting of the 'big picture' still provides a very complex area of study, so the intention now is to present a useful definition of child development and to indicate the issues surrounding this that will facilitate any future debate.

Child development as an arena of study is attempting to provide a systematic and scientific understanding of how the individual grows and changes, from the moment of birth until death, that will enhance the ability of practitioners to make suitably informed decisions. To think about all the influences on an individual from birth to death is a considerably complex task; therefore developmental processes are often grouped into domains, such as cognitive (linked to thought processes and intellectual abilities), physical (to do with internal and external body changes) and social and emotional development, which considers relationships and feelings. This in itself only goes so far to reducing the complexity, as each of these domains contains a large body of ever-changing knowledge. What is proposed here is to deal with the issue raised early on in the chapter – how to understand the world of the child. When we attempt to understand the world of young people we endeavour to problematise the situation, which involves considering the problems of understanding child development rather than immediately applying theory. If this process is carried out on child development a number of familiar themes are raised. These are:

- defining what childhood actually is;
- continuity and discontinuity;
- nature and nurture;
- objectivity and subjectivity;
- similarities and uniqueness.

Each of these will now be discussed briefly. Together they provide a useful framework to examine the many domains and theories of child development; the issues addressed relate to childhood experience and allow the reader to reflect and not become 'bogged down' in theory. Any theory that is encountered can be critically evaluated and related to childhood experiences using one or more of the above issues.

Defining childhood

This issue may not initially appear problematic, as surely we all know what it is to experience a childhood. The concern to be raised is related to how we construct childhood (James and Prout 1997). This concept debates the notion that understanding childhood is not a simple physical, psychological or physiological proposition; for instance, childhood experiences may be affected by historical periods and cultural influences. This explanation of childhood is often referred to as social construction as this theory places more importance on the nurturing effect of society. This may sound extreme but Postman (1983) announced that childhood was over! The rationale for this was related to the influence of television and the economic power that children now have. Postman suggests that the child–adult boundary has been blurred as children are seeing into the adult world via television, which can also give them economic influence – what we may refer to as 'pester power'. Two of the features of childhood, for Postman, have been reduced as children can now see into the adult world and they also manipulate the spending of adults. Aries (1962) also questioned our understanding of childhood and claimed that it was actually a fairly recent concept and one not observed until at least the end of the fifteenth century. At this time childhood seemed to emerge as a distinct condition that would evolve into the child-centred family image of the nineteenth and twentieth centuries. The difficulty faced when reflecting historically is to get an accurate representation of what life was like. Aries did this by looking at medieval art and interpreting the roles represented by children in the images. As a methodological technique this process leaves much to be desired but the legacy of the debate set up by Aries has been a valuable one. It is also important to consider not just the perceived experience of childhood but what the prevalent theoretical understandings were in certain periods of history. This has, to some extent, been exemplified by the philosophies of Locke and Rousseau but it is also notable how major theorists have had an impact at certain times; for example, the effect of Darwin's theories on child observations, the popularisation of behaviourist theories in the early twentieth century and the rise of cognitive explanations, such as Piaget's, in the 1950s and 1960s.

While considering the alternative view that childhood experience may be socially constructed as a result of historical events, it is also logical to comment briefly on the influence of culture. It is hard to imagine a child developing entirely independently from any cultural input, although it is possible to regard the 'Wild Boy' as having had such an experience. Yet the vast majority of children will be 'inducted' into the rituals and traditions of their culture as part of the normal nurturing process. The result of this is to provide the child with a set of values and assumptions that frame their way of thinking and 'being'. We are sometimes made aware of this when we travel and experience a 'culture shock'. In this situation what we experience does not reflect our expectations and we feel uncomfortable and out-of-place. It is as if our development so far has not equipped us to deal with this new experience. What this incident shows could be that the impact of the social world is more significant than, say, cognitive or emotional development. Therefore the dominant position of using psychology to understand child development may not be as secure as previously thought.

This is not intended as a 'things aren't what they used to be' section, but clearly life experiences have changed. The question to grapple with is, 'How is this impacting on childhood experience and therefore developmental processes?'. Ultimately, within this summary, the debate on the nature of childhood experience allows us to frame and debate the role of psychology more accurately on the developing child.

Continuity and discontinuity

If we accept that we are confident with our understanding of childhood experience and how this may cause us to think differently about child development, the next step is to consider the process of development itself. In general, psychologists have two main viewpoints of what they call 'ontogeny' (how individuals develop over time). One is that children develop in a gradual way or continuously; the other is that they develop discontinuously, and this process is noted to have stages of change and plateaux. The twentieth century has been dominated by discontinuous or stage theories and if the debate in the previous section is taken into account this may be due to the dominant way of thinking (paradigm) of this period in history. The theoretical legacy of Darwin and the evolutionists can still be seen to have influence today. The purpose here is not to present one theory as being more insightful than another but to consider what insight each theoretical stance can offer to our understanding of ontogeny.

Continuous theories emphasise the gradual and quantitative, measurable changes that occur, including features such as the development of memory, vocabulary or even the increased complexity of brain structure. Analogies are often provided that liken ontological events in humans to those of seeds growing into trees, as the changes are gradual, measurable and lead to an increase in complexity. Theories from diverse domains of psychological thinking can be aligned to this view of continuous change. Behaviourists such as Pavlov and Skinner attempted to demonstrate how the use of rewards linked to external stimuli could gradually modify behaviour; Bruner (1990) highlights how individuals build up their own narratives that help make sense of their world. This narrative is constantly changing to respond to the ever-changing external world. The social constructionists, such as Vygotsky, explain the development of skills and behaviours as being accumulated gradually, over time, in a social environment.

The more dominant stage theories note that ontogeny is punctuated by periods of little change interspersed with sudden time-limited qualitative development. The analogy drawn here is not that of the seed and tree, but instead, the caterpillar becoming a butterfly, as over a short period of time new observable patterns of behaviour emerge. This paradigm has dominated recent child developmental theory and seeks to explain why certain functions of 'human being' are not obvious in the early stages of life, and also to make some link between structure and function. Classic examples are well known and include Piaget's stages of cognitive development, where accommodation and assimilation of new material is required before the next stage can be reached, and the ability to do this is correlated with age. The psychodynamic theories of Freud and Erikson propose that significant conflicts or life events need to be resolved at specific ages (although Erikson has a broader view of the time periods required) to enable appropriate personality development.

Each of these paradigms has a significant group of adherents and this does not help us to understand the messiness and complexity of child development, for if they cannot agree then what is the fate of those of us who read their works? What is required is to be inquisitive or critical about these two ways of describing ontogeny in order for them to be evaluated. Reasonable points to consider could be: Are these viewpoints influenced by how the observations or data collection have been carried out? For example, will observations over longer periods highlight sudden changes not seen in shorter periods of observation? Are there two types, or more, of development? Why should ontogeny only be gradual or staged? Are individual differences in children taken into account? Are the skills and abilities that children bring to tasks masking a developmental process that could have occurred, yet the psychologist carrying out the research cannot 'get inside the mind of the child'?

Nature or nurture

This is a debate I imagine many are familiar with as it provides another fundamental context in which to debate the process of development. Essentially, the argument debates the impact of nature (the role of biology) and nurture (the influence of the environment) and centres on the underlying causes that shape and guide our development into individuals with very different cognitive abilities, personalities, social skills, body shapes, sizes and growth rates. The question is how or why these differences may be affected by the hereditary influence of genetic material or the physical and social world a child is nurtured in. It is of particular importance as it can influence decisions on how we treat children. If this sounds extreme, then consider the 'Wild Boy'. From the hereditary perspective, this boy was like his genetic material, therefore there is no need to intervene as his fate has already been cast. If development is considered to be influenced by nurturing events then it is worthwhile trying to help the boy, as it may be possible to bring about change. From the historical accounts it appears as if both perspectives are correct; the boy did change, he became affectionate and could recognise a few words; yet he never reached the stage where he could be fully integrated into French society. The lesson provided is an important one in the search to understand how development takes place. Both the nature and nurture protagonists seem to have got it right. Present debates are therefore focused, not on which one is correct but on how the two interact to influence the differences we see in the development of individuals.

Nature or hereditary views of development emphasise the influence of genetic material from the parents on the child's development and, particularly, comparatively stable features such as personality traits and intelligence. There is an argument that the role of genetics is very influential within psychological thinking as it provides a 'respected' and scientific explanation for the complexity of the human condition during these times when the principles of scientific understanding are particularly influential. Nature debates framed examples of maturational processes (those that follow a clear pattern of development) and Gesell and Thompson (1929) illustrated this in a classic study on identical twins. They found that each twin was capable of developing a particular skill independent of whether they had been trained or not, therefore suggesting the powerful influence of inherited material.

Theories of child development that consider nurture to be more important are gaining in popularity as it is easier to explain the role of culture within this context. Nurture explanation of development include Bowlby's attachment theory, where the powerful early events of being cared for are seen to cause behavioural patterns in adults. Also included here is Watson's behaviourist technique, where he claimed that almost any child could be 'shaped' to become capable of any skill, even up to the point of determining an occupation. What nurturing theories also provide is the possibility that changes in the developmental process are possible, and given the right enriching environment children can increase their academic abilities, improve their social skills and even change their physical features. This ability to change the pattern or end-result of development is referred to as 'plasticity' as it suggests that there are periods when change is possible. The 'Wild Boy' was able to gain a number of skills, and yet others remained elusive, and the suggestion is that, for example, with language development a 'critical period' had been missed during which this process would be sensitive to normal development.

It is very difficult to assess the influence of each of these views of development as both can be supported by a substantial body of knowledge. What is imperative, though, is to consider how each of the views present the nature of childhood and how this can be used to influence how we react to young people.

Objectivity and subjectivity

An objective view of the world is one that sees the world as it is, based on observable and measurable facts. Once these facts have been distorted by our own preconceptions and assumptions the world view is now tainted by our subjectivity and therefore may no longer represent a 'truth'. The debate on objectivity and subjectivity is another fundamental issue to consider as we attempt to understand child development, and we can apply this to our existing thoughts and also to the assumptions made by past theorists.

The influence of science as a methodology on the study of young people has already been alluded to briefly in the discussion on the influence of Darwinian thought and theories that were prevalent in certain periods of history. Just as the understanding of child development is a complex process, so too is the understanding of the development of theory, but it is a fruitful discussion to have as it will also help clarify in our minds what we mean by the nature of childhood and the developmental processes involved. It is not necessary to divide this section into separate parts for objectivism and for subjectivism as the debate is often simply an opposite. For example, the objective researcher seeks to remove all trace of both their own feelings and preconceptions and those of those being researched; while the subjective researcher acknowledges these and includes them in the process of finding out.

The very nature of child development as a discipline to study can be seen to be influenced by the desire to be objective and to present the reality of children's experiences and not just subjective notions. Studies on children can be said to have begun at a time when the scientific method was in ascendancy and Darwin had presented his theory of evolution. This created a climate of respectability for scientific explanations and the young discipline of psychology was only too willing to join this esteemed club and so concentrated on using scientific methodologies. Aligned to this was evolutionary theory that strengthened the view that natural development is one from simple to complex via a series of readily observable stages. Walkerdine (2004) adds an interesting dimension as to why science and child development became so closely linked; she sees this as the part of the need to deal with children working in factories during the Industrial Revolution. At this time the 'end-point' of development was assumed to be a 'rational civilised adult', yet long hours of work were having an effect on children and the concern about their moral development was raised. To counter this, child studies were carried out to measure the effects of working and how successful schooling programmes were developing the children's moral character. So from this very early stage the scientific paradigm and child development were inextricably linked and this had the effect of reducing the role of the thoughts and feelings of young people, ironically, in studies about them.

The problem with children is that they are hard to understand. How do we know they are telling the truth? For the objective researcher this is extremely problematic and, as a result, early studies on children probably became more focused on method and how to record the experience of childhood rather than on the real 'construction' of childhood experience. These theoretical developments may actually tell us more about the researcher's views of children than it does about the children themselves. Bringing the focus back to subjectivity, it should be noted that recent research, often within a sociological framework (James and Prout 1997), has attempted to allow subjective values to emerge so that the complexity of early development can be seen. Objectivity should not be seen as misleading, as it may enable some of the threads of this complex world to be 'unpicked' and then maybe the rest will unravel a bit faster?

Similarities and uniqueness

The final issue for debate involves thinking of children as unique or similar, and as with the other issues raised there is not a right or wrong response. What I hope is becoming clear is not the idea that theories can be rejected because they are 'wrong', or accepted as 'right', but instead that some level of reflection is applied to identify what particular feature(s) of a theory provide useful insight. The problem faced by researchers is to provide evidence that appears to have the potential to be applied to a fairly large section of the community, as opposed to insular, parochial findings that can only be applied to one setting and then only at a particular time. Historically, the research into child development has been embedded within a scientific paradigm that has attempted to identify universals or generalities; more recent research has attempted to deal with the complexity of variety, and the idea that there are many constructions of childhood is now becoming more widely known.

A simple, and I suppose fairly obvious, statement is that both viewpoints have something to offer. We all share some similarities and also a number of differences. The vast majority of humans follow similar cognitive, social, emotional and physical developmental patterns and any deviation from these is deemed abnormal. How big the deviation has to be before the distinction between normality and abnormality is clear is problematic. Even identical twins who share an identical genetic make-up are perceived by their parents as displaying different characteristics. 'Normality' and 'abnormality' are frequently used terms within child development and they do have a confident 'feel' but they hide an array of difficult issues.

The average 'normal' child probably does not exist as each of us will have some feature, some process, that, for whatever reason, has not developed as expected. Is this normality referring to cognition, emotional development or physical development? Or is being normal a summary of all of these? The 'normal' child is the one who, statistically, equates to the expected measurements or observations based on past research, research that may be using contentious assumptions about the nature of childhood, based on historically approved notions that may not reflect the child of today, or even research that was so focused on the methodological issues of studying children that it failed to provide a space to hear their voice. Childhood experience is elusive and, for many, to suggest that a normal child exists is to challenge the very assumption that all children have qualitatively and quantitatively different experiences. It is difficult to ignore the argument that we all have competing realities for the same moment in time. The counter-argument to be made is, why does the abnormal child need to be identified? If the focus of research is on the individual, and practitioner advice is also aimed at the individual, then is it not just a matter of observing his or her needs? Or is the focus on the normal, universal, easy-to-generalise child a reaction to admitting that understanding the complexity of childhood experience is such an unattainable goal that the best that can be done is to provide vague averages? These comments should not detract from the exceptional work done to try to understand childhood; they merely aim to provide a focus for debate. It is the continuation of this debate that will allow us to use the theories of the past and present to move towards a clearer understanding of child development.

Conclusion

This chapter does not aim to provide a summary of the major theories of child development; there are many other excellent texts that give far more detail than this chapter is able to. The function of this piece has been to provide a framework to consider the issues that surround the study of the complex and ever-changing processes involved in child development. The ground-breaking work of the likes of Piaget, Freud and Bowlby contains a huge theoretical resource, and knowledge of these would be no bad thing, but the modern student needs to go one step beyond simply knowing what he or she 'found out'. To do this it is essential to question where the theory came from and to evaluate how it can be applied to the child of today. It is hoped that by highlighting the debates concerning the nature of childhood this process has been initiated. Surely this is a fundamental position to take, for unless we have a clear (or even a basic!) understanding of a child's experience then the value of any theory is questionable.

The arrival of psychology as a new discipline of study coincided with a period of considerable social, economic and intellectual change and this placed it in the unique position to initiate studies of children that have influenced much of the research discussed in this chapter. The role of psychology as the dominant discourse within child development has also been analysed, as within this subject area there are many assumptions about the nature of childhood and developmental processes that require consideration. It is not an unreasonable assumption to make that findings from this research base will be used to determine how we treat young people, and it is therefore important to deal with the issues they raise. Do we view children as victims of their genes and so provide little extra assistance, or do we regard the influence of the environment as more important, and so justify intervening action? If the influence of environmental factors can overcome a genetic disposition, how should this effect the development of early years policy? If development is a continuous process or one characterised by periods of relative inactivity, would this influence the timing or process of beginning to teach children to read? The issue of objectively based research highlights many issues for early years professionals who are well acquainted with the individualistic and subjective behaviours of the children in their care. If Piaget attempted to remove subjectivity from his research methodology then are these findings going to be ones you would like to see promoted in your workplace? The final comment can be brief and to the point: there are no simple solutions to understanding child development, but take the knowledge that has been provided 'down the years', evaluate this and apply it to your experience, and do not be scared to question the big names.

Questions for reflection

1. Not all early years professionals study child development in any depth. According to their original professional background, their studies emphasise particular aspects. Is it important that they should study the child development holistically? What is your own experience?

2. What are your personal beliefs about how children develop? What have you already learned from a study of child development? What else do you think you need to explore and how can you do this within your role as an early years professional?

3. In reflecting on what you know about child development, how does your current knowledge impact upon your everyday practice? How do you balance the needs of the individual and the group in response to the comments in this chapter?

References

Aries, P. (1962) *Centuries of Childhood: A Social History of Family Life*. London: Penguin.

Bruner, J. (1990) *Acts of Meaning*. Cambridge, MA: Harvard University Press.

Gesell, A. and Thompson, H. (1929) 'Learning and growth in identical infant twins: an experimental study by the method of co-twin control'. *Genetic Monographs*, **6**, 1–24.

James, A. and Prout, A. (eds) (1997) *Constructing and Reconstructing Childhood: Contemporary Issues in the Sociological Study of Childhood*. London: Falmer.

Postman, N. (1983) *The Disappearance of Childhood*. London: W.H. Allen.

Walkerdine, V. (2004) 'Developmental psychology and the study of childhood', in M. J. Kehily (ed.) *An Introduction to Childhood Studies*. Maidenhead: Open University Press.

5

Children's learning

Alan Bainbridge

CHILDREN'S LEARNING IS an enormous topic and has been well studied and documented for many years. Ironically, rather than the picture becoming clearer, it now seems more confused than ever. As we endeavour to gain more insight into the process of children's learning, what becomes apparent is the complexity of the situation and this complexity only serves to create distractions in our thinking, to an extent that at times it is difficult to really know what it is that we are sure about. The focus of this chapter is to provide a means of thinking about the learning events that young children are involved in. By the end of it you will not have an in-depth knowledge of all the major theories; instead, you should have a number of academic 'hooks' to inform your own debates on children's learning.

It is expected that we all, at some stage, become independent, rational adults who are capable of looking after ourselves. This will involve obtaining a suitable job, maintaining a healthy lifestyle and developing happy and secure relationships. To a greater extent, this is fortunate, as we humans seem to be very good at this. Over the millennia we have been able to adapt to the many physical and social changes that have occurred. Part of what it is to be human is to do with the ability of our species to survive the changing nature of our environment, and this has happened due to the ability to learn. Humans are very good at learning, and if this were not the case our dominance as a species may not have endured. The mature, rational and independent adult is one who has learned to cope with the world he or she is living in and the significant issues that have to be addressed are those related to how this process is initiated and sustained. Without attempting to provide an all-encompassing definition of learning, it is fair to say that learning is linked to bringing about change, or at least coping with change. As this chapter progresses it will be seen that this change can manifest itself in a variety of ways in many different environments and situations and not just in what are normally regarded as traditional learning environments, such as a school or playgroup. This chapter will first consider learning as adapting to a changing environment and then review four theoretical concepts that provide an insight into how learning may be understood. These four areas shall be: biological processes, which consider the role of genetic make-up and the structure and function of the brain; environmental influences, that take into account how an individual's responses can be manipulated by external stimuli; constructivist theory, such as Piaget's views of staged development; and the role of culture and context, which will emphasise the importance of considering the society and culture on the learning experience.

Adapting to change

Young children begin to learn very quickly. From the moment they are born they respond to sounds and faces and begin to develop patterns of activity related to those around them. The very young child who cries to be fed will soon make the association between the feelings of hunger and the comforting and satisfying arrival of the mother. The cries of hunger do not persist after being picked up, as the child has learned to associate the sound, touch and smell of the mother or father with the imminent arrival of food. This mental link has been made and a change in behaviour has occurred as the child is adapting or learning to survive in this new world. Over the next few months there will be evidence of a greater degree of control of behaviours to provide certain effects as the young child learns to have an impact on his or her surroundings. Young children will make noises or pull faces to get a response from others around them and gain pleasure from pushing or pulling toys. This new world is being explored, and from the feedback, behaviours are being adapted to allow the experience to be a far more pleasant one. The child has yet to open a maths book or do a spelling bee but he or she is nevertheless actively learning and beginning the journey to becoming an independent adult.

Wood (2002) makes a clear distinction between two main types of learning encounter: one is similar to that outlined above, where learning events occur in an informal and often social context, and as such we may often be unaware that learning has taken place; the other he regards as 'contrived encounters' (p.16), and these are the occasions that we would more regularly regard as learning. These take place in schools and are linked to educational objectives and outcomes. What is important in our debate is that we open our minds to the widest view of what learning is and where it takes place and attempt to locate learning in an understanding of the whole child, not just the pupil or the child in society. These two views place learning within certain situations or environments, yet we can also consider the type of learning that takes place, as learning to stop crying just before being fed may not necessarily be the same process as multiplying two numbers together. Although not intended as an exhaustive list, learning could be viewed as: the accumulation of knowledge or generally accepted truths, such as when young children learn to name and identify animals and can put things into categories; the development of skills to enable processes such as dressing, talking or turn-taking; and more abstract concepts such a respect for others and the appreciation of stories or songs.

Another major consideration for a discussion of children's learning is that of the role of language as it allows a richness of communication that facilitates the ability to think and reason. Language will also be seen to be fundamental in understanding the role of society and culture in learning, as it provides the mechanism for the transfer of ideas and values. Whether learning is to be considered in a school setting or home environment, conversation between the adult (teacher) and the child (learner) is the normal mode of information transfer. The ability for humans to learn within complex social, cognitive and abstract situations, and for these to be transmitted to others, is unique within the animal kingdom and language as a means of communication is thought to be responsible for this. One way to deal with the complexity of these learning situations is to identify the ways in which the changes in behaviour can be explained. Each one of these approaches provides some level of insight but none is seen to provide the complete picture. The conceptual areas used to discuss the complexity of learning – how changes in behaviour are brought about – are: biological processes; environmental influences; constructivist theory; and the role of culture and context.

Biological processes

The biological perspective provides a view of the child that is linked to an understanding of the physical development of the brain and how this may have been influenced by genetic factors and findings from a relatively new discipline of neuroscience. The explanation of behaviour is very mechanistic and has given rise to an area of understanding known as information processing. The brain of the child rapidly develops in size (about 400 grammes at birth, 700 grammes at six months and to over 1 kilogramme by two years) and complexity in the first years of life and it is thought that this mirrors, or is mirrored by, changes in behaviour. Very early behaviours such as sucking and crying are thought to be controlled by reflexes. This means that the reaction is controlled by the brain stem and not the larger brain structures. Children with severe brain damage may still carry out sucking and crying behaviours yet not develop, if at all, much beyond these. More complex behaviours are observed at about the same time as the brain becomes larger and more intricate. As the brain develops, the individual nerves (neurones) within it make close connections, synapses, with other neurones and it is this increased number of neural connections that is said to enable more complex behaviours to be exhibited. Normal development of the structures of the brain could be controlled by the genes and therefore will always follow a particular pattern; or alternatively, it may be that the brain is dependent on environmental influences to trigger certain neural links. Such views could explain why certain behaviours appear to be present in most individuals from birth, and yet others, such as when the child stops crying when picked up, need to be experienced to be learned.

The increased understanding of the structure of the brain occurred at about the same time that computer technology was developing and the effect of the two was to provide an explanation of human behaviour in terms of information processing. The brain was seen to have specialised areas of activity and computers were programmed by using logical sequences of instructions, and so the information processing perspective of human behaviour attempted to model events within the brain into logical sequences to provide an explanation for behaviour. Human behaviour was understood by considering structures that processed information, and the usual way this was done involved the store model. The store model had three main parts: a sensory register; a working memory and a long-term memory. The sensory register operates like a memory that briefly stores incoming sensory information, such as sound and images. Once aware of this input it is passed on to the working memory. At this point 'thinking' occurs and information is held here for up to about thirty seconds. This area only has a limited capacity and cannot hold much more than seven pieces of information (try to recall a series of seven words, letters or numbers). The arrival of new information will 'push out' the information presently being processed; it is forgotten, and the important aspect here is that there is a limited capacity as to how much can be held and dealt with at any one time. Individuals are thought to develop various strategies, such as chunking, where letters or numbers can be combined. This is probably how we remember phone numbers: 135792468 becomes 135 792 468. After 30 seconds the sensory input is either lost or passed on to the long-term memory, where it is suggested that information is added to the body of permanent knowledge. The link with brain structure suggests that this long-term memory stores information for permanent recall. It does so due to the forming of neural connections and networks.

The biological and information processing perspectives of understanding how changes in behaviour can be brought about provide a number of issues for debating children's learning. The general notion is one of determinism where behaviour develops in response to maturational processes from within the brain and this may incline some to view the prospects of children's learning as fixed. It would be possible from this viewpoint to argue that learning experiences should be limited, as in the early years more intricate learning situations may be out of sequence with the number of neural connections required to cope with this level of complexity – learning needs to be matched to our knowledge of brain development. I can also see the case for arguing that learning environments for young children need to be as play-based as possible and far removed from formalised learning, as these would be the conditions most children would expect to find themselves in, rather than some contrived encounter. The information processing focus on the capacity of the various stages may encourage us to question how much new information to provide young people with and to consider the length of time required on a task before new information is provided. The very busy sessions with lots of competing sensory inputs may present an environment that simply cognitively overloads children and causes anxiety. The process does suggest that new skills or knowledge can be placed in an area for permanent recall (and we can question if this is learning) if neural connections are made. Therefore the more opportunities to make connections in a variety of ways, the more likely it will be that information has been permanently stored. The information processing perspective suggests that this 'laying down' of information is thinking, and the greater the number of neural connections, the easier recall will be. In this situation practice, repetition and training are all suitable methods to change behaviour or encourage learning.

It is not too difficult to see how a biological understanding of learning can be applied to young children, but this must be done with some caution. Neuroscience is still very much a young discipline and the application of its findings to education still requires more evaluation. For example, the brain is far more 'plastic' than the theories suggest and victims of brain damage often do not completely lose an ability, particularly young children, which would question the clear-cut idea of learning linked to neural connections. More complex types of learning related to abstract thinking and language acquisition are difficult to explain using these theories, although Chomsky does suggest that humans possess a defined area of the brain that is responsive to language. Whatever our views, biological explanations provide a useful way to conceptualise learning.

Environmental influences

In the introduction to this chapter it was suggested that because humans have survived and have had a considerable impact on the planet, they are good at learning. The inference is that humans have adapted and responded successfully to the environment around them and so learning is associated with responding to demands placed on the individual by the environment. This is a very passive view for it assumes that humans are waiting for a change to the surrounding environmental conditions before they respond with a change in their behaviour. One of the reasons for the success of mankind could be that humans possess the ability to be proactive, that is, to deal with an issue before it arises. However we decide to look at the relationship between man and the environment, what is clear is that there is a connection between the two. For example, there is a suggestion that our behaviour is influenced by the seasons and in some people with Seasonal Affective Disorder this can create problems. The previous section on information processing discussed the influence of neural connections in learning and suggested that these may be influenced both by genetic predisposition and also by the environment. This interplay between human behaviour and the environment, between genetic predisposition and experience, is thought to provide the mechanism for our gradual increase in learning and the ability to learn more. We are successful because we have become adapted to our environmental conditions, and the inherent reflexes that are present from birth have been matched and co-ordinated to provide appropriate and successful responses. The child has learned when to cry and when to suck in such a way that its needs are met.

At the turn of the twentieth century, Freud's theories on the mind were becoming dominant and although he claimed his psychoanalytical theories were based on scientific principles, many found them too vague. As a result they were not open to the normal scrutiny within the academic community. What began to emerge was a body of knowledge that attempted to understand human behaviour in a more scientific and reductionist manner. This area of study was to become known as behaviourism and had philosophical links to the ideas of John Locke, who eschewed the notion of the child as a *tabula rasa*, as an empty vessel waiting to be filled up with knowledge from the experiences presented to it by helpful adults. Much of the work carried out was related to changing the behaviour of people, especially young children, and was also often referred to simply as 'learning theory'. Three behaviourist areas of learning theory are discussed here: classical conditioning; operant conditioning and social learning theory. These areas all deal with associative learning experiences where a stimulus, real or perceived, is connected to a response that is responsible for a change in behaviour.

The Russian scientist Pavlov carried out research on the reflexes responsible for salivation in dogs and he noticed that some dogs, the older ones, would be salivating as their keepers were bringing them their food. The younger dogs would only start to salivate as the food was presented. What Pavlov attempted to show from this observation was how two stimuli could be associated to cause a certain response. He famously started to present food alongside a ringing bell. After a while, the sound of the bell alone would initiate salivation in the dogs. This was called classical conditioning as the dogs' behaviour had been conditioned or changed. What Pavlov also noted was that if the food was not presented with the bell, the conditioned behaviour, salivating, soon disappeared. The learned behaviour in this example has been developed from an existing reflex response (salivating in the presence of food) to produce the same response in relation to an inappropriate stimulus (the bell) that has then rapidly been 'forgotten' once the bell fails to indicate the arrival of food. This technique of changing behaviour was taken up by Watson who conditioned a nine-month-old baby to fear a neutral stimulus (a cuddly rat) by associating it with a loud clanging sound. These findings led the way for further investigation into the links between stimulus and response, and learning in humans.

Pavlov provided a link between a stimulus and reward but Skinner devised a process of operant conditioning where the animal (often a rat) had to do something before being rewarded. This most regularly involved a rat pressing a lever and then receiving a reward, so in this case the rat's behaviour led to the reward. It was due to an operation it had carried out; hence operant conditioning. Like Pavlov, Skinner also found that new behaviours could be taught rapidly but in this case the new behaviour could be made to last longer by not always providing a reward. Skinner suggested that continuous reward was not as effective as a variable reward. Despite the research focus being based on animals, these two theories have often been applied to the learning of young people and it is also worth noting that young children can be conditioned in similar ways described by Pavlov and Skinner. The major criticism of these approaches relates to the use of animals, extrapolating these findings to a human population, and then to the inability to consider the complex nature of learning.

Associative learning may have applications to learning related to knowledge and skills development but, as with information processing views of learning, it is difficult to consider how abstract thought or language could be developed by these means. They do provide some advantages, though, and this is the desire to be more scientific, to look for valid and reliable methodologies and also to try to highlight some of the features that may be involved with learning. The role of affect on learning has not been considered as this would be regarded as subjective and not suitable for scientific study, and certainly not a factor for animal investigations.

The next theorist to be considered is Albert Bandura who attempted to use behaviourist theories within a real-world context that took the individual's thoughts and feelings into account. Bandura proposed the theory of social learning where the stimulus and reward operate in a social environment. New behaviours occur as a result of modelling the behaviour of others. Bandura claimed that young people will observe and imitate others; they did not have to receive a reward themselves but could simply see others obtain some sort of recognition for their behaviour, and young children were more to likely imitate adults, especially those of the same gender. Social learning theory offers advantages over classical and operant conditioning by simply acknowledging the role of a social world in learning and not as a simple, biological, reflex-driven event, and as such is far more closely linked to a real learning situation. The influence of role models on learning can be accounted for, whether these are good or bad, and certainly young children in a nursery environment spend a lot of time observing others before they carry out a new action. This theory offers far more contextual insight into learning and Bandura has recently begun to review this theory by suggesting that cognition has a far greater role to play. Children are thought to be more analytical and evaluative about modelling than had previously been thought, and new behaviours are not just copied from others.

The seemingly harsh views of the classical and operant conditioners are often disregarded in academic debate as not applicable to young children, but many practitioners will be only too familiar with the use of rewards to control or shape children's behaviour. What may be more pertinent is not simply how we can change behaviour but how long this may last and, taking a lead from Bandura, how this relates to a real social world that assumes children are thinking about learning.

Constructivist theory

The previous two theoretical areas regarded the child learner as a passive subject as the learning events happened to him or her, either as a result of biological maturation that enhanced information processing ability or as a mechanistic response to stimuli received from the environment. Constructivist theories consider the child to be an active participant in the learning process and therefore this presents a very different perspective of children's learning. By far the most famous proponent of constructivist theories of learning is Jean Piaget, a Swiss biologist who investigated the link between the development of knowledge and logical thought. Despite the fact that most of his work was carried out and published in the 1940s, it was not until the 1960s that his theories began to have a huge impact on educational practices. By this time there was growing unease with both the dominant biological theories that failed to take the role of the environment into account and the environmental learning theories that rejected the active child's role in learning. Piaget's ideas, based on many hours of careful observation of children, were able to provide a new insight into learning that would have an impact that lasts until this day. This influence is especially noticeable within child-centred education, particularly linked to the importance of play in the early years.

Piaget observed that children actively acquired, or constructed, knowledge by interacting with the external environment through a process of discovery and control as they were intrinsically motivated to explore the world around them, and would engage in self-directed problem-solving. This understanding of the world by constructing knowledge begins for the individual at the moment of birth via simple reflex responses through the development of more complex thought processes. His observations also led him to suggest that cognitive development took place in clear and definable stages that were closely linked to age. The two stages of most concern to the early years professional are the sensorimotor (between birth and 2) and pre-operational (between 2 and 6) stages which shall be discussed later.

One of the significant contributions made by Piaget was how he theorised the acquisition of knowledge, and the use this made of the existing biological and environmental learning theories. Knowledge is organised in the mind as schema. These are mental structures, or ways of thinking, that can be applied to similar situations. Very early schemas would be based on reflexes such as sucking or crying. Then as the child matures and the brain becomes more complex the schema must be modified to meet the needs of the ever-changing external environment. Piaget referred to this modification of the schema as adaptation, a term clearly taken from his biological background. The old schema would only work successfully for the environment in which it was originally constructed; when this changed, the schema had to be adapted to suit the new requirements, and this occurs by the processes of accommodation, assimilation and equilibration. The route to a newly constructed schema involves new knowledge or information being mentally taken in, and when this is incorporated into the existing schema assimilation is said to have occurred, after which the old schema must be modified to account for the new and old experiences. This is accommodation. The child actively investigating the external world will move between new and old schemas to find a mental structure that works, and Piaget referred to this as equilibration. Adaptation is therefore an active process controlled by the child to make sense of the world.

Piaget observed that children's intellectual abilities appeared to be similar within age-defined stages and this led to the opinion that certain learning events could only occur within these critical periods. The two stages of interest to the early years professional are the sensorimotor and pre-operational stages. The sensorimotor child uses sensory perceptions to interact with the external world that include activities such as sucking and using images and words to represent the external world. The pre-operational child can acknowledge the existence of an object or event, even if it is not present. He or she confuses appearance and reality – for example, wearing a mask causes the person to change. The child is also unable to conserve physical properties, which results in the child not being able to recognise that if an object's physical shape is changed, the quantity that remains may not. An example of this would be transforming a big ball of clay into many smaller balls which the pre-operational child would perceive as being a larger amount of clay. There are many such findings within Piaget's work and the detail of the stages is sufficient for each to have its own chapter. Our function is not to look at the fine details but rather to provide a focus for reflection.

Piaget's work has been published for many years now and has attracted a substantial body of criticism. Penn (2005) claims that his theories now belong to history, yet such has been their impact that they must still be addressed. Much of the focus for the criticism has been based on the methodology of Piaget's work and, for some, simply the attempt to look at childhood experience through a cold, objective scientific gaze was unsatisfactory and fails to reflect the complexity of learning. The use of clinical interviews as the main experimental technique relies heavily on verbal instruction and contrived scenarios set up to be discussed between adult and child. When more child-friendly language (Samuel and Bryant 1984) or tasks (Donaldson 1978) were used, researchers found children to be far more capable than Piaget suggested. The general criticism is that children were being expected to show their abilities in situations that were too far removed from their own social experience. Studies such as these have suggested that the stages are not as fixed as Piaget would claim and may in fact show development to be stage-like, simply as the measures of children's developmental abilities were taken between long periods of time.

This argument is reminiscent of being greeted by a relative whom you have not seen for some time. They see you as having 'suddenly grown', yet your own family have failed to notice. The theoretical concerns are related to three issues: the vague nature of the concepts involved in adaptation; the emphasis on intellect more than affect; and viewing all cognitive functions within a similar model. The positive contribution of Piaget to understanding learning has been huge and the debate he has fuelled is indeed a worthy lasting legacy that has provided some of the most detailed observations of childhood development in recent times. As a theoretical perspective it can be applied to learning knowledge, processes and more abstract concepts, while also placing language as central to each of these.

Culture and context

Contextualist theories of learning and development share similarities with Piaget but differ fundamentally over the role of social influences and culture on this process. Both the constructivist and contextualist theories highlight the importance of the child acting on the environment and they also emphasise the role of biological mechanisms and experience on shaping learning. Piaget sees the child as learning from within as he or she interacts with the environment, enabling the production of schemas that help them to make sense of the world. The contextualist theory regards learning as taking place outside of the individual due to the influence of others from within that society; who, in turn, are influenced by the cultural values that have accumulated over time. This theory acknowledges the particularly unique role that social life plays in child development. Certainly the first reflexes of an infant are those attuned to communication, as babies will respond to faces and voices, especially their mothers'. During the early stages of care there are culturally agreed norms as to how to 'bring up' the child. For example, some years ago babies were left to cry when hungry, then they were fed on demand and now mothers are told to feed when it suits both mother and baby. The process of growing up will involve the negotiation of large numbers of socially accepted rituals that have developed historically and contextualist theorists would suggest that this also applies to learning. To learn in society is to gain the skills, attributes and knowledge that have been agreed as worthwhile. The knowledge that we decide to pass on has been validated by the test of time and so is constructed within that particular cultural framework.

The normal everyday activities and organised events of cultures are observed by the young members as they develop, and in doing so they gain the contextualist version of schemas. These are scripts. The scripts are mental ways of representing events and highlight the role of self and others within these and so they begin to act like guides for social interaction. As the developing child experiences the outside world the scripts provide an internal model of what they and others should do; as more experience is gained these scripts are revised to suit the new conditions.

Piaget's schemas involve the lone learner, but in this context the learner is socially constructing knowledge, and proponents of this theory would claim that this is how learning takes place – as a socially constructed activity that involves the input of others, who we may decide to call teachers. The most influential theorist to support such views is Vygotsky. He was writing and researching at about the same time as Piaget and indeed the two would correspond, but for mainly political reasons his work was only translated in the early 1960s and his ideas only began to gain influence since the 1970s.

Vygotsky was mainly interested in the evolution and transmission of culture and endeavoured to provide a theory for human consciousness, or the activity of the mind, which led him to consider educational issues. While working with children with learning difficulties he demonstrated that it was possible to teach them to perform well beyond the level that would be expected of them if they had carried out the task alone. This was crucial for Vygotsky, as he claimed that knowing what a child was capable of when working alone was simply a measurement of what they had achieved and not what he or she could achieve. For children to reach the level of which they were capable, they needed to be guided by other individuals who had already reached that level. The term for this process has now become as famous as any of Piaget's concepts. Vygotsky referred to this process of achieving at a higher level, due to the assistance of another, as moving through the Zone of Proximal (or next) Development. It is the involvement of the other person that is significant, as they are able to guide the child and suggest ways that the task can be completed. This guidance is based on culturally bound communication that transmits what is the acceptable and correct way. The child will have been guided through a thought process that is embedded in the culture by the meanings of the words the language uses. To put this very simply, the process of making a cup of tea in London will not be the same as making tea in Beijing. The words used and the actions taken will be specific to each culture.

For the social constructivist, the child is a novice who needs to be guided from what he or she already knows towards understanding socially constructed concepts by the continued and intentional instruction towards accepted norms. It is this instruction that lies at the heart of learning and it is the use of language within this that distinguishes contextualist theories from the others covered so far. Vygotsky also indicated that play was an important feature in a child's learning, as he noticed that during play children tend to 'become' older, that is they play out roles of adults, or certainly play at a level that is beyond them. During this time children talk to themselves and each other and imagine future roles that enable them to anticipate future possibilities, but all the time within the accepted social norms. The views of Vygotsky have provided a valuable antidote to the dominant Piagetian position and have allowed the social child to have an influence on our understanding of learning. The contextualists have provided a theoretical framework for many of the 'new' theories of learning, such as scaffolding, reciprocal teaching and co-operative learning. The comparatively short time during which Vygotsky's theories have received attention has limited their amount of critical analysis compared with the other learning theories covered here, and at present these views are certainly in the ascendancy. A regular criticism is the almost complete focus on social aspects of learning, despite Vygotsky claiming that learning has a biological basis. The concept of learning provided by Vygotsky is complex and takes into account the abstract and culturally based features of learning, particularly how language plays a role in developing the minds of young children.

Conclusion

Each of the approaches to understanding a child's learning that has been presented provides valuable insight into what is certainly a very complicated process. Learning takes place all the time and not just in the contrived places of education, but whatever theory we feel helps to explain this process, it needs to be one that can account for the learning events – in the playground, around the dinner table and in the classroom. The human condition can be defined by our unique ability to not only learn but also to be able to control the learning situation. Individuals who successfully navigate the learning process will clearly be at an advantage in the near and distant future compared with those who find this more challenging. If we seek to enable children to maximise their potential and opportunities then it is essential that our understanding of how their learning takes place is based soundly in theory.

Questions for reflection

1. Think back to your own early childhood and discuss the situations in which you consider your learning was most effective. What sort of experiences were these and how, as an early years professional, could you ensure that the children in your care have similar, rich opportunities?

2. How important is it that early years professionals, whatever their original professional backgrounds, understand how children develop? What happens if we have no, or only partial, understanding of these theories?

3. How does your knowledge of how children learn impact upon your practice as an early years professional, especially how you organise your provision or programme to meet the needs of children?

References

Donaldson, M. (1978) *Children's Minds*. London: Fontana.

Penn, H. (2005) *Understanding Early Childhood: Issues and Controversies*. Maidenhead: Open University Press.

Samuel, J. and Bryant, P. (1984) 'Asking only one question in the conversation experiment'. *Journal of Child Psychology and Psychiatry*, **25**, 315–18.

Wood, D. (2002) *How Children Learn and Think: The Social Contexts of Cognitive Development*. Oxford: Blackwell.

Children learning: a practical point of view

Pamela May

The links between theory and practice

OFTEN WHEN STUDENTS have visited an early years setting I ask them what they have seen. When we have listed the sand and water play, the home corner and the outside area, and all the recognisable areas of learning, we go on to consider what the children and adults are doing. A rich debate usually follows as answers are sought to questions such as 'Why is there a home corner in the nursery?' 'Why are the children moving around and playing so much more than at key stage one?' 'How can the adults plan and assess this busy place?'

The answers to these and similar questions are to be found in educational theory. Yet most research into practitioners' beliefs finds that there is a gap between what they think they do and what they actually do. One example of this gap between rhetoric and reality would be the claim that practitioners believe in active learning and yet their children are required to sit on the carpet for long periods of time. Practitioners may say that they believe that children learn best independently, yet they provide only ready-mixed paints that restrict children's opportunities to experiment with colour. The rhetoric that is used to explain practice is often very different from what actually happens to children.

Educational theory, which is taught as part of practitioner training both at NVQ level 3 and at QTS level, seems often to be a case of what Stones (1984) calls 'galloping through the gurus' with little regard for how the gurus' work has impacted on current practice. Adults working in settings will often say that they are too busy doing the job to consider deeply what lies behind the daily routine. They teach the way they do 'because it works' or 'because of the school policy' or 'because of the Foundation Stage requirements', rather than because research and theory suggest that children learn best in particular ways. The reason that this is said is that it is only research and theory that give a sound basis for effective practice. Robust research provides evidence that holds firm among the changing opinions of governments and other agencies who are in positions of power. Basing teaching on a secure foundation of evidence gives practitioners confidence that they know why they teach in certain ways and helps them to be articulate to parents, colleagues and trainees.

Educational theory, like every other form of human activity, evolves over time and is influenced by a range of factors. The perceptions and interests of the individual theorists, the contextual situation of politics and culture and the image of the child and childhood all have an influence on thinking. Often when a theory is suggested, it is challenged and a lively debate follows, demonstrating that theory is not static. However, some certainties underpin the ways in which most teachers teach. To arrive at these certainties and to answer questions such as 'Why do we have sand and water in nurseries?' it is helpful to consider a brief history of the educational theories that have been pivotal in influencing practice in early years settings.

In Table 6.1, a range of theorists are linked to their key beliefs and then to the implications that these beliefs have had for which activities and provision are available in settings, and how they might be used. To a greater or lesser extent all these theories have regard to children's developmental progress and the assumption is that effective teaching will link with the level of development that the child has reached.

The theory of constructivism was one of Jean Piaget's major tenets and centred on the idea of a child actively and personally making sense of his or her world. This came to influence what was offered in settings. Although Piaget was a biologist and not an educationalist, his experiments and research on several aspects of children's development became the basis of what is currently thought of as 'good practice'. His key beliefs can be summarised as follows:

- Knowledge does not originate in innate programming, neither do external influences predominate. Each child constructs his or her own unique view of the world from his or her experience of it.

- All children, irrespective of culture, interpret information from their experiences from birth.

- Children are active agents in their own learning and they use both their innate capabilities and their experiences to interpret the world around them.

- Conceptual growth occurs by a process of gathering new information and *assimilating* it into existing knowledge. Sometimes a child needs to change what he or she believes to allow the new knowledge to fit with his or her understanding. This is known as *accommodation*. When this process is complete we say that *adaptation* has taken place.

- The child moves through several stages of development that are known as the *sensory-motor*, the *pre-operational* and the *formal-operational* stages. Culture and environment may affect the age of transfer through these stages but the sequence is universal and linear.

TABLE 6.1 Summary of developmental theories

	Maturationism	Behaviorism	Psycho-dynamic theory	Constructivist theory I	Constructivist theory II
Key theorist	G. Stanley Hall Arnold Gesell Frances Ilg	Ivan Pavlov John Watson Edward L. Thorndike B. F. Skinner	Sigmund Freud Erik Erikson	Jean Piaget	L. S. Vygotsky Jerome Bruner
Key ideas	Development is the unfolding of genetically determined traits.	Development is the result of environmental influences. Operant conditioning: Reinforcement Learning is based on prerequisite knowledge.	Influence of the early years on mature personality Importance of mental health in early childhood Psychosexual stages Psychosocial stages	Stages of cognitive development Assimilation + Accommodation = Equilibrium (self-regulation) Importance of play for cognitive development	Cognitive development + natural development + cultural development Zone of proximal development Cultural tools
Curriculum implications	Readiness Developmentally appropriate practices	Task analysis Identifying prior knowledge Teaching complex tasks in small steps (simplifying) Reinforcement	Art, music as forms of expression for young children Play as a form of expression for young children	Teaching to the stages (readiness; developmentally appropriate practice) Hands-on learning activities for young children	Teaching cultural content Teaching beyond children's development level Scaffolding

The implication of Piaget's theories

It is with these theories in mind that we can begin to see why there is so much emphasis on activity, such as the sand and water trays, in early years settings. If children are thought to learn through first-hand experience (Piaget likened the exploring child to 'the lone scientist') there must be interesting things for them to engage with. Activity must be offered at a level that is appropriate for children, although Piaget's view that children could not be moved on in their learning until a 'readiness' to progress had been reached has long been disputed. The 1960s was full of infant classrooms with 'pre-readers' who were not given books to read as they were not deemed to have reached the stage of readiness to begin reading. I remember, as a young teacher, issuing these unfortunate children with tobacco tins full of tiny flash cards instead, which had to be learned before a reading book was offered. The fact that many of these children were experiencing books at home was not thought of as having any significance at all in the days when it was considered that children came to school knowing very little.

Piaget's stage model of development can be thought of as 'intellectual milestones' and can help practitioners to match the curriculum to the levels of thought and understanding a child has reached. In practical terms, this means that planning for teaching a concept such as distance needs to be varied to match children's different thought forms. Teaching this concept at the Foundation Stage would consist of a range of activities and provision, of rolling and throwing games, of songs, of building tracks and roads, of introducing the vocabulary of 'long and short', 'far and near', and of noting the distances covered first in non-standard and then standard measures. Differentiating teaching by type of task, by the level of support or by the end-product are all recognised ways to ensure this match.

Piaget's theory of 'readiness' states that if children's progress through stages of development could not be influenced, the role of the teacher was purely one of installing a suitable environment and then observing and recording the children's activity. This view has been challenged as the view of the adult's role as central to learning has been emphasised. The notion of stages of development being, invariably, linear led to an ideology of negativity. Instead of building on what children can do, Piaget's stages theory tended to emphasise what children cannot yet do. He likened it to a brick wall, each layer needing to be firmly cemented in place before the next layer could be added.

Despite the refuting of many of Piaget's ideas, it is to him that we owe the basic theory of children as constructors of their own knowledge, which is quite fundamental to traditional practice. His idea of the brain working rather like a 'cognitive jigsaw', with children constantly trying to fit pieces together so that they make sense, is clear to anyone who knows young children and has experienced them asking questions constantly, Very young children can be heard suggesting that the sun goes to bed at night because that is what happens to them, and they are, as yet, developmentally tied into an egocentric way of thinking. These rather endearing misconstructions of knowledge are due, we now believe, not to children's inferior levels of intelligence but to their lack of experience.

Some Vygotskian theories

Vygotsky's research was founded on Piaget's observations of these stages of development. Although Piaget had identified children's *actual* levels of development, it was on the level just beyond what they knew and could do that Vygotsky's interest lay. He found that children differed in their ability to learn new concepts and to grasp new ideas if help was given by a more experienced child or an adult. If this 'expert other' provided what is often called the 'apprenticeship approach', offering less help as the learner becomes more experienced, the learner will acquire new knowledge more quickly and effectively than if he or she learn alone. What the child can do on their own he named the 'zone of actual development', and what he or she could do with the assistance of the expert other he named the 'zone of proximal development'.

This research had huge implications for the role of early years teachers who began to move away from the Piagetian *laissez-faire* approach of providing for, observing and recording children's progress, to an active role of supporting children's efforts to learn new knowledge.

It was at this point of endeavour, just beyond what children had understood, that Vygotsky suggested teachers should concentrate their efforts. He believed that children learned through teachers' 'instruction', which he defined as demonstration, asking leading questions, responding to children's questions and offering peer group support. This view accords well with current research, which suggests that a 'learning journey', or co-construction of knowledge undertaken by the learner and the teacher, is the most successful way of securely understanding new knowledge.

One of Vygotsky's other significant contributions to this debate was the role of language and communication as tools for learning. Whereas Piaget considered language as external evidence of what children knew, Vygotsky saw language as a mechanism by which thought was processed in the mind. Communication was an intrinsic element of learning and, far from Piaget's view of the learner being isolated (or 'a lone scientist'), Vygotsky saw learning essentially as a social activity, with learners watching and asking questions and teachers supporting and extending the child in his or her zone of proximal development to move him or her into his or her new zone of actual development.

Jerome Bruner and children's learning

Jerome Bruner (1986) was much influenced by the work of Vygotsky and understood learning as 'a communal activity, a sharing of the culture' (p. 127). He defined instruction as 'an attempt to shape intellectual growth' (Bruner 1966) by negotiation and sharing between teachers and learners. Children's learning was totally reliant on their interactions with others and their learning was innately focused on making sense of their world. Bruner and Vygotsky understood that there is order and logic in the ways in which people act and behave and it is of critical importance that they learn about these social systems if they are to function successfully. Bruner believed that children's innate initiative means that they are constantly learning not necessarily what teachers are teaching them but what they themselves perceive as important to them for survival in a social world.

Bruner felt that Piaget's theory of stages of development limited children's learning if it was assumed that children could only be taught at a level they had already reached. He suggested that anything could be taught 'in some intellectually honest form' to any child at any stage of development. In practical terms this freed teachers to take up the professional challenge of making new knowledge available to young children by teaching it in appropriate ways. Thus it built on what they already knew and took them into the zone of proximal development that Vygotsky had already defined. Significant learning did not have to wait until children were 'ready' but could be taught by sensitive and supportive adults.

Bruner used the notion of a 'spiral curriculum'. Instead of Piaget's linear description of learning by stages, Bruner believed that as children visit and revisit experiences they bring increasing knowledge and understanding to the experience until they have achieved mastery. Another way to describe this process would be by practising something. An implication of this theory is that equipment must be available to children consistently so that they can visit and revisit it at their increasing levels of competence.

Bruner suggests that there are three major different ways of representing new knowledge and that adults generally have access to all three of them. These are:

■ the enactive mode – through action;

■ the iconic mode – through visual imagery;

■ the symbolic mode – through words.

Children can be said to prefer to learn through the enactive mode as their ability to represent images and use symbols is less well developed. In this, Bruner agreed with Piaget that active, first-hand experiences are an appropriate way to present new knowledge to young children.

Theory into principles

The theorists that have been considered in this chapter are collectively known as 'constructivists' as they have the common belief that children construct their own understanding of their world. Their ideas build on and interlink with some of the greatest pioneers of early years education whose work with children has come to form the basis of what is known as the 'traditional' or 'kindergarten' type of education. Tina Bruce (1987) formalises the thinking of these pioneers into principles that define high-quality practice (Table 6.2). These principles range across the whole spectrum of children's learning, whereas the discussion above has concentrated primarily on children's cognitive development.

The responses quoted here were made by Lesley Grundy who as head teacher of an Oxford nursery school in the 1980s and 1990s, sat on the Committee of Inquiry funded by the DES. The principles are echoed in *Starting with Quality* (DES 1990) – or, as it is more popularly known, the Rumbold Report – by the statement:

> The educator of the under-fives must pay careful attention not just to the content of the child's learning but also to the way in which that learning is offered to and experienced by the child, and the role of all those involved in the process. Children are affected by the *context* in which learning takes place, the *people* involved in it and the *values and beliefs* which are embedded in it. (DES 1990:9)

Principles, then, become guidelines for teaching and these are based on evidence gathered from research. The responses that practitioners make to these principles will provide firm foundations for high-quality practice. As Sir Christopher Ball (1994) commented in his report to the Royal Society of Arts, 'quality of learning depends on a set of principles, not a favoured type of provision' (p. 59).

Learning from the pioneers

The reason that early years settings look the way they do is because of beliefs and principles. It was Maria Montessori who designed a miniature house for children (the 'Children's House'), complete with authentic tools for them to use when cooking and cleaning. It is also to her that we owe the traditional 'named drawer' for each child and the good-quality wooden toys and bricks that form the core of traditional nursery provision. Other pioneers, such as Rachel and Margaret McMillan, established 'open air' nursery schools. They believed that fresh air would halt the spread of TB and other infections that were rife in inner cities such as Bradford and London in the late nineteenth and early twentieth centuries. They concentrated particularly on providing a healthy environment for young children and considered young children's bodies and souls to be every bit as important as their minds. Thankfully, the outside area in early years settings is gradually regaining its rightful place at the heart of provision.

TABLE 6.2   Principles of early childhood (*Source*: after Bruce (1987), Chs 2, 3)

Principles	Response
Childhood is seen as valid in itself. It is a stage of life and not simply a preparation for the future.	Enrich the process of being a child.
The whole child is considered to be important; social, physical, intellectual, moral and spiritual aspects of development are related.	Consider all aspects of the child in planning our provision and interactions.
There is potential in all children that will emerge powerfully under favourable conditions. Each child is unique and special, with individual ways of learning.	Get to know each child. Have high expectations of all children, based on our knowledge of them. Support each child's developing self-esteem.
Learning takes place in a variety of settings. Home is the most powerful setting. We acknowledge parents as the first and continuing educators of their children.	Develop a partnership with parents – and carers – that is based on mutual respect and a shared interest in the child.
Learning is holistic and interconnected. For the young child, experience is not usually separated into different compartments.	Provide broadly based experiences that are rich contexts for learning, and which have real meaning for the child.
Young children learn through exploration, talk and play.	Provide an interesting, relevant environment and wide opportunities (people and places) in which children can be actively involved in their learning, i.e. in exploring, in talking, in playing.
Our starting points are what children *can* do, and what they can nearly do.	Help children to identify their own, and others', achievements. Provide a context that enables children to set their own targets. Support children in finding ways to achieve their own success.
Autonomy (physical, social and intellectual) and self-discipline are emphasised. Child-initiated activities and self-directed learning are valued.	Foster intrinsic motivation (i.e. curiosity and the innate drive to make sense of experience and to achieve control), through children's involvement in planning, making choices and decision-making.
The people – both adults and children – with whom the child interacts are of central importance.	Support children in working together. Develop their skills in supporting children's learning. Be aware of ourselves as models, and as partners in learning.
The children's education is seen as the total experience of, and interaction with, their environment.	Consider the implications of all aspects of the provision we are making, i.e. the choice and presentation of equipment and resources; the organisation of time and space in relation to equipment and resources; the relationships and interactions – between children, between staff, and between adults and children.

Susan Isaacs (1932) stated that, 'When we ask children not to move, we should have excellent reasons for doing so. It is the stillness we must justify, not the movement'. She studied children's cognitive development and encouraged their active discoveries in a nursery school environment. For her, the teacher is vital in the interpretation of the world. (The above statement should be incorporated on every planning sheet!)

These pioneers had in common the belief that children needed to engage with their world to interpret it and they understood that children's emotions formed a vital part of this process. The emotional and playful aspects of learning played a key part in the thinking of Friedrich Froebel and Jean-Jacques Rousseau, the philosophers who have had such a profound influence on modern educational theory. It is their understanding of childhood as valid in itself, of each child's unique and holistic development and of the importance of self-directed and social learning, that has given us the basis of the modern good practice.

Issues for today's educators

There are many dilemmas for today's trainees and practitioners who, during the course of their training, have understood the principles of traditional good practice, debated their own responses and look forward to putting them into practice. As discussed earlier in the chapter, reality is often far removed from rhetoric as settings struggle to maintain an environment that reflects their principles.

Research commissioned by the Association of Teachers and Lecturers in 2002/3 found that 'Everyday practice in classrooms does not appear to reflect adequately the principles of early childhood education' (ATL 2004). ATL constructed a framework of dimensions that show a huge variety of practice in the following areas:

- children's activities and behaviours;
- the educators' priorities, key constructs and activities;
- the learning environment and working conditions; and
- the conceptual structures of schooling.

This latter dimension, with its attention to practitioners' beliefs and understandings, would seem to set the scene for everything that follows in terms of children's early school experiences. As a set of bi-polar constructs, it starkly reminds us that all educational settings reflect the institution's perception of its purpose and intentions.

A study of these extremes provides an excellent starting point for self-evaluation for teams of professionals who are determined to hold fast to the principles they have studied.

One should ask, 'How has this come about?'. Why are such comprehensively articulated principles from such a widely respected range of philosophers, psychologists,

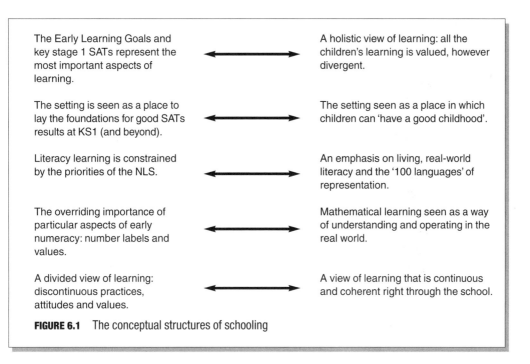

The Early Learning Goals and key stage 1 SATs represent the most important aspects of learning.	A holistic view of learning: all the children's learning is valued, however divergent.
The setting is seen as a place to lay the foundations for good SATs results at KS1 (and beyond).	The setting seen as a place in which children can 'have a good childhood'.
Literacy learning is constrained by the priorities of the NLS.	An emphasis on living, real-world literacy and the '100 languages' of representation.
The overriding importance of particular aspects of early numeracy: number labels and values.	Mathematical learning seen as a way of understanding and operating in the real world.
A divided view of learning: discontinuous practices, attitudes and values.	A view of learning that is continuous and coherent right through the school.

FIGURE 6.1   The conceptual structures of schooling

biologists and educators from the last 200 years so difficult to abide by in today's settings? The answer is, of course, multi-faceted and has much to do with the status and training of early years professionals. However, the overriding struggle has been the ideological one between the 'kindergarten' educationalists of the traditional kind (who espouse the values on the right of the table above), and those of the 'elementary' tradition who believe that schooling is about instruction in 'the basics', namely numeracy and literacy. In fact, so extreme did this trend become that when my early years PGCE SCITT was inspected by Ofsted in 1998, its remit was to inspect only 'number' and 'reading'; the narrowest aspects of Maths and English that it was possible to identify. This posed significant problems for trainees who were teaching holistically and yet had to provide standard lesson plans with these aspects highlighted. Young children's learning does not, of course, lend itself to this style of teaching and it became a huge challenge to hold fast to the principles of an integrated curriculum while achieving compliance at inspection.

How children learn

We know from educational theory, and from our own observations of young children, that they learn most effectively in certain ways. One of the most significant difficulties about teaching them in the formal ways advocated by the elementary, or 'skills and drills', tradition is that this approach is, plainly, ineffectual and potentially damaging. It is sad to see trainees who have learned about active learning still bemused when young children struggle at being told to sit for long periods of time on the carpet. We know that children learn by asking questions and by being active and we also know that by issuing the two commands, most often heard in classrooms, 'Sit down' and 'Be quiet', we are removing from children their two most basic means of finding out new knowledge. We can see that children engaged mainly in child-initiated learning with access to knowledgeable and sensitive adults will remain concentrating at a high level for long periods of time. Ferre Leavers described these children as looking like 'fish in water' as they use a stimulating environment in the same way that a scientist uses a laboratory or a craftsman uses a workshop. Csikszenlmihayli (1979) suggests that 'there is evidence to show that an "involved" child is gaining a deep, motivated, intense and long term experience'.

There seems no reasonable doubt, therefore, that the theorists were right and that the ways in which young children are taught do matter, and matter very much. It can be no coincidence that the levels of disaffection to education in schools is increasing and that a worrying number of children no longer believe that school learning is anything to do with them.

Contexts for children's learning

The issue of engaging children and engaging with children is central to effective teaching, and the Rumbold Report (1990) was right to claim that the *context* in which a child learns is every bit as significant as the body of knowledge being taught. Where should practitioners look to find contexts that best support children's learning? They would do well to look at children's homes, where children have already gathered many of the strategies they need to find out new knowledge and where the environment supports their preferred ways of learning. Here there are adults who answer questions rather than ask them. Theorists tell us that children learn what *they* want to know much more effectively than they learn what *teachers* want them to know. Families live in the real world of supermarkets, grandparents and paying the rent, rather than the school world of the Literacy Hour, lining-up and worksheets. This real-world context has meaning for children who can relate academic skills, such as reading, to environmental print, and writing to shopping lists, and this provides a purpose that makes sense to them. Thus learning is linked to intrinsic motivation, which is key to persistence and concentration. Families also love and care for their children. This provides the emotional element so vital to successful learning, and which is so powerful a motivator.

Children with a healthy self-image believe that they are successful and worthwhile people. These are the children who will persist, struggle and concentrate on learning because their life experience has taught them that there will be a successful and worthwhile outcome to their endeavours. Their families have encouraged and supported their curious enquiries and helped to create children with a secure sense of identity and an ability to value their achievements. Rosemary Roberts (1995) describes two children with high self-esteem; 'They knew what they wanted, and they went about the task with confidence, energy and enthusiasm'.

Sadly, however, this 'confidence, energy and enthusiasm' often ebbs when young children reach school. Schools are institutions where children have to turn themselves into pupils. They have to follow the agenda of others and learn in ways that are passive and decontextualised. Motivation falls away as they are required to answer questions that are inside adults' heads rather than inside their own. Their resilience to the uncertainty involved in learning new knowledge weakens. If little time is given to reflection and if watching others is seen as 'time-wasting', young children lose the impetus to struggle with new learning. This is because their school experiences begin to teach them that they are often unsuccessful and the new learning is sometimes not worth the struggle. In everyday terms, the practitioner needs to ask themselves whether the four-year-old running eagerly to the setting is looking forward to completing the model started yesterday or waiting on the carpet for a registration session.

Implications for teaching

It can be seen that understanding educational theory and the sound principles for early learning matter hugely, as it is the youngest children in our schools and settings who are the least able to recover from inappropriate teaching methods. Practitioners committed to a career in early years invariably become campaigners as challenges arise from many quarters. Often head teachers, from understandable motives of whole-school consistency, try to fit the Foundation Stage, with its untidy part-time provision and different curriculum, into the model that runs so successfully for the rest of the institution. The response to this must be, 'Is it appropriate for the children?', as their needs must prevail against those of the institution. It takes courage on the part of the new practitioner to reason that it is inappropriate to take large numbers of very young children to the school hall for a whole-school assembly. It takes courage to address whole-staff meetings and parents' evenings on the subject of 'learning though play', but this is the role that the practitioner must take on with confidence and enthusiasm if young children's rights are to be safeguarded. It is an understanding of the underpinning theory and the knowledge of how to implement the principles that have been drawn down from this theory that provide the early years specialist with the evidence on which to base a practice that can be explained and defended with impunity.

Views of childhood

In conclusion, the question needs to be asked, 'What is our image of the child and of childhood?'. It was a question asked with passion by Peter Moss at the 2004 international conference at Reggio Emilia as he linked education to ethical and political choice. This is a question echoed by other professionals. Ruth Lister, a professor of social policy writing in the *Guardian* in October 2005, makes the same point: 'In the language of the sociology of childhood, the construction of the child as citizen-worker of the future means that children are valued as "becomings" rather than as "beings" '.

It is a worry that government concentrates its resources on training very young children to achieve highly in a narrow range of academic skills that they do not currently need, rather than promoting policies that would support children's well-being and enable them to flourish in the here and now. The 'strong' child, in the words of *Birth to Three Matters* (DfES 2002), needs policy-makers who understand the importance of a high-status profession so that resources can be allocated to make this vision a reality. Either children are human beings with rights and entitlements or they are not. They cannot be treated as 'citizens in waiting'. It might be argued that this is not an 'either/or' question and that priority can be given to achieving both high academic progress *and* to well-being. But, as we have seen in this chapter, it is only through the process of exploration, independence of thought and developing a high self-image that children stand any chance of fulfilling their potential in academic terms. We, as a society, have a choice to make.

We will leave the last word on this to Jerome Bruner, spoken via video-link at the 2004 international conference at Reggio Emilia:

> There are many ways to destroy human rights – the most effective is to deny children their childhood. We say to them, 'You have lost your opportunity to develop your mind but you now have the right to be an effective, coping adult'.

We need to listen to the theorists and choose wisely.

Questions for reflection

1. What are the elements that are essential to a good early years setting? Why are these crucial to young children's learning in the early years?

2. Where can practitioners find other contexts whose philosophies and practice best support children's learning? What are the factors that identify 'good practice'?

3. Why are research findings and the principles of a variety of respected investigators into early childhood in danger of being, effectively, bypassed in developing the early years system we have in the UK today?

References

ATL (2004) *Inside the Foundation Stage: Recreating the Reception Year*. London: Association of Teachers and Lecturers.

Ball, C. (1994) *Start Right: The Importance of Early Learning*. London: Royal Society of Arts, p.59.

Bruce, T. (1987) *Early Childhood Education*. London: Holder and Stoughton.

Bruner, J. (1966) *Towards a Theory of Instruction*. Cambridge, MA: Harvard University Press.

Bruner, J. (1986) *Actual Minds, Possible Worlds*. Cambridge, MA: Harvard University Press.

Bruner, J. (2004) Spoken address via video-link, international conference at Reggio Emilia.

Csikszenlmihayli, M. (1979) 'The concept of flow', in Sutton Smith, B. *Play and Learning*. New York: Gardner, pp. 257–73.

DES (1990) *Starting with Quality* (Rumbold Report). London: HMSO.

DfES (2002) *Birth to Three Matters*. Nottingham: DfES.

Isaacs, S. (1932) *The Children We Teach*. London: University of London Press.

Roberts, R. (1995) *Self-esteem and Successful Early Learning*. London: Hodder and Stoughton.

Stones, E. (1984) 'Supervision in teacher education: the first years at school', in Anning, A. (1997) *The First Years in School*. Buckingham: Open University Press.

Birth to 3

Pamela May and Angela D. Nurse

Where are we now?

IN WRITING THIS chapter we acknowledge that our practical experience, as teachers, with the very young is limited mainly to our own families and friends. That is not unusual, however, in the rarified setting of a university where the study of babies and very young children, until very recently, has rested with those in medical and psychology departments. As we foresee and welcome developments in this field, we can draw on the professional knowledge of colleagues and start to bring together academic resources that will underpin our understanding and help us to develop a philosophy that can then be shared with, and augmented by the experience of, our students.

The view has been expressed that the period between birth and age 3, in educational and care (if not health or psychological) terms, has been a 'dark age'. Although there has been much more focus recently on very young children, Elinor Goldschmied and Sonia Jackson (2004: 1) counsel in the introduction to the second edition of their book *People Under Three*, in the past five years: 'The landscape of early childhood services has been transformed, but the trees are still quite sparse and most of them are only saplings, vulnerable to the winds of economic downturn or the whims of politicians'.

In the UK, the names of researchers and renowned practitioners who have specifically explored this field and impacted on practice have been few in comparison with research into the development of children beyond age 3. Particular aspects of early development, such as language, have been explored and guidance has been given to parents. Dr Sally Ward published *Babytalk* for parents in 2000, following more than two decades as a speech and language therapist and researcher. She had researched language development in very young children and implemented a programme aimed at ten-month-old babies with varying degrees of language delay, their parents worked with them closely for half an hour each day, and then Ward followed these children periodically to see if improvement was maintained.

Goldschmied's work has looked at interaction between babies and counteracted the generally held view that babies do not recognise, or need to make contact with, others as young as they are. By introducing 'treasure baskets' she has demonstrated that providing stimulation to babies is not difficult and babies can share with each other in their play. Peter Elfer *et al.* (2003) have investigated the crucial role of key persons in the nursery and explored the sometimes difficult boundaries between parents and professionals. They conclude that:

> The evidence about the nature of human relationships and the longing to form individual attachments, particularly for very young children, is overwhelming. For us the arguments against individual attachments, to do with feelings and organisation, become challenges to be overcome rather than reasons not to develop the key person approach.
>
> (Elfer *et al.* 2003: 6)

Overall, however, the emphasis until recently has not been on a comprehensive programme that ensures quality for under-3s in group care. This illustrates the dilemma in the UK that focuses on whether nurturing very young children is purely a family affair or a responsibility with the state.

In 2002 the DfES published *Birth to Three Matters*, which provides guidance for all those working within this age-range. Professor Lesley Abbott, who has championed the cause of the under-3s for many years, led the team that developed this. The pack includes a comprehensive literature review, compiled with the assistance of Professor Tricia David and Kathy Goouch from Canterbury, as well as training materials. This publication, distributed to all settings providing for this age-range, is potentially seminal. The quality of the materials is such that it meets both the practical and academic needs of those working in the field at all levels and reveals the world of very young children and their potential to a wide audience.

Aspects of infant development

Why has the age-range birth to 3 been introduced? Has three years been adopted as a cut-off point because it has been the traditional entry point to school nursery classes in the UK, or is there a more complex reason? What is it about three-year-olds that indicates a milestone in a child's journey? Is it to do with their developing skills and knowledge, though incomplete, about how the world works, their gradual movement away from total dependence on adults and their ability to negotiate using language? At what point could children of 3 survive without adult support if circumstances were as severe as those we have seen recently as a result of a series of cataclysmic natural disasters? This is an interesting debate because it reveals how strong and resourceful young children can be. Yet we tend to view children as vulnerable and in need of adult protection, even though in different times and places they have been anything but powerless and fragile.

It has been a common reaction throughout our society to consider small babies as passive, and less interesting than older children who can do things or talk to you. Consider this incident:

> Amy brought her new baby to the last university session before Christmas as her usual childcare arrangements had broken down that morning. In the bustle of settling ourselves into the class, none of us noticed at first that May was with us. She was just nine weeks old, but already, as she sat propped in her pushchair, constantly looking around at the new environment in which she found herself. A continuous stream of people went up to see her. As befits a group of mature students studying the early years at this level, each engaged her in a conversation. May watched each carefully, making strong eye contact and clearly smiling in response to each person's interest. As the conversation continued, May joined in, taking turns in trying to talk back. Her mouth and hands moved to the rhythm of each conversation, punctuated by smiles as she enjoyed each encounter. She stayed awake and alert throughout the four-hour session, only whimpering a little when people's attention moved elsewhere.

As the event above illustrates so well, babies are not passive, and research by Trevarthen and others in recent years has demonstrated that babies come into the world far more capable than they have generally been given credit for. Researchers have shown that babies initiate communication and adults respond. Babies understand a number of moods that are reflected in facial gesture, reacting, for example, to sadness in a parent's face by mirroring that emotion in their own expressions. Experiments have shown that babies respond to music heard before they are born by calming and listening more attentively to tunes with which they are familiar, whether intentionally introduced to the mother for the purposes of the research or because the sounds they hear represent the musical patterns of their particular society. A personal incident illustrates this well. My daughter, Eleanor, was induced at eight months, yet already clearly recognised my voice. At three days old, a nurse was cradling her as I joined other new mothers for lunch. She accepted this peacefully, but as soon as she heard my voice, despite the general background noise in a busy maternity ward, she turned towards me, even though I was several feet away from her. This movement was so powerful that it astonished both the young nurse and myself.

The first five years of a child's life are seen as the most crucial to later success, although we are now recognising that, if the environment is right, human beings continue to learn throughout their lives. If the foundations are secure, then a person's motivation and ability to learn will be enhanced. The idea of 'imprinting' and 'critical periods' for learning, a concept that developed from the work of researchers, such as Konrad Lorenz, in the 1960s and 70s, has been criticised, but it is recognised that it is easier to acquire certain skills, particularly language, in the early years, even if the plasticity of the brain enables different parts to take over functions for which they were not primarily intended. As we begin to understand the way in which the brain's structure is developed, the importance of good relationships, communication and environment becomes crucial in ensuring optimal development. Babies do not just eat, sleep and fill their nappies; they are constantly searching for stimulation and interaction with parents and caretakers, most of whom supply this naturally. Bowlby (1953), working at the same time as Lorenz and other researchers in the same field, introduced the concept of bonding, that is the primary relationship a baby forms, then usually interpreted to mean the mother. Bowlby's theories need to be set in context because they were disseminated at the end of World War 2 when they were used politically to make a case for women to return to the home. They were also developed and generalised from observations of a group of children who were hospitalised rather than from a mainstream sample. Although his theories were developed further in later years, this original linking of theory to political expediency (resulting in many women feeling frustrated by being expected to stay at home after the experience of work) worked to undermine the importance of what Bowlby was saying. His work stressed the importance of attachment to specific people to ensure emotional security.

Bonding is not always an immediate and natural process; birth should be a natural experience but often is not so. A difficult delivery and poor health can lead to adjustment difficulties and depression. Personal circumstances may be problematic or there may be issues to do with gender or special needs. Professionals need to recognise this and support, rather than condemn, parents who find it difficult. They need to respect any confidences that they are allowed to share and not make judgements. There are other family members who can provide lovingly for the child and support the mother, as well as people in the wider community. One of our responsibilities as early years professionals is not to judge but to build trusting relationships so that we can offer advice sensitively when parents are struggling and are prepared to accept it. Often we can share our own experiences. Some parents, particularly mothers, feel intense guilt because of the failure, in their eyes, to match up to their own perceived ideals of perfect parenthood.

The introduction of a 'key worker' system, where a baby is assigned to the care of a specific practitioner, leads from Bowlby's work, but we need to ensure that the system ensures emotional security and does not become purely a means to assess and keep records. Nurseries need to be sure what their philosophy is and how to put it into practice. There has been debate as to the *depth* of the emotional relationship that develops between a baby and his or her key worker, on the grounds that staff should avoid replacing the mother or becoming the preferred adult. This caters more for the adults' needs than the child's. Elfer *et al.* (2003: 9) are very clear:

> We believe, however, that the evidence about the nature of human relationships and the longing to form individual attachments, particularly for very young children, is

overwhelming. For us, the arguments against individual attachments, to do with feelings and organisation, become challenges to be overcome rather than reasons not to develop the key person approach.

Recently there has been a growing emphasis on children's emotional development, in recognition, perhaps, that this has been neglected in schools where the push towards academic standards has had priority. Following on from the publication of *Every Child Matters* (2003), The Children Act 2004 highlights five principles, put together with the aid of children, which should impact on practice. These include 'being healthy' and 'enjoying and achieving'. It has been established for many years that emotional neglect has a physical consequence in 'failure to thrive'. The importance, particularly of touch, in the healthy physical and emotional growth of the baby has been explored by Lise Eliot (2000) who reminds us that a baby's sense of touch is the most developed of the senses at birth. Gerhardt (2004) explores how affection shapes a baby's brain. In contrast to the experience of many children placed in orphanages or cared for on hospital wards until the 1940s (or in Romanian children's homes much more recently), the importance of touch has been acknowledged in special care units for a number of years in establishing the bond between babies in incubators and their parents and in improving physical status. At a recent conference (2005), Dr Patricia Champion recalled an incident in a hospital in New Zealand where pre-term twins were being cared for in separate incubators. The smaller twin was struggling and, against hospital guidelines, a nurse placed his stronger sister next to him in his incubator. She immediately put her arm around his shoulders and he visibly calmed, the positive effects registering on the monitoring apparatus. In countries where high-tech resources are not readily available, premature babies have made significant progress when cradled directly next to their parent's skin, able to hear and feel his or her heartbeat. This is now being adopted in more economically developed countries which are also reconsidering whether the use of incubators is always the best course. Eliot (2000: 142) describes how 'nests' are created within incubators that 'mimic the comforting confines of the womb'. These examples contradict some of the strictures placed on professionals, especially teachers, in touching children because of fears to do with child abuse (explored further in Chapter 10).

The ability of researchers to view the working of the brain by ever more sophisticated scanning techniques has demonstrated how appropriate experience enables synaptic connections to be made which increase the power of the brain. Without appropriate experiences at a suitable time, the ability to make those connections becomes harder, if not impossible. This is particularly true in the case of visual development and language acquisition. The case of Genie illustrates this well. Genie was kept restrained and isolated from her family by her father until she was 13. Although she managed to retrieve some functioning, her language levels remained at around the equivalent of a two-year-old. Enhanced knowledge of how the brain develops and functions has resurrected the debate that climaxed in the 1960s and 70s which considered the relative importance of 'nature' (the potential a child is born with) and 'nurture' (how the environment or context into which the child is born supports or diminishes this potential). In parallel, research into genetics is revealing how much of our functioning may be governed by the genes we inherit. Twin studies, particularly those where identical twins are separated soon after birth and raised in different families, have often seemed to reveal an eerie similarity in the lives they lead and the choices they make, but few pairs of twins in these circumstances have been studied and, as Eliot (2000: 424) points out, they spent the months before, and often soon after birth, together. As a consequence, the environment we create for the youngest children must take this interplay of 'nurture' and 'nature' into account.

Acceptance

If, then, we are now beginning to recognise that babies bring into the world many attributes that enable them to recognise their own families and thus add to their chances of survival in a complex world, the time a baby spends *in utero* has to be seen as part of the continuum from conception onwards. Birth is a milestone in this journey, but not a completely new beginning.

One area of argument centres on termination of pregnancy. Currently, the timing of an abortion and the use of foetal material for research and for medical reasons are under debate. These need to be considered by all those who work with children and families because personal philosophies will colour responses to other families' experiences and thus to their children placed in our care, if details of the family history become known. For example, some may consider that because a number of conditions can be tested for prenatally that parents who have a child with Down's syndrome have been irresponsible. Others may, for religious, cultural or personal reasons, see the termination of a pregnancy for this or any other reason as morally wrong.

Other medical advances have made it possible for many more babies and their mothers to survive than would have been feasible in earlier times. Some of the babies who survive may have complex problems. In a world where economic value seems frequently to be more highly prized than the right to live, practitioners must be wary of disturbing the relationship between parent and child, when there are issues of disability or delayed development, particularly in the early days as parents respond to the impact of a child who has additional needs. It has to be stated that the possibility of a baby with complex needs being cared for beyond the family home, whatever the parents' expectations had been before the birth, are minimal, as few settings are willing to accept the responsibility of caring for a baby with additional needs. To meet the parents' and professionals' need for information, the government has sponsored the 'Early Support' (DfES/DH 2004) project which has produced a wealth of materials aimed at those caring for infants, particularly parents, from birth to 3.

As practitioners working with very young children we need to work with parents closely, recognising and complementing what they do. As professionals, we need to reflect deeply on our own beliefs and recognise how they make us respond. It is not always easy to remain objective, but part of our professionalism must be to accept that others may choose to live their lives in ways that do not accord with our own, but neither do they impact upon the well-being of their children. In the end, however, we must work with the situation as it is presented, not make moral judgements, value the child and his or her family and the right of families to make their own decisions.

How the UK system evolved

Traditionally, because it was thought to be 'natural' work for females, those who cared for babies were generally young, poorly trained and poorly paid. There were, and are, some exceptions, such as the Norland nannies who are highly trained professionals sought out by the more wealthy in our society. The cost of care within the home for the majority, where relatives are not available or willing, has led to the employment of young girls as carers, perhaps in a gap year or from overseas, gaining experience of living in a different community and learning the language. This whole area has been poorly regulated compared with other aspects of modern life, even though the quality of these young people's work and the understanding of young children's development they bring to it could impact upon the futures of the infants they care for. Outside of the home, other parents may choose group care in day nurseries or other people's homes. Childminders have long provided care. Although the quality of the care has been debated and researched, for example by Jackson and Jackson (1979), Mayall and Petrie (1983) and Elfer *et al.* (2003) among others, registered childminders have been regulated and subject to yearly inspection, transferring from local authority responsibility in 1948 to social services departments which undertook regulation and inspection. Training and support are available to ensure good practice and childminders bring to the care of babies experience, comfortable home environments and the opportunity to bond well.

Although day nurseries were established during World War 2 to enable women to work, these were mainly closed afterwards, as women were encouraged to revert to homemaking to release jobs for men returning from the forces. Those that remained tended to be located in inner-city areas, to provide for the children of families who were severely disadvantaged and often in trouble. Nursery nurses who were often very young and not well paid, but dealing with some of society's most complex problems, staffed these state-provided day nurseries. Since World War 2, we have never decided that, as a nation, we have a shared responsibility for small children, particularly babies, except in exceptional circumstances. Unlike many of our European neighbours, who have established a state responsibility, we have seen the care of children as a family affair, unless children are truly at risk. Consequently, what is accessible to parents is patchy. Choice is limited by availability and ability to pay. In the past two decades some attempt has been made to unify the system, though it still depends on a mish-mash of private, voluntary and state provision, regulated by quite complex – and ever-changing – rules and regulations. The growth in private nurseries, or, as Peter Moss defines it, the 'for profit' sector, has provided further challenges. In the UK, care for under-3s in the private sector is funded entirely by families. The ratio of staff to children for babies in the UK is 1: 3. Even if qualified staff members are relatively poorly paid, the costs of this are substantial. In other European countries there is often a sliding scale for fees, taking into account parental income and 'ability to pay'. The overall costs to a family tend to be much lower than here because there is a state or local subsidy. This is the system in Reggio Emilia, renowned for the quality of its preschool provision. Costs increase because nurseries remain open for long hours throughout the year. Many nurseries, therefore, particularly if they are individually owned, have a very narrow profit margin, enabling them to remain viable. Extra regulatory demands from government or, for example, a change in employment law can remove this viability. A number of daycare providers initially disappeared when the minimum wage became a reality, but now nursery ownership offers a very popular small-business opportunity. As costs need to be kept as low as possible in the symbiotic relationship between parent and provider, wages often remain at the national minimum, risking the stability of the setting as practitioners leave in order to find better-paid employment elsewhere.

A commitment to quality and training

More issues become evident as we start to talk about enhancing the quality of practice in nurseries and other forms of daycare. There are choices we have to consider in raising standards, and all have implications for funding. These centre on:

- initial professional training as an entry requirement to the profession;
- the level of initial training;
- ongoing 'in-service';
- continuing professional development.

The funding implications not only involve the costs of a full-time college or university education, or financial support for short courses, but also in paying for cover for those released to improve their qualifications. Over the past four years the DfES has developed and, at first, generously supported Foundation Degrees in Early Years, which have included a pathway for those who work with children aged from 0 to 3. As the funding the participants receive has decreased, difficulties have arisen for many, particularly from the private and voluntary sectors, who wish to further their knowledge and understanding, as the availability of support for them is restricted. This is particularly pertinent to childminders, where organising free time during the working week to attend courses is often practically impossible unless programme providers organise crèches. As it is childminders who provide much of the available provision for our youngest children, any attempt to introduce higher qualifications to them – and their needs should not be ignored – has to take this into account.

The whole area of education and training for those who work with the very young is currently under consideration as this book is being written. We know there are debates about the nature of the 'professionals' who will be responsible for our youngest children in the future. This centres on the level and kind of professional training they will receive and who will be responsible for it. We have reviewed the current situation in the Introduction. A number of us, represented by the Early Childhood Studies Degrees Network, have worked tirelessly for nearly two decades to ensure that there are graduates in the field who would raise the quality of practice and the educational aspirations of those who work within it. At the moment of writing we are considering what our stance is. One way forward would be to create a new kind of professional – a 'pedagogue' – whose background will be in a broad, transdisciplinary understanding of children and families even though individuals may opt to undertake postgraduate study that will lead to qualifications in a more traditional profession. Another option may be to qualify as teachers, if the decision is to incorporate the under-3s into the Foundation Stage, though this will be a new venture for the majority of teacher-trainers who have little, if any, experience with under-3s and few qualifications. Our fear, however, is that we will, as a nation, miss this opportunity to think in new ways and make radical decisions that will really enhance the provision for our youngest children.

Changing times, changing expectations

There is no uniform system of day care and education (in its fullest sense) for babies and very young children within the UK. Care and education have been traditionally separated, with responsibility split across the statutory authorities of health, social services and education. Until recently, the latter has played a minor role in the lives of those who are under age 3. The National Childcare Strategy, in 1998, the ensuing centralisation of care and education within the DfES, the introduction of Sure Start and the extension of Ofsted's role in inspection and regulation have been an attempt to co-ordinate and bring some degree of cohesion to a fragmented service. This is not a particularly smooth transition, welcomed by everyone. Just as those who worked in state-maintained nurseries have been concerned in the past about the 'educational' content of day nursery programmes, now there are concerns that the emotional, 'care' aspects will lose out in the greater emphasis on education. One fear that could unite both is opposition to government intentions to introduce more formal expectations, as they have done with older children, which seems to many to rely little on research and knowledge of very young children and how they learn and develop. The Post Report (June 2000) contained a wealth of references to research into very early infant development and examples from practice across the world. Those in the profession greeted this very favourably, but the recent publication of the interim *Rose Review of Reading* (December 2005) once again raises issues that potentially confront the beliefs of the majority of those who practise within the Early Years. The *Review* stresses (para 38) that 'an important, albeit obvious, early marker needs to be entered here that listening and speaking are the roots of reading and writing'. This is rarely disputed (perhaps in the cases of some children with special needs) but the later emphasis on introducing 'a systematic programme of phonic work by the age of five', followed by 'there is no good reason for delaying it beyond this age', contradicts what we know and believe about starting from the child's interest and strengths. Of course, the approach could be through songs, nursery rhymes and stories, but our experience has been that a phonic approach is not always embedded in children's real-life experiences and often makes no sense at all to those teaching reading purely in this way. It is also very early to teach children reading formally. The government's own Post Report (2000: 12) stated in its summary:

> Other skills such as reading, writing and maths require teaching, but there is no convincing evidence that teaching these skills early (before about six) is advantageous. International studies suggest that a later school starting age (six or seven) might be beneficial, if school is preceded by high-quality pre-school provision.

Why have we included this in a chapter on the under-3s? The fear derives from the government's intention to create a new Early Years Foundation Stage which will incorporate both *Birth to Three Matters* (DfES 2002) and the Curriculum Guidance for the Foundation Stage (DfEE 2000). This is outlined in the DfES publication (December 2005) *Early Years Foundation Stage: Direction of Travel Paper*. Although it is too early to judge professional reaction as this chapter is written, initial fears centre on the creation of a 'top-down' model where under-3s are introduced to educational approaches that are not in line with their level of development. This is not an anxiety without roots. For a number of years, institutions such as the Institute for the Achievement of Human Potential (IAHP) in the USA have worked with parents to accelerate very young children's learning. The programmes include one focused on early reading which, according to the IAHP's developmental profile, can produce children in the 'superior range' who can read with 'total understanding' by the age of 3, with an average of 6 years. This may be so, but some of the methods from programmes such as these have been to introduce flashcards to babies within their first year of life. This makes little sense to those whose understanding of child development rests on first-hand experience and a holistic approach. Pushing down the start of formal education into infancy, because there is so much to learn in a complex society, is an anxiety many share. It is interesting, however, that the IAHP's approach to successful early reading rests on 'visual competence' and phonics are not mentioned, rather an 'understanding of complete vocabulary and proper sentences'. While suggesting that neither method alone is certain to enhance most children's development, it is easy to see how a very selective approach to research and practice can impact on how we care for our youngest children.

The future?

All of this has implications for the environments in which we place babies and the status we offer to those who care for them outside the home. The DfES (2004: 7), in its *Five Year Strategy for Children and Learners*, includes as one of its five key principles 'a major commitment to staff development with high quality support and training to improve assessment, care and training'. This needs to include those such as childminders who, by the very nature of their job, can be excluded from the training on offer to others. This has become crucial at a time when, following the British political tradition of issuing contradictory advice and legislation, mothers, particularly those raising children single-handedly, are exhorted to return to paid employment. In a joint department document published by HM Treasury at the end of 2004, while declaring that 'children benefit from spending the first year of their life in consistent one-to-one care', the document firmly supports employment of lone parents particularly, as part of 'its commitment to eradicate child poverty', setting a target for 70 per cent of lone parents to be in work by 2010 (p.9) The DfES (2004: 7) document, highlighted above, states that parents with children from birth to 2 are to be offered 'more opportunities and support', while there is said to be an element of 'choice' in taking maternity (or paternity) leave in the child's earliest years and being supported financially to do this . . . 'to stay at home with their children if they want to'. Whatever the government's intentions, the implication is that we will need more care outside the home for our youngest children.

We have discussed in the first chapter how quickly birth rates are falling across the developed world. Additionally, women are delaying starting a family until later in their lives, and some decide to have children by artificial means and bring them up alone. If they are older mothers without nearby families to support them, then the support of a good preschool centre becomes crucial to their own well-being as well as their child's. The French have for many years supported families generously, offering financial incentives to those who have children because they recognise the value to society as a whole of maintaining the birth rate and supporting children. If UK mothers are expected to work, in the absence of childcare assistance from relatives, the state must surely have a duty to ensure not only that there is sufficient provision for families to have choice, but also that the quality of what is provided is enhanced and safeguarded. Quality, as evidenced by resourcing and staff knowledge and understanding, must surely take priority.

Questions for reflection

1. Should parents of very young children be encouraged to work outside the home?
2. Should the care, welfare and education of very young children be seen as a state or private family concern? What is the state's role and responsibility in raising children?
3. What is your individual stance on the termination of pregnancy?
4. What level and kind of qualifications should be required for those who work with the very young?

References

Abbott, I. and Langston, A. (2005) *Birth to Three Matters: Supporting the Framework of Effective Practice*. Maidenhead: Open University Press.

Bowlby, J. (1953) *Child Care and the Growth of Love*. London: Pelican.

Champion, P. (2005) 'The challenge from the children to early childhood', at conference: Early Childhood Intervention: National Developments: European Perspectives. International Conference Centre, Birmingham, 28–29 November.

DfEE (2000) *Curriculum Guidance for the Foundation Stage*. London: Qualifications and Curriculum Authority.

DFES (2002) *Birth to Three Matters*. London: Department for Education and Skills, Sure Start Unit.

DfES (2003) *Every Child Matters*. Norwich: The Stationery Office.

DfES (2004) *Five Year Strategy for Children and Learners*. London: Department for Education and Skills.

DfES (2005) *Early Years Foundation Stage: Direction of Travel Paper*. London: Department for Education and Skills.

DfES/DH (2004) *Early Support*. London: Department for Education and Skills.

Elfer, P., Goldschmied, E. and Selleck, D. (2003) *Key Persons in the Nursery*. London: David Fulton Publishers.

Eliot, L. (2000) *Early Intelligence*. London: Penguin.

Gerhardt, S. (2004) *Why Love Matters*. Hove: Routledge.

Goldschmied, E. and Jackson, S. (2004) *People Under Three* (2nd edn). Abingdon: Routledge.

HM Treasury (2004) *Choice for Parents: The Best Start for Children: A Ten Year Strategy for Childcare*. London: HMSO.

Jackson, B. and Jackson, S. (1979) *Childminder: A Study in Action Research*. London: Routledge.

Mayall, B. and Petrie, P. (1983) *Childminding and Day Nurseries*. London: Kogan Page.

Post Report (2000) *Early Years Learning* (no.140). London: Parliamentary Office of Science and Technology.

Rose, J. (2005) *The Rose Review of Reading*. London: DfES.

Ward, S. (2000) *Babytalk*. London: Century/Random House.

Websites

'Early Support' materials – **www.earlysupport.org.uk**

The Institute for the Achievement of Human Potential – **www.iahp.org**

Play and creativity

Pamela May

Definitions of creativity and play

CREATIVITY IS GAINING a foothold in our schools after many years of being banished to the shadows. Government documents such as *All Our Futures* (NACCCE 1999) and *Excellence and Enjoyment* (DfES 2003) respond to policy-makers' recommendations that 'human resources' need to be developed urgently and that what is needed in the twenty-first century is a workforce that can respond to policies that 'promote creativity, adaptability and powers of communication' (p. 29). To this end, approaches are needed that will emphasise motivation and high self-esteem. *All Our Futures* defines creativity as an 'imaginative activity fashioned so as to produce outcomes that are both original and of value' (p. 29). It goes on to state that creative processes require 'freedom and control'; the freedom to experiment and the control of skills, knowledge and understandings' (NACCE 1999).

There is then, a tension between the *freedom* elements and the *control* elements of creativity that needs to be resolved in the classroom and which lies at the heart of any good teaching. Happily for the early years practitioner, play is a process that lends itself to creative learning and the issue around freedom and control in play is a key theme that this chapter will explore.

If creativity is hard to define, play is even more of a challenge. The slippery nature of play makes it difficult to describe in words, particularly if we, as practitioners, are looking for play that we can identify as a vehicle for high-level learning rather than the low-level 'playing about'. High-quality play is rather like an elephant; impossible to describe but instantly recognisable when seen. Because play emanates from within the child, it is not subject to adult controls and it is this quality that makes it such an uncomfortable process in today's culture of measurable outcomes and formal schooling. Play has been described as having many possible purposes, with recreation, practice and preparation being but a few of them. However, what interests educators is the purpose of play as a vehicle for learning, and it is this aspect that we will concentrate on in this discussion of the links between play and creativity.

Pellegrini (1991) offers a useful definition of play as consisting of three dimensions. He stated that play is considered:

- as a psychological dimension;
- according to contexts that elicit playful behaviour;
- as observable behaviour.

The dispositional aspects of play include intrinsic motivation, concentration, exploration, flexibility, non-literal behaviours and active engagement. The contexts that elicit playful behaviour normally involve freedom of choice, control by the participant and a familiar and stress-free setting.

Observable behaviour has been defined as the three levels of Piagetian play. These are the functional level, the symbolic level and games with rules. These were later refined by Tina Bruce (1991) into exploratory play, representational play and free-flow play. Bruce argued that 'play' is too broad a term to be useful here, preferring to use 'free-flow' play to describe the child truly 'wallowing in ideas, thoughts, feelings and relationships'. This description of play as an integrating mechanism whereby children bring all they know, feel and believe to their play begins to make clear links to what might be thought of as creative behaviour.

In today's climate of accountability it may be thought that too much 'wallowing' has aspects of non-rigorous Plowdenism, which was a feature of preschool provision in the 1960s and 1970s. It may be more helpful to consider this high-functioning process in terms of disposition, which should happily link across to what might be termed 'attitudes to learning'. In using disposition as a defining feature of play – which is perhaps the most secure in the current educational climate – we have found ways into a consideration of the features of play that bridge the tension between freedom and control in creativity.

High-level play

High-level play shows children displaying features of learning that practitioners and parents alike recognise as valuable. Ferre Laevers (1994) uses the following aspects to describe children learning effectively:

- concentration
- energy
- creativity
- facial expression and posture
- persistence
- precision

- reaction time

- language

- satisfaction.

Children displaying these aspects of behaviour are usually playing. Within these aspects there are elements that are both 'playful' and 'work-like'. Children who are playing at this high level of involvement are persisting, concentrating, trying to solve problems and refining skills, as well as being creative and energetic. This may be helpful in moving practitioners' thinking away from the notion of play and work as being necessarily at opposite ends of a continuum, with play being purely a low-level reward for completion of formal tasks that are thought of as work.

Loris Malaguzzi in his poem 'The Hundred Languages of Children', quoted by Filippini and Vecchi 1996, makes this point eloquently by saying of schools that:

> They tell the child
> that work and play
> reality and fantasy
> science and imagination
> sky and earth
> reason and dream
> are things
> that do not belong together.

The complete poem from which this is a quotation follows:

No way. The hundred is there.

The child
is made of one hundred.
The child has
a hundred languages
a hundred hands
a hundred thoughts
a hundred ways of thinking
of playing, of speaking.
A hundred always a hundred
ways of listening
of marvelling, of loving
a hundred joys
for singing and understanding

a hundred worlds
to discover
a hundred worlds
to invent
a hundred worlds
to dream.
The child has
a hundred languages
(and a hundred hundred hundred more)
but they steal ninety-nine.
The school and the culture
separate the head from the body.
They tell the child:
to think without hands
to do without head
to listen and not to speak
to understand without joy
to love and to marvel
only at Easter and at Christmas.
They tell the child:
to discover the world already there
and of the hundred
they steal ninety-nine.
They tell the child:
that work and play
reality and fantasy
science and imagination
sky and earth
reason and dream
are things
that do not belong together.

And thus they tell the child
that the hundred is not there.
The child says:
No way. The hundred is there.

Loris Malaguzzi
(*translated by Lella Gandini, from the catalogue of the exhibition* The Hundred Languages
of Children © *Preschools and Infant-toddler Centres – Istituzione of the Municipality of
Reggio Emilia, published by Reggio Children 1996*)

This brings us to a consideration of the creative process that has far wider implications than the curriculum area of 'creativity' as described in the *Curriculum Guidance for the Foundation Stage* (DfEE 2000).

We can begin to realise that creativity exists in every part of the curriculum and that science and maths are creative and can be taught creatively. We see that a creative approach to learning reaches far beyond the art easel and the cutting and sticking area. This creative approach provides a bridge that links aspects of children's experiences such as science and the imagination, which, in turn, reflect the holistic ways in which good learning happens.

Once, when discussing this very issue with a distinguished physicist, the author described an average day in the nursery. Children would be moving around, discussing ideas, seeking help, experiencing failure, taking a break to reflect and then trying out different solutions to their problems. (Think, for example, of trying to make a car from a cardboard box and wanting wheels that turn.) The physicist listened carefully to this and then suggested that, although the end-results might vary, the process was identical to the one he went through each day in his laboratory. The difference is the label; in early years practice this process is called 'play' and at the level of post-doctoral science it is called 'experimentation'.

One of the joys of working with very young children is that their ability to think creatively is highly developed. It is easy to have a negative view of the young child as there are so many things that they cannot yet do. Yet their very youth and egocentricity can protect them from too many constraining experiences of failure and the depressing notion that many things are, in fact, impossible. All things are possible to the young child; reality and fantasy are fused, and, as Malaguzzi suggests, 'reason and dream' are things that can, and should belong together.

Reason and dream

To achieve the freedom to reason and dream children need to be allowed independence and autonomy in their actions. Distinguished physicists have autonomy, without question, in their laboratories but young children in educational settings very often do not. If early years professionals do not have a secure grasp of the sound principles that underpin their teaching, they may fetter creativity on the grounds that it is not easily assessed and measurable, or they may be uncomfortable that the control of ideas is, of necessity, with the creator rather than with the practitioner. The *Curriculum Guidance for the Foundation Stage* (DfEE/QCA 2000) wisely reminds us that 'Creativity is not about pleasing adults' (p. 118). Again we come back to issues of control and freedom. The easy answer might be that play is the key way to ensure that creativity and control stay in the hands of children, yet this is to oversimplify what is actually required to ensure that high-level creative learning happens. Creativity is always responsive to its context and will only flourish in the very young if the culture supports its development. As young children lack experience to think otherwise, they will make assumptions that the adult's values are the correct ones and are therefore vulnerable to a setting's ethos.

Guy Claxton, in an unpublished lecture at Canterbury Christ Church University in 2003, suggested a number of disincentives to children's creativity:

- create a chaotic environment;
- be over-controlling;
- sow the seeds of compliance;
- be over-protective;
- be over-helpful;
- don't give children 'meaty' projects; stick to 'McNugget' activities;
- make a strong distinction between 'work' and 'play';
- hook children into clarity;
- keep them busy;
- emphasise symbols;
- do not model 'confident uncertainty';
- do not allow 'downtime'.

This list points to a number of constraints to creative learning that are both physical and philosophical. An environment that is either chaotic or over-controlling in the ways that, for example, time and resources are allowed to be used will limit children's opportunities to be inventive and imaginative. A setting that has, as part of its cultural make-up, the attitude that knowledge is either 'right' or 'wrong', or that children are incompetent and as such need protection from challenge, will give powerful messages that young children are not expected to achieve highly. It is a truism that one of the most powerful adult attitudes that will support creative thinking in children is that of 'confident uncertainty'. By this Claxton means that it is acceptable, even preferable, for adults to be uncertain, and by being 'confidently uncertain' they will encourage a range of other possible solutions to a problem.

'Downtime' is a vital element of creativity. In the current educational climate it is often difficult to justify time when children do not appear to be busy. Although the *Curriculum Guidance for the Foundation Stage* (DfEE/QCA 2000) is clear in stating that creativity is not about pleasing adults, the culture of many settings is just as clear to children. They know that they have to look busy. Despite our own professional aspirations to become 'reflective practitioners' we find it very hard to encourage time for reflection in our children. Claxton compares our western culture with that of the eastern world and suggests that the attributes associated with eastern culture, such as meditation and calm reflection, are vital to the creative process. In fact, a consideration of many of the 'Eureka' moments in scientific discovery reveals that they often happen when the scientist's mind is far away from his discovery. Newton was probably not thinking of gravity as he sat beneath the apple tree and Archimedes was probably not thinking of displacement theory as he enjoyed his bath. 'Eureka' moments often 'pop up' from nowhere after ideas have been mulled over, forgotten and absorbed into the slower-acting brain after having been tossed around in the fast-paced logical mind. For the most part our schools are locked into fast-paced logical thinking, as exemplified by the Numeracy Strategy and the Literacy Hour, with little value attached to giving time for the reflective downtime aspects of learning.

Here again, play is a useful process. The very nature of play rejects the notion that successful learning consists of a piece of academic knowledge being taught just once in a didactic format. We know that new knowledge needs to be encountered several times, sometimes many times, before the concept is fully embedded and understood. We only have to think of an adult equivalent, such as learning to drive, to know that once is not enough. While not suggesting that play is a helpful process in learning to drive, practice is certainly essential, and one of the most valuable aspects of play is that it provides opportunities for children to rehearse and practise a new skill or piece of knowledge at a level appropriate for them, and in a range of different ways, to ensure a secure multi-embodiment of what is being learned.

Being creative

Children are sometimes expected to 'be creative' but may not have the necessary skills and competence. Bennett *et al.* (1997), in their research into children's learning through play, found that 'Some of the activities were virtually content free, as the children were engaged in a hands-on capacity, but were chatting generally with little "brains-on engagement" ' (p. 121). A setting needs to retain control over teaching the children specific skills to ensure that they have the competence needed to use their creativity. Being creative needs full 'brains-on engagement' as well as the ability to use tools and equipment safely. This suggests that planning needs to incorporate the teaching of both physical skills and thinking skills. What needs to be taught is, first, physical dexterity. Tools that enable children to be creative are sometimes thought of as problematic as they need to be effective and not toys or plastic replicas. Real hammers, staplers, clay and musical instruments can be noisy, messy and challenging when children are learning to use them, but with constant access and with supportive direct instruction they will be invaluable in aiding high-quality creations. Together with the physical prowess to use equipment, practitioners need to teach thinking skills to encourage children in the major tenets of creativity. Bernadette Duffy (1998) defined these as:

- the ability to see things in fresh ways;
- learning from past experience and relating this to new situations;

- thinking along unorthodox lines and breaking barriers;
- using non-traditional approaches to solving problems;
- going further than the information given;
- creating something unique and original.

Teaching children to think creatively in the ways Bernadette Duffy describes has been problematic of late. Recently a group of children's authors published a series of essays called *Waiting for a Jamie Oliver: Beyond Bog-standard Literacy* (Powling 2005). They complained that their books were being used to teach the deconstructing of print and for comprehension exercises rather than being enjoyed and experienced as creative and imaginative experiences. As Michael Rosen said in his essay, 'We can't ever lose sight of the purpose of literature: enjoyment, pleasure, intrigue and excitement'. This quote complements the sentiments of Csikszentmihalyi (1997) who said that 'if the next generation is to face the future with zest and self-confidence we must educate them to be original as well as competent'. This is where the balance must be considered between the competence of the process of writing (or drawing or painting); the 'penmanship' and the disposition to be creative; and the 'authorship'. It is pointless having children who can write correctly but cannot think of anything to write about or to have children who can deconstruct print but who do not want to read. When considering this balance it may be helpful to remember that 'enjoyment, pleasure, intrigue and excitement' are probably more powerful motivators than is the satisfaction gained by being able to recognise adjectives and capital letters. Peter Ashley (2005), in his contribution to *Waiting for a Jamie Oliver*, reminds readers, 'Often the excitement of a story, in a weird, wonderful way, can take a child along a line of print'. Perhaps we should have more faith in the power of positive dispositions to motivate children to be both creative and competent.

Teaching children the thinking skills they need to be creative helps them to capitalise on this enjoyment and excitement. In many European countries the teaching of these skills through play and games is what happens in the very early years of schooling, so that when formal learning begins at the age of 7, children are able to use these skills to learn to read and write quickly. The idea of teaching 'how' rather than 'why' (teaching how to learn rather than the teaching of academic bodies of knowledge) is growing in popularity as governments realise that skills for living together with the creativity necessary to be inventive and divergent are what twenty-first-century societies need. In fact, the present ITE Futures debate, being hosted by the Teaching and Development Agency, has highlighted the perceived need for a different type of teacher for 2020 and beyond. Muriel Robinson, one of the contributors to a conference held in April 2004, expressed the specific concern that the current teaching force, who were educated through the National Curriculum, tend to be compliant and risk-averse. She declared that a prime need was to encourage those people who could think along unorthodox lines and who could see things in fresh ways to train as teachers.

Self-concept and creativity

The ability to 'see things in fresh ways', to 'think along unorthodox lines' and to 'use non-traditional approaches to solving problems' has roots in a child's view of herself. In her report on the Headstart research conducted into children's early learning in the USA in the 1960s, Kathy Sylva (1994) makes the statement that 'The style of helpless or mastery-orientated behaviour is not related to intelligence; rather, it is a personality characteristic, a way of viewing oneself and one's capacity to be effective with things and people'.

Emotional intelligence, rather than intellectual skill, then, is the main driver in the process of giving children the concept that they are 'can do' people. This, therefore, becomes a key issue for early years managers and teachers to consider when implementing a culture in their setting. The setting not only has to have interesting things to engage children's curiosity but it also needs to be a place where children's ideas, views and preferences are treated with respect and acted upon. The Steiner philosophy of early childhood education emphasises the development of the whole child, including spiritual, physical and moral well-being as well as academic progress. A very creative and artistic environment is provided for the children who can develop their own interests and abilities in naturalistic surroundings. There is a strong emphasis on social abilities as well as the natural development of early numeracy and literacy skills, but formal learning begins much later and usually follows the teacher's and children's own interests. The aspects of the Highscope settings in the Headstart research, which had such a positive and long-lasting impact on children's lives, were, first, a well-trained workforce and, second, a good adult–child ratio. The staff encouraged a process of learning that involved planning what was to be learned and reflecting on what had been learned. This 'plan-do-review' model provided vital opportunities to teach children the thinking skills and the practical skills they needed to operate at a high level of thoughtfulness, while at the same time being secure in the understanding that their ideas and projects were valued by the adults. Recent comments heard from students that their setting 'does Highscope in the afternoons' become problematic, for if children understand that they have autonomy and that their ideas are respected for only half a day each day, how can they develop a consistent view of their 'effectiveness with things and people'? Sometimes students have been unclear as to the nature and purpose of the 'review' part of this process, observing it being used as a teacher-initiated time rather than a time for children to take the lead and talk about their ideas and other aspects of the setting that are important to them.

Risk and resilience

All new learning involves risk. A child's view of his or her ability to withstand the trauma of the uncertainties involved in struggling towards new understanding will determine whether he or she feels able to take the risk of not succeeding. Young children trying to saw large pieces of wood or counting the number of cakes needed for all their friends will often have their tongues stuck out in that characteristic pose of children deep in concentration. The commitment to the struggle is clear to see and the sensitive adult will also know that a reasonable number of successful outcomes are important to children's self-esteem. Here again, play is a useful process as through play children can rehearse new understandings that are important to them but without the associated failure that can be so damaging to a positive self-image. In play it is possible for children to refine their ideas by experiencing what did not work as well as what did. The creative process is not valid if everything is straight-forward or if the answer is known at the outset. By struggling with alternative strategies and possible solutions children gradually move closer to a successful conclusion and the satisfaction of a completed project is significant and a cause for general rejoicing. This process reflects the 'confident uncertainty' discussed above as well as the aspects of children learning effectively that Ferre Laevers (1994) describes in his Leuven Involvement Scale.

The early years setting is the ideal place to help children develop their creative abilities. The *Curriculum Guidance* (DfEE/QCA 2000) reminds practitioners that 'Children do not make a distinction between "play" and "work" and neither should practitioners' (p. 11). The gaining of new knowledge has aspects that reflect both work and play. By devising activities and provision that engage children's curiosity, but which is at a level and in a format that does not cause anxiety, practitioners can help the less courageous child to embark on the business of risky enquiry. Fearful children who can be persuaded that failure is but a step on the road to success will have learned possibly the most valuable life skill of all; that they have the ability to see themselves as 'can do' people.

Children's compulsive play patterns also contribute to the creative process. Schematic play, in which children repeatedly practise a concept they are currently en-gaged in, allows them to make connections between what they know already and new, related understanding, and is a significant part of the concept formation and embodi-ment process. By being practical and playful, it has the flexibility to be used by the child at exactly the appropriate level. Schematic play sometimes annoys and confuses practitioners who are unaware of its significance; particularly when, for example, chil-dren exploring an enclosure schema empty the contents of the workshop each day and use all the contents to fill small boxes; or boys exploring a trajectory schema enjoy squirting water around the classroom. Athey (1990) identifies a range of schematic preferences and discusses their implications in depth together with the benefits to children of working with parents to support children who are learning in this way. Schematic play would seem to provide opportunities for children to engage in creativity by allowing them to try out new ideas associated with a concept with which they are growing increasingly familiar as they repeat and extend their play patterns.

Controls and freedoms

We have considered some of the major ways in which play and creativity are linked and suggested that, philosophically, control and freedom are issues that underpin the successful implementation of provision in ways that allow children to learn creatively. We will now look in more detail at the sharing of controls and freedoms to debate the issue of what might be called 'Whose classroom is it anyway?'.

Control can be thought of as being exercised over children's play in the following ways:

- control by resources;
- control by adults;
- control by peers;
- control by the child.

It is important to consider the implications of these controls on children's freedom to have autonomy, and thus creativity, in their learning.

Control by resources

The resources that are provided for children to play with are always chosen by adults, but the ways in which they are used can be in children's control. In general, learning is more effective when resourcing is generous and can be used flexibly according to children's wishes.

Some play, such as water play, for example, is often a source of anxiety to practitioners who see it in terms of its problematic wetness, and control its use by constant reminders to children to 'be careful'. Research has shown (May 2000) that water play curtailed either by its positioning in cramped conditions or by adults' attempts to keep children dry, had a significant effect on the level of the involvement of the playing children. Children who were not in control of how or where the water was used were seen to engage in casual, haphazard and unplanned activity that often resulted in significant spillage. Water play that was positioned in generous proportions and placed outside where dryness mattered less, gave rise to deep-level play where children engaged in co-operative imaginative scenarios, setting their own rules of engagement and using complex language to accompany their play scripts. A lessening of control by the adults not only gave rise to higher-level learning but also lessened so-called 'behaviour problems' as children were far too engrossed to wish to misbehave.

Control by adults

Adults, of course, control most aspects of early years provision, either explicitly or implicitly. Explicit control is evidenced by an adult agenda that allows for little autonomy on the part of the children. This may be seen in following ways:

- access to the outdoor area is limited;

- children are encouraged to engage in particular activities that the practitioners value more highly than others;

- the sessions are divided into short allocations of time to allow for snack times or visits to other parts of the building;

- children are encouraged to stay at an activity until it is 'finished' or to produce a completed piece of work or object to take home;

- adults ask 'closed' questions related to the assessment of children's knowledge rather than answer questions that children have;

- adults value symbolic representation over creative activities;

- adults spend much of their time managing low-level clearing up rather than talking to children about their learning;

- children are given templates to use when drawing or painting;

- adults assess by completing tick-sheets rather than by observing children at play.

The points above reflect a setting where creativity will probably not flourish as children's agendas are of secondary importance to those of the adults. The child who asks, 'Have I finished yet?' has no control over his or her activity, and children who are given templates to draw round are given the clear message that adults' images are 'right' and that those of children are 'wrong'. This type of control is often known as 'top-down' and allows for little freedom for the children.

Implicit control over settings is based more securely on principles and beliefs and is founded on a secure understanding of child development. Practitioners will base all aspects of their practice, from choices of resources to the ways in which staff spend their time, on their professional knowledge of how to support and extend creative learning. This is often referred to as the 'bottom-up' model and necessitates a subtle sharing of control with children so that it is the children's agendas that take priority. This is often the more complex system to operate as it requires all members of staff to understand clearly why the setting is organised in the way that it is. They need to be secure enough in the sharing process to relinquish significant elements of control to the children. In practical terms, organising the setting to offer freedom to children can be thought of as requiring a 'sandwich effect' in which the 'top and bottom' sections of planning and assessment are carefully thought through and implemented, leaving the middle, or 'filling', section to be flexible and open-ended.

This implicit control recognises that while the adults are responsible for everything that happens in the setting, both the overt and the hidden curriculum, the ownership of ideas, preferences and processes stay with the children.

Control by peers

One of the most complex and yet valuable lessons that can be learned in the early years setting is how to work collaboratively while being creative or solving problems. Where adults are not present in children's play, the control of the 'script' or agenda remains with the children. Children do not assume control equally but exert control over, or acquiesce to, their peers. Because of the slippery nature of play it is often a hard activity to join, especially if there is already a strong fantasy theme being enacted. A child with a controlling script can often be unremittingly dominant and without an adult present to exercise some positive discrimination in favour of the weaker players, some harsh lessons are learned about how difficult it is to join a group. Genuine negotiation is rare among very young children and support by practitioners is one of the most valuable actions that can be taken to ensure that ideas and creations of the more timid children come to fruition. It is here that the 'review' part of a 'plan-do-review' system is so valuable as it provides the opportunity for children to verbalise their creative ideas and processes to a small group.

Control by the child

The extent to which children exert control over their own play would seem to depend on several unvarying factors. As Tina Bruce (1987) says: 'Giving control to children requires us to understand children from the inside looking out rather than from the outside looking in'. From the inside looking out, we can imagine children asking themselves questions as they approach the activity or provision they are about to join and making a decision about whether to become involved in what is happening there. Questions could include:

- 'Is this an activity that I understand?'

- 'Is there something here that interests and challenges me?'

- 'Have I something that I can contribute to this activity?'

These are not, of course, articulated by children but are implicit in what we understand about the ways in which children engage with learning. These and other similar questions are enshrined in Te Whariki, the New Zealand early years curriculum, as it considers the curriculum from a child's viewpoint.

Children who are uncertain about the ground rules of play, such as how long they are able to play or whether the adults have a learning agenda, are those who play with less purpose. When a setting gives mixed messages about the reason for, perhaps, the water play (is it for a purpose of the child's choosing or is to teach about floating and sinking?), children do not commit to the play with the certainty that they will if they know they have ownership and control. Alongside lack of purpose goes lack of creativity.

Children's construing, both of the play on offer and of their relationship to it, seems to depend on their view of themselves as effective learners. Butler and Green (1998) suggest that the confidence to approach an activity is dependent upon a match between how the child expects to perform and the reality of the performance. Repeated performances with consistent results begin to confirm a child's view of themselves as competent or incompetent and become a validation of the child's self-image. Consistency of high-quality provision would seem to offer the best chance to promote successful encounters with play that help children see themselves as people who have enough confidence to be creative and imaginative players.

Children's self-image is made up of the 'super skills' referred to by Sir Christopher Ball in *Start Right* (1994). These super skills – aspiration, socialisation and self-esteem – seem to enable children to take control of their play experiences and to profit from them. This could well lead on to what Margaret Donaldson (1987) describes as the notion of choice between what children might have done as opposed to what they have done. Here lies the beginning of real choices as children direct their thoughts along the lines of 'if not this, then, that'. Independence of thought is control indeed.

Play and creativity in society

A final thought needs to be directed to the value society attaches to children's playful activities as a way of encouraging creative thought in the next generation. Worryingly, although children seem, like the rest of the population, to be ever busier, times for recreational play, which can be structured and directed by children themselves, appear to be infrequent and given low status by parents.

Families are worried about allowing their children freedom to roam or 'play out' in the ways that their parents and grandparents did and toys are increasingly single-purpose and 'educational'. Entertainment for children tends to appear in cartoon format and families are encouraged to buy edited reading scheme books for young children instead of stories written by real authors that will inspire their imagination. Opportunities for creative and imaginative thinking and doing seem to be closing down rather than being opened up, thus placing an ever heavier burden on the early years setting to redress the balance. It may well be that it is in the educational settings of the twenty-first century that Loris Malaguzzi's vision of the many creative ways that are available to know are made available to children:

> The child . . . has a hundred thoughts
> a hundred ways of thinking
> of playing, of speaking
> a hundred, always a hundred
> ways of listening
> of marvelling of loving
> a hundred joys
> for singing and understanding
> a hundred worlds
> to discover
> A hundred worlds
> to invent
> A hundred worlds
> to dream.

(quoted by Filipini and Vecchi 1996 – see p.97 for complete text)

Questions for reflection

1. What are your views on the nature of play and its value? How do you define it and how would you explain your philosophy to parents and colleagues?

2. Do we impose limitations on children's thinking through creating common curricula which have expected, adult-driven, outcomes? How can we place young children and their ideas at the centre of early years education? Should we?

3. How can we ensure that children have opportunities to explore and learn from their environments in a world which seems increasingly adult-controlled?

References

Athey, M. (1990) *Extending Thought in Young Children: A Parent–Teacher Partnership*. London: Paul Chapman.

Ball, C. (1994) *Start Right: The Importance of Early Learning*. London: Royal Society of Arts.

Bennett, N., Wood, L. and Rogers, S. (1997) *Teaching through Play*. Buckingham: Open University Press.

Bruce, T. (1987) *Early Childhood Education*. London: Hodder & Stoughton.

Bruce, T. (1991) *Time to Play in Early Childhood Education*. London: Hodder & Stoughton.

Butler, R. and Green, D. (1998) *The Child Within*. London: Butterworth Heinemann.

Claxton, G. (2003) *Serious Frivolity; laying foundations for a creative life*. Unpublished keynote conference presentation; Canterbury Christ Church University College, 21.06.2003 *Play, Creativity & Learning*.

Csikszentmihalyi, M. (1997) *Creativity*. New York: Harper Perennial.

DfEE/QCA (2000) *Curriculum Guidance for the Foundation Stage*. London: QCA.

DfES (2003) *Excellence and Enjoyment: A Strategy for Primary Schools*. London: DfES.

Donaldson, M. (1987) *Children's Minds*. London: Fontana.

Duffy, B. (1998) *Supporting Creativity and Imagination in the Early Years*. Buckingham: Open University Press.

Filipini, T. and Vecchi, V. (eds) (1996) 'No way, the hundred is there', by Loris Malaguzzi (trans. L. Gandini), in the catalogue of the exhibition *The Hundred Languages of Children: Narrative of the Possible*, p. 3. Reggio Emilia: Reggio Children s. r. l., Via Bligny 1/A, 42100 Reggio Emilia, Italy (www.reggiochildren.it).

Laevers, F. (1994) (ed.) *Leuven Involvement Scale for Young Children EXE Project*. Leuven, Belgium.

Leuven Involvement Scale for Young Children (1994) EXE Project. Leuven, Belgium.

Malaguzzi, L. 'No way, the hundred is there', in Filipini, T. and Vecchi, V. (eds) (1997, 2nd edn) *The Hundred Languages of Children: Narrative of the Possible*. Reggio Emilia: Reggio Children.

May, P. (2000) 'Waterplay in early years settings'. Unpublished MA thesis. Oxford Brookes University.

NACCCE (1999) *All Our Futures: Creativity, Culture & Education*. London: DfEE.

Pellegrini, A. D. (1991) *Applied Child Study: A Developmental Approach*. Hillsdale, NJ: Lawrence Erlbaum.

Powling, C. (ed.) (2005) *Waiting for a Jamie Oliver: Beyond Bog-standard Literacy*. National Centre for Language and Literacy, University of Reading.

Robinson, M. (2004) *Themes for the future of initial teacher education*. TTA *ITE Futures* Conference, Radisson SAS Portman Hotel 22/04/2004.

Sylva, K. (1994) 'The impact of early learning on children's later development', in Ball, C. *Start Right: The Importance of Early Learning*. London: Royal Society of Arts.

Te Whariki (1996) New Zealand Ministry of Education, Wellington, Learning Media.

The new health visitor

Sally Robinson, Jane Arnott and Jane Greaves

Public health workforce

SINCE THE LATE 1990s the British government has pushed forward a major reform programme with an agenda to reduce poverty, social exclusion and health inequalities between people (Department of Health 2003). The prime method by which it has striven to achieve these goals has been through a revitalisation of public health. Public health today, as in Victorian times, recognises that the origins of many health problems are environmental and social, not medical; and many, such as illegal drugs and tobacco, can only be tackled through international consensus by governments. In 2002 Derek Wanless reported that the National Health Service could not afford to continue to treat the sick at its current level indefinitely, the solution was the prevention of illness and the promotion of health (HM Treasury 2002; 2004). Public health has become an economic imperative.

Public health is being carried out by an army called the public health workforce. According to the Chief Medical Officer this includes those who have a role in health improvement, such as social workers, teachers and doctors, and those who spend a major part of their work in public health practice, such as environmental health officers, health promotion specialists, community development workers, school nurses and health visitors. The public health workforce is led by public health specialists and 'defined specialists' who have, for the first time, their own professional register, which is managed by the Faculty of Public Health. Public health practitioners and public health specialists are being required to become competent albeit to different levels, in the National Standards in Public Health (Skills for Health 2004; Faculty of Public Health 2005).

The public health workforce is directed by national targets set out by the government in white papers such as *Choosing Health: Making Healthy Choices Easier* (Department of Health 2004a), and by local interpretations of such targets set out in Local Delivery Plans written by primary care trusts. Their work remit spans working with individuals, families and the community, and, most of all, it demands inter-professional working.

The specialist community public health nurse

As part of this public health revival, the professional register of the Nursing and Midwifery Council (N&MC) was reorganised in 2004 to include specialist community public health nurses. Existing health visitors will continue to be called health visitors and will be registered as specialist community public health nurses (health visitors) (Nursing and Midwifery Council 2004a). However, those who undertake the new programme of education and meet the Standards of Proficiency for Specialist Community Public Health Nurses (Nursing and Midwifery Council 2005a), which are based on the National Standards in Public Health, will, in future, be registered and called specialist community public health nurses.

The Nursing and Midwifery Council explains that:

> Specialist Community Public Health Nursing aims to reduce health inequalities by working with individuals, families and communities promoting health, preventing ill health and in the protection of health. The emphasis is on partnership working that cuts across disciplinary, professional, and organisational boundaries that impact on organised social and political policy to influence the determinants of health and promote the health of whole populations.
>
> (Nursing and Midwifery Council 2005b)

Implications for family-centred health visiting

The expectations resting on these new public health professionals are enormous and present a number of challenges. One challenge is how to take on the extended role without losing the elements of the job that are currently recognised as being appreciated and worthwhile. For many families, health visitors are perhaps best known for their work in supporting parents, carers and families, and for acting as a co-ordinators of care on behalf of families (Department of Health 1999a). Health visitors are notified of the birth of all babies within their GP practice population. At about fourteen days, health visitors visit the families, carry out an assessment of their needs, noting medical, social, psychological and cultural circumstances. The assessment helps to determine the level of support that is put in place until the child enters school.

A key feature of the work with families is child health surveillance, a universal service for all children focused on screening and developmental checks. It has been criticised for being a professionally driven, inflexible programme of care based upon the detection of defects (Elliman 2005). The move to a wider child health promotion model began with the fourth edition of the health visitor's 'bible', *Health for all Children* (Hall and Elliman 2003), and has been further developed into the Child Health Promotion Programme within Standard One of the *National Service Framework for Children, Young People and Maternity Services* (Department of Health 2004b). The latter aims to provide a universal but also targeted service based on a partnership between professionals and parents. It aims to be flexible, to give priority to mental and emotional health as well as physical health and to include the welfare of the mother and family (Elliman 2005).

The more holistic aims of the health promotion programme, and indeed other parts of the National Service Framework, partly reflect what John Bowlby asserted half a century ago, that investing in the emotional health of a young child can reap rewards in terms of social behaviour later on (Bowlby 1953). Home visiting is associated with improvements in parenting skills, child behaviour problems, child intellectual development, the detection of postnatal depression, social support, rates of breastfeeding and a reduction in unintentional accidents and injuries (Elkan *et al.* 2000).

The National Service Framework stipulates that all primary care trusts and local authorities need to include targeted programmes for vulnerable children and community-based programmes. This means that the new specialist community public health nurses have to assess the needs of the community, not just the family. In practice, this means accessing and analysing local epidemiological, social and environmental data produced by regional offices of public health. Furthermore, the government has set out national targets to reduce smoking, obesity, teenage pregnancies and binge drinking within their overall aim to pay particular attention to people living in areas of deprivation and to reduce health inequalities (Department of Health 2004a). So just as the evidence to support the importance of home visiting and traditional family-centred health visiting is growing, and other countries such as Australia seek to emulate this valuable work (Alperstein and Nossar 2002), the public health agenda in the UK is pulling the new specialist practitioner public health nurses in another direction (Weeks *et al.* 2005).

Working together to address health needs

The challenges of trying to address the individual needs of a child and the needs of a community, let alone a government, are evident. This is why government white papers (Department of Health 1997; 1999b) have set out that the new public health agenda is to be met through established methods of working that are collectively called public health practice. Public health practice means assessing the health needs of local communities using epidemiological and socio-economic measures. It means working across agencies such as education, housing and health. It means working alongside other professionals (multi-professional working) in a way that one professional respects and learns from another professionals (inter-professional working).

Health visitors are experienced in working with other agencies on behalf of families. For example, they liaise with postnatal support groups, fathers' groups, teachers of infant massage, nurseries and social services. The Laming Report (Laming 2003), which resulted from the inquiry into the death of Victoria Climbié, is a lamentable reminder of the tragedy that can ensue if agencies fail to work together. Increasingly, health visitors are now working with other agencies on behalf of both families and communities.

Sure Start is an example of a multi-agency community development strategy that aims to intervene at a young age in order to improve children's physical, intellectual, social and emotional development, and to try to promote social inclusion. Focusing on geographical areas of deprivation it has provided services to support a wide range of children's needs including the Home Start home-visiting programme alongside parenting classes, literacy, play schemes and more. While some are cautiously optimistic that the research evidence supports the Sure Start strategy (Roberts and Hall 2000), it has also been described as being about a therapeutic state wishing to erode the privacy and autonomy of the family by prescribing emotional and behavioural correctness (Bristow 2005). As specialist practitioner public health nurses move out of the safety of family work into a wider, and more political, arena, they will need to call upon the support and skills of other agencies.

Health visitors are experienced in facilitating inter-professional working on behalf of families (Sines *et al.* 2001). This became a necessity in the light of anecdotal reports of families being visited by up to 16 individuals, generating multiple interventions and excessive stress. Health visitors contribute to integrated nursing teams whereby community-based nurses from different disciplines, such as paediatric nurses, school nurses and nursery nurses, work together to co-ordinate and plan care (Wright 2001). They also work with other health professionals such as doctors. For example, Davis and Spurr (1998) explain how doctors and health visitors were trained in parent counselling and worked together to help parents of preschool children with multiple psycho-social needs. The outcomes included improvements in parental self-esteem and their perceptions of their own children; decreased levels of parental stress and child behaviour problems; and improvements in the home environment. Sometimes inter-professional working may mean that professionals collaborate in order to allocate the most appropriate professional to address a particular need. In this way, inter-professional working is perceived to benefit clients by reducing professional overlap and client confusion (Robotham and Frost 2005).

School nurses are also to be called specialist community public health nurses, but unlike the health visitors, they are being asked to produce a portfolio of evidence to demonstrate appropriate experience first. This is questioned by some who recognise that many school nurses have extensive relevant experience (Madge and Franklin

2003). The profile of school nursing has been boosted in recent years by the National Healthy School Standard (Department of Health/Department of Education and Skills 1999), and the government sees school nurses as playing a leading role in the new National Healthy Schools Programme (Department of Health 2004a). The public health agenda should help to strengthen the historical link between health visitors and school nurses in order to provide a seamless service for children.

Every Child Matters (DfES 2003) proposed the move towards increased inter-agency working in the form of Children's Trusts, and inter-professional working through the use of a common assessment framework. The underpinning legal framework was provided in The Children Act 2004. This means that the responsibility for families and children is now shared across agencies such as health, education, social services, Sure Start and neighbourhood services, and how well these services are working together to improve the health and well-being of children will be reported in annual performance assessments and joint area reviews.

Learning together to meet health needs

Successful inter-professional working is complex and relies on a deep, mutual understanding and respect for different professional perspectives and models of working, and, to this end, the government has been a driving force behind inter-professional education (Department of Health 1999; Barr and Goosey 2002). A key aim is to promote a better understanding of each professional's role and responsibilities through learning together. Some of the barriers to inter-professional education include issues such as differences in professionals' histories, culture, language and status, which can lead to fears of losing professional identity (Headrick *et al.* 1998).

Evaluations of inter-professional learning that have taken place to date suggest that the desired outcomes are not being achieved because of factors to do with the length of courses and styles of teaching and learning (Sines *et al.* 2001; Freeth *et al.* 2002). The Learning and Teaching Support Network for Health Sciences and Practice, a section within the Higher Education Academy, undertook a critical review of inter-professional education. They question how much inter-professional learning can take place in a classroom setting and whether what is taught in the classroom is supported, or undone, by what students see in the workplace (Freeth *et al.* 2002). Inter-professional working and learning is more about a profound attitude change and understanding rather than a superficial understanding of differences in roles, and its achievement would be a major step forward for all early years professionals.

Practical and ethical challenges

While inter-agency and inter-professional working seeks to reduce professional overlap, save money, use resources more efficiently and reduce confusion for the client (Robotham and Frost 2005), it can also raise tensions around client confidentiality and about what information should or should not be shared between professions in the interests of the client. Health visitors are professionally obliged to communicate effectively and share knowledge with others for the benefit of their clients (Nursing and Midwifery Council 2004b). The new specialist community public health nurse may have concerns about a family, but hasty or inappropriate sharing of information with others could lead to the labelling of a child or a family as 'difficult,' 'untrustworthy' or 'unstable'. It could lead to unnecessary harm through an inappropriate intervention. The ethical challenges of child protection work, for example, are advertised through the media on a regular basis. A suspected perpetrator can be believed to be guilty until proven innocent, and health and social care professionals are quickly blamed for not intervening earlier when another tragedy comes to light.

Four widely accepted ethical principles (Beauchamp and Childress 1995) are: respect for autonomy; beneficence (doing good); non-maleficence (doing no harm); and justice (being fair and equitable). Consider these ethical principles alongside the practical challenges that are illustrated in these three case studies.

Case study 1

Peter was born to a 37-year-old woman called Josephine. Prior to giving birth, Josephine held a good job at executive level in a large multi-national company. Her pregnancy was unplanned, and her relationship with Peter's father ended before Peter was born. Consequently, Josephine found that her social circumstances changed from being an independent career woman and homeowner, to being reliant on benefits and living in poor-quality rented accommodation with mounting debts.

In addition to feeling stressed about her change in circumstances, Josephine was trying to cope with additional problems within her wider family as well as recover her poor physical health following childbirth. The health visitor offered support, but Josephine and Peter did not attend their GP surgery often and Josephine missed appointments that had been set for Peter, believing them to be unimportant.

Josephine continued to maintain contact with Peter's paternal grandparents and his father, for Peter's benefit. When Peter was two years old, Josephine became concerned about Peter's behaviour and her ability to respond appropriately and effectively to him as a mother. Meanwhile, other members of the family were also voicing their concern about Peter's behaviour, and this was causing rifts in the family. During this time, the health visitor reviewed Peter's development and behaviour at regular intervals and supported Josephine with her parenting and stress reduction. The health visitor also referred Josephine for debt counselling to Home Start, and to a self-help group for a medical problem.

When Peter was nearly three years old, Josephine was still finding Peter's behaviour challenging in the company of others; for example, when they went out shopping, or when he was playing with other children. Although the health visitor's developmental assessment at age 2 had indicated little cause for concern, Josephine felt that Peter was not listening to her. The health visitor carried out a hearing screening test, which was normal. This was also an opportunity to observe Peter's speech and language skills, which were well developed, and it was noted that Peter was co-operative in this one-to-one situation.

Josephine wanted Peter to attend nursery, and the health visitor was able to advise on local nurseries. Josephine decided on a nursery that was convenient to home and offered the opening hours that suited Peter and her. Peter started to attend nursery three or four times a week. However, within a few weeks of starting, the nursery school teacher asked Josephine to attend a meeting about Peter's behaviour. The nursery teacher said that he was behaving aggressively towards other children, and that he had a short attention span. The nursery had to assign one assistant to be with him at all times and he was frequently excluded.

The health visitor was invited to attend meetings with the nursery teacher and the local authority preschool adviser to discuss Peter's development and health. Further support was put in place and it was agreed that the health visitor would refer Peter for a developmental assessment with the community paediatrician, and a social communication assessment with a speech and language therapist. These assessments were inconclusive, but eventually Peter was diagnosed with Asperger's syndrome before he commenced primary school.

Questions for reflection on case study 1

1. How might Josephine's resilience have been challenged by the birth of her son?

2. Draw a spider diagram in which Peter is at the centre. Draw lines from Peter to all the professionals and agencies that have been involved in supporting him. Why have they supported him? Can you suggest any missing professionals or agencies?

3. How might Josephine feel about the system of support that has been set up for herself and her family?

4. List three benefits of collaboration between professionals working in health and education (statutory) and non-government organisations (voluntary) in this case study? Consider three threats to effective collaboration.

5. What ethical issues arise within this case study?

Case study 2

Sylvia's three older boys were born in quick succession before Sylvia was 22 years old. Their father left the family home when the boys were all quite young. Sylvia had spent most of her childhood in children's homes and at some stage was sexually abused. She suffered from an obsessive need to clean which caused chronic dermatitis on her hands. She was not supported by a mental health team and she rarely attended appointments. Following an incident when the boys were left alone, the children were taken into care with a foster family.

The family were eventually reunited with regular support from social services, which included practical support and monitoring through child protection procedures. It was during this time that the eldest boy disclosed that he had been sexually abused during the foster placement. He was referred to community child and mental health services. A few years later, the social services team withdrew their support.

Sylvia met Phil and they had three more children. Phil worked as a labourer and adopted a paternal role towards all six children. Sylvia provided basic care for the family, including regular meals and clean clothes, but the environment provided limited intellectual stimulation for growing children. Phil was keen to formalise the family arrangements, and the couple got married.

The three older boys attended the local primary school, but their behaviour was difficult to manage, and at times the school could not cope with them. Sometimes they were only allowed to attend for part of the day. The head teacher struggled to maintain an appropriate level of educational support for the children. Eventually the boys were assessed as being suitable to attend day and weekly boarding schools for children with emotional and behavioural difficulties.

Throughout this period of several years the health visitor was consistently involved with the family, and supported the parents through marital breakdown, births, parenting skills and an unwanted pregnancy. The parenting and care afforded to the younger children were enhanced by this ongoing engagement with a health visitor.

Today Sylvia is much more responsive to services such as play groups and nurseries, which will enhance the children's development and their preparation for early learning. More opportunities for the children to play at home are evident, and the family attend appointments, including speech and language therapy, much more consistently than before. Moreover, Sylvia demonstrates an increased confidence in her parenting skills and the children are demonstrating secure attachments.

However, last year the eldest boy was excluded from school due to his violent behaviour. Now all three older boys are linked to local criminal acts and are known to the police. The probation service is involved.

Questions for reflection on case study 2

1. Reflect on how Sylvia's early life experiences have affected her style of parenting.

2. Consider how parenting activities prepare children for learning. For example, having regular meal times, contact with an extended family, bedtime routines, going out for walks and playing in the park. What other parenting activities prepare children for learning?

3. How can parenting activities build children's confidence and self-esteem?

4. Place the three older boys at the centre of a spider diagram. Draw lines from the boys to all the professionals and agencies that have been involved with them. Consider how well this inter-professional and inter-agency collaboration has worked. Could it have been improved? If so, with what outcomes?

5. What are the ethical issues that arise in this case study?

Case study 3

Mike, a specialist community public health nurse, analysed the local statistics produced by the local director of public health. He noted that there had been a sharp rise in childhood obesity during the last five years within his local community. As a member of the local public health network he worked with representatives from the health promotion service specialising in diet and physical activity, representatives from children's services, local food wholesalers and the local council on a local plan of action. Mike's remit was to disseminate his own increased knowledge and skills about healthy eating and physical activity to fellow public health nurses, and to the families attending their clinics. Mike takes every opportunity to introduce the subject. His objective is to deliver a measurable reduction in the number of overweight children within two years, and thus meet the local target to reduce child obesity outlined in the Local Delivery Plan written by his primary care trust.

Here are some of the families in Mike's community.

Keith, who has an overweight three-year-old child called Nathan. Keith seems to talk about little else but food. Keith will not touch anything that has been processed or is not organic. He washes all food very carefully and is reluctant to allow Nathan to eat anything that has not been prepared by himself. He always makes sure Nathan eats everything. Keith confides that he feels guilty that Nathan's mother has left him.

Daisy, who became a mother four years ago, is 5ft 6in. and weighs 5 stone. She began aerobic exercise after her daughter was born in order to regain her figure. She becomes highly anxious if she cannot complete her six hours of exercise per day.

Lily is four years old. She does not eat chips, potatoes, chocolate, biscuits or bread. She says that they will make her fat. Her mother reports that she doesn't want Lily to go through the teasing that she endured as a fat child.

Hilary and Winston are overweight and have overweight twins aged 3. Both parents have been unemployed for more than five years and rely on state benefits. They are slowly paying off a number of debts. The hot chips from the fish-and-chip shop are their usual main meal in the evening. The twins tend to eat biscuits and crisps during the day, bought at the newsagent across the road. It is two bus rides to the nearest supermarket.

Questions for reflection on case study 3

1. List all the factors that are influencing the health and well-being of Mike's families.
2. What ethical dilemmas does this case study present?

Conclusion

There seem to be four key challenges facing the new health visitors. First, how to become specialist community public health nurses who can successfully meet the health and well-being needs of the individual child, the family and their local community while contributing to national health targets, in a way that avoids coercion and respects the autonomy of individuals.

The second challenge is for health visitors to confidently adopt their new role. Studies that have investigated health visitors' perceptions of their new specialist community public health nursing role show that they are concerned about the lack of clarity of their new role, about how to put it into practice, how to manage the broad range of work and how this might translate into a need for different levels of practice within the profession (Smith 2004; Carr 2005).

Third, the challenge is the need to strive towards making inter-professional working work on behalf of children, their families and their communities. This includes the achievement of successful inter-professional education of early years professionals so that they are confident and competent in their own profession, within a culture of mutual respect, to a degree to which they are able to share generously with other professionals.

The fourth challenge is dealing with the practical and ethical dilemmas that arise from the work of the new specialist community public health nurse.

References

Alperstein, G. and Nossar, V. (2002) 'Can the Families First initiative contribute to reducing health inequalities?' *Public Health Bulletin*, **13**(3), 38–41.

Barr, H. and Goosey, D. (2002) *Interprofessional Education: Selected Case Studies*. CAIPE. Commissioned by Department of Health, London.

Beauchamp, T.L. and Childress, J.F. (1995) *Principles of Biomedical Ethics*. Oxford: Oxford University Press.

Bowlby, J. (1953) *Child Care and the Growth of Love*. London: Pelican.

Bristow, J. (2005) 'A sure start for the therapeutic state'. 22 September. Available at: http://www.spiked-online.com/Articles/0000000CAD72.htm [Accessed 16/06/06].

Carr, S.M. (2005) 'Refocusing health visiting – sharpening the vision and facilitating the process'. *Journal of Nursing Management*, **13**, 249–56.

Davis, H. and Spur, P. (1998) 'Parent counselling: an evaluation of a community child mental health service'. *Journal of Child Psychology and Psychiatry*, **39** (3), 365–79.

Department of Health (1997) *The New NHS: Modern, Dependable*. London: HMSO.

Department of Health (1999) *Saving Lives: Our Healthier Nation*. London: HMSO.

Department of Health (1999a) *Making a Difference: Strengthening the Nursing, Midwifery and Health Visiting Contribution to Health and Healthcare*. London: HMSO.

Department of Health (1999b) *Working Together to Safeguard Children*. London: HMSO.

Department of Health (2003) *Tackling Health Inequalities: A Programme for Action*. London: Department of Health.

Department of Health (2004a) *Choosing Health: Making Healthy Choices Easier*. London: Department of Health.

Department of Health (2004b) *National Service Framework for Children, Young People and Maternity Services*. London: DoH/DfES.

Department of Health/Department of Education and Skills (1999) *National Healthy School Standard: Getting Started: A Guide for Schools*. London: DfEE.

Elkan, R., Kendrick, D., Hewitt, M. *et al.* (2000) 'The effectiveness of domiciliary health visiting: a systematic review of international studies and a selective review of the British literature'. *Health Technology Assessment*, **4** (13).

Elliman, D. (2005) 'From child health surveillance to child health promotion: clinical perspective'. Key note speech at From Health Surveillance to Health Promotion: Promoting Standard 1 of the Children's NSF. The Barbican Centre, London, 26 April.

Faculty of Public Health (2005) *UK Voluntary Register for Public Health Specialists*. Available at: http://www.publichealthregister.org.uk/ [Accessed 28/10/05].

Freeth, D., Hammick, M., Koppel, I., Reeves, S. and Barr, H. (2002) *A Critical Review of Evaluations of Interprofessional Education*. London: LTSN.

Hall, D.M.B. and Elliman, D. (2003) *Health for All Children* (4th edn). Oxford: Oxford University Press.

Headrick, L.A., Wicock, P.M. and Batalden, P.B. (1998) 'Interprofessional working and continuing medical education'. *BMJ*, **316** [online]. Available at: http:bmj.bmjjournals.com/cgi/content/full/316/7133/771 [accessed 16/06/06].

HM Treasury (2002) *Securing Our Future Health: Taking a Long-term View*. London: HM Treasury.

DfES (2003) *Every Child Matters*. Norwich: The Stationery Office.

HM Treasury (2004) *Securing Good Health for the Whole Population*. London: HM Treasury.

Laming, Lord (2003) *The Victoria Climbié Inquiry*. Command paper CMND5730. London: HMSO.

Madge, N. and Franklin, A. (2003) *Challenge and School Nursing*. London: National Children's Bureau.

Nursing and Midwifery Council (2004a) *N&MC News*. July.

Nursing and Midwifery Council (2004b) *The Nursing and Midwifery Council Code of Professional Conduct: Standards for Conduct, Performance and Ethics*. London: NM&C.

Nursing and Midwifery Council (2005a) *Standards of Proficiency for Specialist Community Public Health Nurses*. London: N&MC.

Nursing and Midwifery Council (2005b) *Specialist Community Public Health Nurse* [online]. Available at: http://www.nmc-uk.org/(hekahxrbh5of2j34zzxl1nr5)/aDefault.aspx [Accessed 16/06/06].

Roberts, H. and Hall, D.M.B. (2000) 'What is Sure Start'? *Archives of Diseases of Childhood*. **82**, 435–37.

Robotham, A. and Frost, M. (2005) *Health Visiting Specialist Community Public Health Nursing*. Oxford: Elsevier Science/Churchill Livingstone.

Sines, D., Appleby, F. and Raymond, E. (2001) *Community Health Care Nursing* (2nd edn). Oxford: Blackwell Science.

Skills for Health (2004) *National Occupational Standards for Public Health Practice*. Available at: http://www.skillsforhealth.org.uk [Accessed 16/06/06].

Smith, M.A. (2004) 'Health visiting: the public health role'. *Journal of Advanced Nursing*, **45** (1), 17–25.

Weeks, J., Scriven, A. and Sayer, L. (2005) 'The health promoting role of health visitors: adjunct or synergy?' in Scriven, A. (ed.) *Health Promoting Practice: The Contribution of Nurses and Allied Health Professionals*. Basingstoke: Palgrave, pp.31–44.

Wright, C. (2001) 'Community nursing: crossing boundaries to promote health', in Scriven, A. and Orme, J. (eds) *Health Promotion: Professional Perspectives*. Basingstoke: Palgrave, pp.51–64.

Safeguarding children

Angela D. Nurse

THIS IS NOT a chapter that is solely dedicated to child abuse or protection. Rather it is an attempt to put this whole issue of safeguarding children under debate and to gain a new perspective. It is a complex area of study, involving all the major services, each with its own legislation, guidance and reports, together with impact evaluations of voluntary, local authority and national expectations and extensive media attention. Child welfare also has a long (and not always distinguished) history.

Troubled by high levels of infant deaths, Parliament passed, in 1872, the Infant Life Protection Act. It had little impact on the number of young children dying as the result of abuse or neglect (Corby 2006). The Liverpool Society for the Prevention of Cruelty to Children was established in 1883 and the National Society for the Prevention of Cruelty to Children (NSPCC), based in London, in 1884. Five years later, Parliament tried again to curb the abuse and neglect of children with the Prevention of Cruelty to Children Act (1889), commonly known as the 'Children's Charter'. This Act enabled the state to intervene, for the first time, in relations between parents and children. Police were empowered to arrest anyone found ill-treating a child, and to enter a home if a child was thought to be in danger (Batty 2005). By 1908, 'the main components of child protection law that exist today were in place' (Corby 2006: 26). Further legislation, guidance and reports – covering all major services (early years, education, health, social services and sport) – followed, periodically, over the years. The principal piece of legislation in recent years was the Children Act 1989, passed by Parliament a century after the Children's Charter. Legislative activity over the century has tended to be reactive rather than proactive; high-profile deaths (Kimberley Carlile, Jasmine Beckford and Tyra Henry in the 1980s, and Lauren Wright and Victoria Climbié more recently) providing the incentive for action.

Child abuse is clearly not a new phenomenon – children have been whipped, starved, beaten, abandoned, locked up and sexually molested by their parents and care-givers for centuries. What has changed is our recognition of child abuse as a social problem. Calder (2005) has reviewed the history of child abuse and protection, placing our current concerns in context. He concludes that:

> the chastening truth is that child abuse has always been known about and talked about, that the willingness amongst the public and professionals to do something about it has waxed and waned through the years, and it is by no means clear that the professionals have always been on the more admirable side of the argument.

(Calder 2005: 26)

Furedi (1999, 2002) approaches risk from another perspective and has written extensively on his concerns that our society is becoming fixated on the idea of abuse and, consequently, is placing far too many restrictions on children's activity which 'has predictable consequences for their development'. Through our fears of being sued if children are hurt, 'children's accidents that were formerly understood to be an inevitable part of growing up are now seen through the prism of litigation'.

One of the intentions of this chapter is to help early years professionals clarify for themselves how they should respond to children and families who may be at risk. We have laws, policies, systems and structures intended to offer support and protection for vulnerable groups, but they have often failed. We need to consider the broader perspective of how we view children and how we ensure that they are prepared for independence and able to secure their own safety. Later on there is a discussion on young carers that highlights a number of incongruities in the UK in the way we view and behave with children. In debating these issues it is difficult to reconcile the opposing pictures of children undertaking tasks for which they are not yet ready with examples where children are over-protected and their ability to grow independently is compromised. It is difficult to avoid accusations of putting children at risk if we attempt to alter our society's perception of the dark and dangerous world which awaits our children outside our front doors, though it is well-known that for the majority of children who are harmed, the nightmare is within their family home or another place that we would consider safe. It is difficult to open an honest debate with parents (many of us are, or will be, parents) when incidents happen, such as a two-year-old with special needs who wandered from her playgroup and was drowned in a neighbour's pool. As early years professionals, the balance between 'protecting' and 'stifling' is a difficult one to manage. We can keep children physically safe if we remain alert, but we also need to ensure their emotional well-being is safeguarded too.

Terminology: a reflection of philosophy

The terms we use in considering children's safety are multifarious, sometimes obscuring the central point of the discussion, because it is an area that many people find very uncomfortable. This is not always because of incidents that involve harm to children in their care, but because of episodes from their own lives. This will be discussed later in this chapter. Many of the terms used, therefore, have a very negative impact which stops us from fully exploring what it is that children need protecting from. Terms include 'abuse', 'harm', 'protection' and 'at risk'. The term 'risk' is problematic. Like a number of terms common in education it has different meanings according to the context in which it is used. 'At risk' signals that children are vulnerable and may be harmed. It is our duty as caring professionals to ensure that this harm is at least minimised if not totally prevented. We are governed by legislation and local guidance as well as by our own ethical standards. The idea of 'risk', however, can be seen in a much more positive light if we replace it with 'challenge'. If we remove 'challenge' from children's lives it can also remove motivation and a sense of personal achievement in overcoming challenges. It also can mean that we are not helped to manage this form of risk for ourselves, leading to a reduced ability to foresee dangers and protect ourselves.

United Nations Convention on the Rights of the Child

The Convention on the Rights of the Child (UNCRC) was adopted by the United Nations on 20 November 1989 and entered into force on 2 September 1990. The UNCRC has rightly been described in glowing terms:

> It is the most widely ratified treaty in history, the first virtually universal human rights convention, it is the most far-reaching, the most forward-looking, the most comprehensive, it is the embodiment of a whole new vision for children, a definitive turning point in the struggle to achieve justice for children, and a document with an unprecedented potential to bring about dramatic change.
>
> (Alston and Tobin 2005: 2)

Only two states have not completed their ratification of the UNCRC. One of these is Somalia which has been in a constant state of war for the past two decades. The other is the USA. Though initially supportive (signing the Convention in 1995 during the Clinton administration), the USA has, under Bush, hardened its opposition to the UNCRC. The reasons for the USA's opposition have never been officially spelt out and, consequently, 'are frequently either exaggerated or misrepresented, or are assumed to be synonymous with the views of radical groups of one type or another, whose agenda is wholly antithetical to any reasonable notion of children's rights' (Alston and Tobin 2005: 10). For example, Winford Claiborne's (2003) diatribe against the UNCRC, stating 'some provisions of the convention appear to be innocuous, but most of them pose a great threat to the homes of our world'. Much of his paper is centred on the rights of individual families to use corporal punishment in disciplining their children. This is at variance with the views of many states in Europe where such physical punishment has been banned, both within the home and elsewhere. The UK has partially addressed this, having banned corporal punishment in state schools in 1987, but still allows 'reasonable chastisement' within the home. While asserting that 'many of the arguments invoked by opponents of the UNCRC are unsustainable and easily refuted', Alston and Tobin (2005) have identified a number of issues that need legitimately to be addressed before the UNCRC can fulfil its 'unprecedented potential to bring about dramatic change'. These include what they call

> structural rights such as the balance between children's rights and parental rights, the degree of any resulting public intrusion into the private domain and questions of respective federal or state responsibilities. [In the USA,] specific concerns relate to the Convention's implications for abortion, juvenile justice and corporal punishment.
>
> (Alston and Tobin 2005: 12–13)

Ratification indicates a state's commitment to the comprehensive list of children's rights incorporated within the UNCRC and binds it in international law. Nevertheless, as the UK parliamentary Joint Committee on Human Rights explained in its tenth report (2003), 'unless and until any of its provisions are incorporated [into national law] the role of the Convention within the [state] will be principally as the source of a set of child-centred considerations to be used when evaluating legislation, policymaking and administrative action' (Joint Committee on Human Rights 2003: Summary). The transition from ratification to incorporation has been slow. Few states have incorporated the UNCRC into local laws and compliance with the UNCRC has been patchy. As Kofi Annan (2002), Secretary-General of the UN, was forced to concede:

> The idea of children's rights . . . may be a beacon guiding the way to the future – but it is also illuminating how many adults neglect their responsibilities towards children and how children are too often the victims of the ugliest and most shameful human activities.
>
> (Annan 2002: 12)

It is generally acknowledged that the UNCRC has succeeded in raising our awareness of children's rights but, until its provisions are fully embedded and enforceable within national laws, for many children they will remain rights on paper only.

Our view of children so often focuses on their vulnerability and denies their strengths in looking after themselves and others. The UNCRC enshrines this view in its preamble:

> It reaffirms the fact that children, because of their vulnerability, need special care and protection, and it places special emphasis on the primary caring and protective responsibility of the family. It also reaffirms the need for legal and other protection of the child before and after birth, the importance of respect for the cultural values of the child's community, and the vital role of international cooperation in securing children's rights.

The UNCRC has been criticised for perpetuating a particular vision of children. Its values can seem very much a reflection of those of the western, developed world. The realities of many children's lives – where families and communities have been devastated by disease, war and disaster – bear little resemblance to the lives of the majority of children who live in the more settled and affluent western societies, where poverty is relative, not absolute. When examining our own perceptions of children and interpreting the views of others – whether expressed in official documents or in face-to-face conversations – we should acknowledge that how children are viewed changes with time, place, culture and circumstance. The UNCRC marked a radical shift in our thinking about children. It has provided us with a new vision of children as 'subjects entitled to rights and not only objects of protection' (Alston and Tobin 2005: 8). The UNCRC will continue to impact on the roles of all early years professionals and, hopefully, will inform both their professional communications with colleagues, parents and children and their vision of the future.

Parents' anxieties

It appears we are approaching a situation when many parents see even normal, everyday events – like a seven-year-old walking to the end of the road to post a letter or making a cup of tea – as dangerous. Adults often fear placing their children in such natural situations in case something goes wrong and they are deemed to be at fault. Yet, if children are never allowed to undertake such simple tasks, how will they ever learn to manage more complex situations as they grow older, where quick thinking and decision-making may be crucial? In the UK our concerns about 'danger' may have been heightened as a result of the immediate and often sensational way that the media has reported traumatic events. When children have disappeared, we follow the efforts to locate them hour by hour, feel relieved when they are safe, and are angry and saddened when they are not. Despite how it may seem because of this media attention, these events in the UK are probably no worse than in earlier times. The percentage of children who are murdered here is very small, compared with, for example, the USA where figures were running four times as high in 2000 as in the rest of the western world (Murray 2000). We worry about this yet allow children to watch murder and mayhem thousands of times on TV during their childhoods, not just as drama but also on the news and in documentaries. As a three year old I can remember vividly being very frightened by scenes from the Korean War on our small black-and-white TV. My daughter, at the same age, mirrored my response when watching scenes of violence during the Iran-Iraq War, but on a large colour screen. Each child, however, who dies or is traumatised is a tragedy, especially when warning signs go unheeded and co-operation between the agencies involved is minimal.

Protecting the vulnerable

Is life so much more dangerous to children in the UK now than it was 50 years ago? How can we compare our children's lives with those who live in war zones or areas of the world where poverty and disease are so rampant that daily survival is a challenge? In many ways the media has intensified our fears. We all now know, in quite graphic detail, what has happened to children such as Victoria Climbié, whose appalling death triggered the publication of *Every Child Matters* and the Children Act 2004. The failure of legislation, policies and practices to protect Victoria and the other children who have fallen through our national safety nets is an indictment of our society, not just because such incidents happen but because, in most cases, we *let* them happen. This occurs partly because we are often wary, or embarrassed, about issues to do with child protection. We reassure ourselves that we do not want to make things worse for children (they may be punished more if abusing parents think they have exposed); we are not sure that the evidence is strong enough; we do not want to upset parents as they may then take children elsewhere (and this would make it worse for the children); we are not prepared to put ourselves in a situation that is personally unpleasant: As early years professionals, we have to overcome our reluctance to intervene when necessary and always remember that we have a duty to place the child's interests at the centre of our concerns; their needs are paramount.

I learnt this lesson over twenty years ago and have used the following case study frequently in working with teachers and others in training on issues to do with safeguarding children.

Fay was four and a half years old and had joined the nursery class halfway through the previous term. She took a long time to settle, made no friends and never appeared at ease with either children or adults. The team was extremely concerned about Fay's silence, wondering whether there was any language impairment although she seemed to understand what was said to her within the context of the nursery. They were also very anxious because Fay would never choose an activity for herself, always waiting to be shown what to do. She never moved on to anything else until an adult had suggested an alternative and given her 'permission' to take part. For example, one morning she had been carefully cutting out old greetings cards – not a riveting activity – and managed 13 before the staff could bear it no longer and moved her on to something else. Fay seemed to have more than her fair share of bumps and bruises and staff always asked her parent (usually her mother) what had happened. Her parents were very pleasant and not offended by these questions, always offering plausible explanations. Normally they put it down to 'larking about' with her two-year-old sister or suggested she was just rather clumsy for her age, though this did not match the observations of the nursery staff. Fay, however, was always very happy to see either of her parents, running up to them to give them a big hug when they came to collect her. I was asked to observe Fay as the local advisory teacher.

In Fay's case, because of internal issues to do with the nursery school management, no decisions were made about referral to social or health services, although concerns remained and grew. After three months the newly appointed head teacher called in social services who examined Fay. Their

> reaction was that this was one of the worst cases of sexual abuse they had ever seen. The parents were not the abusers (rather, a male relative with whom they shared a house) but seemed aware of what was happening but powerless to intervene to resolve it because of the family dynamics. It was the gratitude of the parents in seeing the situation end that is part of the tragedy of this case. It also illustrates how easy it is to allow things to move slowly or cave in to institutional difficulties. All our instincts as experienced early years professionals told us that something was very wrong, yet Fay underwent three more months of harm because of our collective inability to act.

In more than twenty years as a practising early years teacher and advisor, I have seen very few cases as disturbing as the one above, but there are other instances where relationships between different agencies working with families did not support a co-ordinated approach to preventing harm. There was, occasionally, an inability to accept the evidence of very young children who were disclosing to us experiences that affected other members of their households. There were also cases where we knew children in the nursery were not living in optimal conditions, but other agencies were under pressure and our concerns were not high on their priority list. Sometimes, it has to be said, children undergoing abuse present, not as silent as Fay and other children I have met, but as difficult and angry, mistrusting adults, and manipulative and challenging in their behaviour because of what has happened to them. These children need our special understanding, care and attention but who among us can say, in all honesty, that they have not sometimes sighed with relief on the days when particularly challenging children have failed to appear. What we have to consider is why they are not there. Regulations to do with attendance of children of statutory school age (the term after the child's fifth birthday) in state schools have been considerably tightened over the past few years, but children attending nurseries and day-care are not always subject to the same scrutiny as older children, particularly in settings outside the state system. Poor attendance linked to other concerns may mask family difficulties which are not to do with possible child harm, but could be to do with a family under stress and in need of transitional support. If we view absence in this way, then we may be able to break a cycle which leads to risking a child's future well-being. We now have the five outcomes from *Every Child Matters* (2003) which encapsulate what children and young people have expressed that they want and not just what professionals have said they need. These are to be healthy, to stay safe, to enjoy and achieve, to make a positive contribution and to achieve economic well-being. All these are significant in the context of this chapter, but two aspects are especially important: to have security and stability and be cared for; and to attend and enjoy school. Schools, or other provision which offers children care and education, should be havens for those whose home lives are difficult, not an additional source of worry and marginalisation.

Young carers

One group of children whose needs have largely been ignored are those who become 'carers' for adults in their families. For many years, young carers were either not recorded or grossly under-reported in official statistics. Awareness of, and support for, these young people, however, have increased since the beginning of the 1990s. The General Household Survey for 1990 (OPCS 1992), which looked at carers, failed to count any carers under the age of 16. In 1995, the Health Services Management Unit at Manchester University estimated the number of under-18 carers to be between 10,000 and 40,000. By the 2001 census, as Dearden and Becker (2004) point out, the figure has risen to 175,000 nationally. These figures are unlikely to include the very young for the simple reason that we do not *expect* to see such young children in the role of family carer. Yet very young children do take on caring responsibilities for adults in their families, particularly when the adults have illnesses, disabilities or are substance abusers. Aldridge (1995) writes that in her research in 1992 she interviewed 11 carers in Nottingham who were aged between 3 and 18. Dearden and Becker (2004), with a research sample of 6178 young carers, established that less than 1% was aged below 5 but 29% were aged between 5 and 10. In exchanging the role of 'child' for the role of 'adult', not only do they have to undertake tasks (like taking care of the household, washing, toileting and dressing dependent relatives, finding food and money) but they could also become responsible for children in the family who are even younger than they are. Through a sense of duty to the family, young – and sometimes very young – carers are compromising their own futures by interrupting the development of social relationships and putting their emotional health and education at risk.

Despite local and national initiatives and a variety of supportive projects, the number of families who rely on young carers continues to increase. The specific needs of these children have to be recognised and addressed by all early years professionals – and not just by those responsible for providing the direct support that their families require. As Baker and Newnes (2005: 38) point out, 'children used to caring for other members of the family need to have their continuing role of carer respected even when acting in ways teachers find challenging', not be subject to further maltreatment. The children themselves often have been loath to ask for support because they fear the break-up of their families; yet we, as adults and as a society, have failed to ask what we can do to help them and to think creatively about the provision of appropriate family support, given that the support the children so willingly offer saves our society millions of pounds each year.

An attitude change

As early years professionals, we can start by reviewing our own attitudes to families who, often through no fault of their own, fail to live up to 'our' standards. Not surprisingly, surveys of professionals employed in the 'caring' services reveal that the majority have come from 'middle-class' backgrounds with little or no experience of living in poverty or being under constant stress. Although this picture may be gradually changing as more mature students enter higher education through the increased opportunities to return to study offered by foundation degrees, for example, many of us (if we are honest) still hold very entrenched views about 'good parenting', even if only subconsciously. In the lectures I give on safeguarding children, I always start with a stark warning to students – don't judge families solely on the grounds of your own experience. There are occasions when, as early years professionals, we are asked to visit families in their own homes. Many of the homes I have visited over the years have been much grander (and tidier) than my own, though some have not. One family I visited lived in rented accommodation in a poor area of North London. The floor in the kitchen had rotted away in the middle and collapsed, leaving a border barely three feet wide around the hole, on which were balanced an oven, fridge, sink and other necessities. The landlord was not prepared to do anything about it as the house was due for demolition sometime in the future. The four-year-old growing up in this decay had cerebral palsy. Other professionals had placed the blame on the parents – why did they not do something themselves to ameliorate their poor housing conditions? But they had exhausted all that was in their power to do and they had no money to affect the repairs themselves. Yet this little boy came from one of the most loving families I have ever met. Other children I have visited were growing up in the most beautiful, expensive surroundings with all that they could want, materially, but they lacked the warm loving relationships with their parents so important for healthy emotional development, being sequestered away in huge rooms of their own without companionship for long periods of time. Which of these children is more 'at risk'? The little boy with cerebral palsy living in deplorable housing conditions but with the support of a loving family; or the children deprived of companionship and closeness with their parents but who had everything that money could buy? To what extent do our own experiences (both as children and as adults) colour our perception of, and response to, these and other children and families in need?

The effect on children: resilience

Children are sensitive to their parents' feelings, pick up on their anxieties and become fearful or sometimes angry about the limits placed on their lives as a result of parental fears. Our difficulty as professionals, when encouraging young children to take more control of their own lives, is that we run the risk of accusations of failure in our duty to protect and care for other people's children if anything happens, however minor.

As professionals we need to consider how we prepare children to take care of their own needs and take control of their own lives. The concept of *resilience*, the ability to overcome adversity and make good out of it, is an important one to explore. Clarke and Clarke (2000: 79–80) ask why some children succeed and others fail. There have been few systematic studies so far and, as they point out, it would be very difficult to design proactive research. Their review of existing studies provides some clues to the origins of resilience in children:

- Constitutional dispositions and a sociable personality which is 'likely to attract positive attention from teachers in school';
- A 'network of affectionate support';
- Schools (or other settings) 'where children are valued and encouraged to learn';
- Friends within a supportive peer group;
- An ability to plan purposefully.

As Corby (2006) points out we are only just beginning to understand what factors are important to the development of resilience and how they can be identified. Until we are sure that we understand, we run the risk of deciding a child is resilient when the child's response may be superficial, masking the hurt that is suppressed. Corby (2006) concludes 'on the positive side it may inform supportive help given to children coping with adverse circumstances, but there are dangers that children could be too easily identified and not helped in an effective way' (Corby 2006: 191). Another way to support children is to ensure that they are always listened to and their fears taken seriously. The Commission for Social Care Inspection (2005) in its second report noted that 'some children feel they are adequately listened to and consulted' (section 2.5) but 'many other children do not have sufficient opportunities to express their views or concerns' (section 2.6). By developing an environment where discussion and debate is welcomed and time is set aside to do this, children's viewpoints can be valued. In this way, other issues can be ameliorated through open discussion, including perhaps bullying and racism.

One aspect that seems to have helped a number of children to come through very difficult circumstances is a positive relationship with at least one other person who has been able to show genuine interest in the child and has restored a sense of worth. There have been examples of this kind of relationship throughout history, some grounded in myth or fairytale (Cinderella, Snow White), but more recently in a plethora of autobiographies that have explored deviant childhoods and seemingly positive, adult, outcomes. These have recently been termed 'misery memoirs' by a number of reviewers in newspapers and on radio and many are harrowing. *Angela's Ashes* (McCourt 1996) has already been mentioned, but there are numerous others by British authors, such as *Ugly*, which recounts the story of Constance Briscoe (2006) who became a barrister and judge; *Once in a House on Fire* by Andrea Ashworth (1999) who graduated from Oxford University and became a research fellow; or *Bad Blood: A*

Memoir by Lorna Sage (2000), which explores the impact of grandparents on family dynamics. An internet search of booksellers will bring up many more titles from the UK and across the world. These can be starting points to try to understand how children rise through their early experiences and may give us a lead into supporting them appropriately. Corby (2006) points out that general ability may play a part in people's ability to come to terms with trauma. Perhaps the ability to write and to use their experiences to give hope and support to others is crucial to personal resolution.

We have to accept, however, that many incidences where children are harmed are suppressed and do not surface for many years, often restricting a person's choices in life because of the deep-seated feelings of worthlessness or anger. These feelings and their causes can be hidden away from family, friends and colleagues, only surfacing when there is a trigger which opens the door to a world they would rather forget. This became apparent to me when a close friend and I attended a day seminar on religious education and child protection many years ago. My friend left the room suddenly and I found her outside in floods of tears. She revealed to me a series of events that had happened when she was living in a village as a very young child. Her reaction was to enter a profession – and a particular field – where she thought she could help children and could regain some sense of self worth by giving back to the community. Each year I am asked to give a number of lectures on child protection and know that there will be students who themselves have issues. We start the sessions talking openly about childhood issues and offer options, so that students can leave the session and find someone they are comfortable with to talk them through in the first instance. They can then decide whether they wish to use the university counselling service. Another way for undergraduates to resolve issues from their own early lives is to ask them to reflect upon their own childhoods. They are reassured that they can select what they wish to discuss in their essays and anything raised will be treated in strict confidence by the lecturers involved. A small number each year choose to use this opportunity to come to terms with personal events, not solely of abuse, but divorce, death and other challenging circumstances that have impacted on their young lives. We consider it important to assist prospective early years professionals to come to terms with these experiences because otherwise they may influence the way they later respond to others in their professional lives. We have an alternative assignment for those who are not yet ready to confront these issues but very few have opted for it in the past ten years. We have wondered, however, whether we had the balance quite right when a couple of students approached us looking very worried about this assignment, because they had had very happy childhoods and did not know what to write about.

Safeguarding children does not just involve keeping them safe from physical harm. Humans are emotional beings, however hard we may try to mask it. The reciprocal relationship between a child and an adult, whether a parent or another from the close family or community, is often only partially explored as we learn to become early years professionals, though the importance of the social and emotional development of infants is now being more fully investigated. At the beginning of the 1950s, as I grew up, many mothers were counselled not to pick up their babies when they cried, nor to feed 'on demand', because this would 'spoil the child'. It is now recognised that the physical comfort of being held closely is very important for a new baby or young child in any society, but it is seen almost as a 'sin' if adults enjoy this too, unless they are very closely related. This dilemma raises important issues for our practice with children, as more and more very young children are placed for longer periods in daycare, at the same time as increasingly restrictive legislation has impinged on family and professional life. Many students now ask 'can I touch children?'

For teachers, unions, attempting to protect their members from accusations of abuse, have normally responded 'no'. This has been particularly difficult for men who work with young children in the UK. Elaborate systems have been established to ensure parents feel secure when leaving their children in the care of men; confident, for example, that there is always a female nursery nurse or classroom assistant available if a child needs changing or washing. Parents have been asked to sign forms either agreeing to the normal practices in the nursery or school or allowing them to express their own reservations and wishes, effectively allowing them to request an alternative approach. This is not a particularly new concern and not always centred on males. This incident occurred at the start of my career, when we used to take the whole school for games each week. As a young teacher, not long married, I was expected to accompany the boys into their changing room, but my colleague who taught in a parallel class was expected to go with the girls because she was unmarried, despite the fact she was also a qualified nurse and had spent much time on male wards.

The scenarios above raise issues about how we work with and support children physically, emotionally and socially. Practitioners and those in training – whatever the student's age – are confused by the messages we are given by professional associations and unions, as well as social services, particularly to do with touching children. Some of this advice is aimed at protecting their members from false and unfounded allegations, but what are the messages we are giving to very young children who crave physical contact because they are feeling anxious or unhappy? Are we saying to them 'I don't want to touch you, I don't have time for this – I do not value you sufficiently, therefore I am turning you aside'? This whole area needs to be revisited and reviewed from a child's perspective, perhaps by talking about what they feel happy with and discussing 'acceptable' and 'non-acceptable' physical contact. They need to feel secure enough to say to an adult 'I don't like this. Please don't do it'. During times when children and families are under stress, it is particularly important that the messages we give do not include further rejection. One way of dealing with the dilemmas this raises for us is to take the lead from the children, responding to their needs, never imposing upon them.

Conclusion

Some of the concerns raised and ideas presented may be controversial and difficult to accept, particularly as readers will come from different personal and professional perspectives. The aim, however, was to raise the level of debate and to start to explore how our society views children and what our expectations are of those we trust to help to raise them. Much of what we should do to protect those 'at risk' is set out by law and we have a professional and moral duty to abide by these rules, however difficult that may be personally. The Children's Services Guidance, *What To Do If You're Worried a Child Is Being Abused* (2003), states clearly in its introduction that:

> All those who come into contact with children and families in their everyday work, including people who do not have a specific role in relation to child protection, have a duty to safeguard and promote the welfare of children'.

There are wider issues, however, to do with how we manage other 'risks' (challenges) in the work we undertake and how we ensure that parents and carers agree with what we do. In the end we have a responsibility to guarantee that our children learn to take care of themselves, because we will not always be there to take care of them. Simon Knight (2002), in a presentation to the Play Wales conference, explored how adult society is restricting many of the opportunities that children have had over time to explore their environments and gain control of themselves physically and emotionally. He writes, 'as adults modelling tomorrow's adults, we should be able to stress that life does and should contain risks. We should know when to intervene in children's lives and when not to interfere, without fear of legislation'.

Questions for reflection

- Is the UK a more dangerous place for children now than it was for our parents, grand parents and previous generations? What evidence is there for your viewpoints?

- What are your views on physical contact with the children in your care?

- How have we come to a point where parents and others are so concerned about children's safety that we may be doing children harm by overprotecting them? How can we resolve this and restore some balance?

- Discuss openly your anxieties about dealing with a child protection issue within your setting. Do you understand the systems in place and what *must* you take into consideration?

References

Aldridge, J. in Becker, S. (1995) *Young Carers in Europe: An Exploratory Cross-National Study in Britain, France, Sweden & Germany*. Loughborough University, Young Carers Research Group.

Alston, P. and Tobin, J. (2005) *Laying the Foundations for Children's Rights: An Independent Study of some Key Legal and Institutional Aspects of the Impact of the Convention of the Rights of the Child*. Florence: UNICEF Innocenti Research Centre.

Annan, K (2002) *We the Children*. New York: United Nations.

Ashworth, A. (1999) *Once in a House on Fire*. London: Picador.

Baker, E. and Newnes, C. (2005) 'The Discourse of Responsibility', in Newnes, C. and Radcliffe, N. (eds) (2005) *Making and Breaking Children's Lives*. Ross-on Wye: PCCS Books.

Batty, D. (2005) 'Timeline: a history of child protection'. *The Guardian*, May 18. Available at http:society.guardian.co.uk/children/story/0,,1219395,00.html

Briscoe, C. (2006) *Ugly*. London: Hodder & Stoughton.

Calder, J. (2005) 'Histories of Child Abuse' in Newnes, C. and Radcliffe, N. (eds) (2005) *Making and Breaking Children's Lives*. Ross-on Wye: PCCS Books.

Clarke, A. and Clarke, A. (2000) *Early Experience and the Life Path*. London: Jessica Kingsley.

Commission for Social Care Inspection (2005) *Safeguarding Children: The Second Joint Chief Inspectors' Report on Arrangements to Safeguard Children*. Newcastle: CSCI. Available at www.safeguardingchildren.org.uk

Corby, B. (2006) *Child Abuse: Towards a Knowledge Base*. Maidenhead: Open University.

Dearden, C. and Becker, S. (2004) *Young Carers in the UK: The 2004 Report*. London: Carers UK.

Department of Education and Skills (2003) *Every Child Matters*. London: TSO.

Department of Health (2003) *What To Do If You're Worried A Child Is Being Abused: Summary*. London: DoH.

Furedi, F. (1999) *Counting Mistrust: The Hidden Growth of a Culture of Litigation in Britain*. London: Centre for Policy Studies.

Furedi, F. (2002) *Culture of Fear: Risk-taking and the Morality of Low Expectations*. London: Continuum.

Office of Population Censuses and Surveys (OPCS) (1992) *General Household Survey: Carers in 1992*. London: Office of Population Censuses and Surveys (OPCS).

Joint Committee on Human Rights (2003) *Tenth Report*. London: HMSO.

Knight, S. (2002) 'What Children Lose When We Make Them Safe'. Paper for Play Wales conference, 12–13 June.

McCourt, F. (1996) *Angela's Ashes*. London: Flamingo.

Murray, I. (2000) 'Juvenile murders: guns least of it'. *Christian Science Monitor*, 27 March.

Sage, L. (2000) *Bad Blood: A Memoir*. London: Fourth Estate

United Nations (1989) *Convention on the Rights of the Child (UNCRC)*. New York: United Nations. Available at http:www.ohchr.org/english/law/crc.htm

Websites

Loughborough University Young Carers Research Group – www.ycrg.org.uk

Carers UK: the voice of carers – www.carersonline.org.uk

The Children's Society Young Carers Initiative – www.youngcarer.com

Winford Claiborne: The Gospel Hour – www.gospelhour.net

Paper 2063: Convention on the Rights of the Child – www.nspcc.org.uk

The National Society for the Prevention of Cruelty to Children: A Pocket History of the NSPCC – www.nspcc.org.uk/documents/history_of_nspcc

Inclusion and special needs: Can education successfully encompass both?

Sue Soan

Introduction

THIS CHAPTER AIMS to explore our practice with very young children with special needs and to provide an understanding of the issues surrounding inclusion, inclusive practice and special needs for early years professionals. As part of the introduction to this area, because it is such a complex field, a time-frame has been included to set developing policy, legislation and initiatives in context. In setting the context, terms will be defined and issues and perspectives reviewed. It will discuss inter-agency and trans-agency working and how these can be particularly pertinent when working with young children with special needs and their families. Educational inclusion may dominate the structure of the chapter, but it will also be of interest to other professionals working within any early years environment. It is anticipated that this chapter will enable readers to examine and debate their workplace practice and professional views critically, taking into account the role legislation, literature and research have on the development of inclusive practice and special needs within individual workplace settings. Through analysis and debate, the effectiveness of specific interventions and strategies within early years learning and teaching can be evaluated, alongside a reflection on how collaborative practice with other individuals supports parents, carers and the children themselves.

Understanding the definition of special educational needs

Special Educational Needs is defined in the SEN Code of Practice (DfES 2001:6) in the following way: 'Children have special educational needs if they have a learning difficulty which calls for special educational provision to be made for them.' However, it was in 1978 that the Warnock Report (DES 1978) first suggested 'special educational needs' (SEN) as an appropriate term to be used for any child needing extra support to enable them to access education. It was a significant and influential report, especially for children with learning difficulties and physical disabilities, and especially for early years education and care, as it also proposed that there was a need for early diagnosis and pre-school support. It also recognised the importance of greater parental involvement and offered an opportunity for parents to be seen as equal partners in the assessment process, though it never gave them the right to decide which type of school their child would attend. It recommended that professionals should focus on a child's potential and how they could address difficulties, rather than on their disability or learning need, though, in practice, in seeking extra funding, a child's difficulties have had to be stressed. The 244 recommendations from the Warnock Report (DES 1978) formed the basis of the Education Act 1981 and introduced the terms still used today within the SEN Code of Practice (DfES 2001) framework, such as: speech and language disorders; visual disability and hearing disability; emotional and behavioural disorders; and learning difficulties (specific, mild, moderate and severe). The main point that the Warnock Report stressed, however, was that 'the aims for education should be the same for all children' (Wedell 1990:22).

This is the most significant point, because it enabled the move away from *segregation* and the introduction of *integration* (see Figure 11.1). The Warnock Report had concluded that there was, at that time, a three-tiered system of integration. These were:

Stage 1: Segregation
Children with special educational needs were taught separately from other children in special schools. Theoretical model informing segregation was biological determinism.

Stage 2: Integration
Integration is a fixed state – children were integrated into mainstream schools if they could, with support, access the school's curriculum and environment. This is still considered a deficit medical model because the child has to change and receive help to support their needs. Theoretical model informing integration was / is social constructivism.

Stage 3: Inclusion
Inclusion is an active process and not a fixed state like integration. Diversity and difference is valued and therefore the school and the teachers adapt the curriculum and the environment so that the child can access, engage with and participate in the full life of a school. Theoretical model that informs this practice is post-structuralism.

FIGURE 11.1 The progress from segregation to inclusion

- Locational – where the site is shared, but special provision is separate to the rest of the school;

- Social – where children may attend mainstream classes for non-core subjects, but return to their class for core subject teaching; and

- Functional – where children with special needs are taught within a mainstream class by the class teacher all of the time (Wall 2003 : 13).

It is still valuable to consider these descriptors today when we are appraising special needs practice within our settings, even though at the time they were identified they referred to school; the concepts can be transferred to other kinds of provision.

During the 1980s and early 1990s the integration of children with disabilities and learning needs into the mainstream became accepted 'good' practice following the Education Act of 1981, which legislated that local education authorities (LEAs) had to provide children with special educational needs with the support they required, from birth if that was appropriate. The term used in the legislation for children with special needs is 'in relation to a child under that age, educational provision of any kind' (Education Act 1996, Part 4, Ch.1 : 312 : 46) and, of course, this is open to interpretation.

It was especially between 1988 and 2002 that legislation continued to influence and develop special educational needs provision directly. The following are by no means all of the acts and guidance to be published, but are the most significant when considering special educational needs provision. The wider educational and social argument about *integration* and *inclusion* ran alongside the legislation and documentation of this era; this will be discussed in greater detail later. Although much of the educational legislation refers to children of statutory school age, it has impacted on our thinking about the needs and rights of younger children. For example, the Education Reform Act 1988 (DES 1988) focused on trying to ensure that every child had equal access to a broad and balanced curriculum. Following this, the Disability Discrimination Act 1995 required schools and preschools to ensure that all children had equal access to the curriculum or activities, as well as to facilities, and that an anti-discrimination policy and ethos existed. Additionally, schools and providers were told to have admission statements for children with physical and cognitive special educational needs. For many schools and preschools their actual physical environments meant that they *could not* actually adhere fully to this Act. The Children Act 1989 placed the welfare of the child as paramount, clarified language and terminology used and emphasised the need for effective multi-professional systems and communication (DoH 1991), although funding was never made available to ensure that this happened. This piece of legislation was a UK response to the United Nations Convention on the Rights of the Child (1989) and it is interesting that the language used here concerning parents is that they have 'responsibilities' as well as 'rights', a term current in other 'educational' legislation. By referring to 'children in need', another dimension to working with children with special needs was introduced by this Act that has not always been helpful when different services are arguing about their responsibilities towards children and families and who funds this work.

Further legislation sought to improve parental involvement, enhance policies and improve assessment procedures. The Education Act 1993 (DfEE 1993) reviewed the Education Act 1981 and tried to rectify the inconsistencies that had been highlighted. This resulted in the introduction of independent special educational needs tribunals, offering parents the opportunity to question decisions made about the education of their children by LEAs.

The SEN Code of Practice (DfEE 1994) offered very specific and comprehensible guidelines to LEAs, practitioners and parents on all aspects of special educational needs. It is important to remember that the Code of Practice was guidance and not a legislative document, with providers needing only to pay 'due regard' to it. Although it was a very positive step forward for children with special educational needs, it must also be recognised that it caused massive additional work and responsibility for practitioners. Schools and preschools were expected to provide for all children's special educational needs and this included:

- the identification of SEN;
- the assessment of SEN using the new five-staged process (the final stage would result in a Statement of Special Educational Needs);
- the planning of the provision for children with special educational needs (Individual Education Plans (IEPs));
- a regular reviewing system of provision, statements and, importantly, progress;
- the establishment of a special educational needs co-ordinator (SENCo);
- the establishment of an SEN register.

Early years providers were not excluded from this and were also expected to follow this guidance for the children with special educational needs below the age of 5 as detailed in Section 5 of the Code of Practice (DfEE 1994). This again supported the philosophy of early identification and effective provision and intervention within a multi-professional framework. It was from this point, therefore, that early years settings had to establish special educational needs documentation and systems to ensure that parents were aware of the SEN Code of Practice and similar documents. Staff members needed to be informed and knowledgeable about special educational needs intervention and provision. Settings needed to ensure that they had a working knowledge of all agencies working with families and with children with special educational needs. The Nursery Education and Grant Maintained Schools Act 1996 (DfEE 1996) acknowledged the work and importance of early years provisions but also increased the expectations on providers who wished to obtain government funding, including allowing Ofsted to inspect their provision (Schedule 1 : 6 (1) a).

In 1997, with a change of government, *Excellence for All Children – Meeting Special Educational Needs* (Green Paper) (DfEE 1997) was introduced. This was the initial strategy for developing effective inclusion and for removing barriers to education, setting out a programme of action with targets to be met by 2002. As one of its highlighted 'policies for excellence', early identification and early intervention were established as crucial:

> The best way to tackle educational disadvantage is to get in early . . . early diagnosis and appropriate intervention improve the prospects of children with special educational needs, and reduce the need for expensive intervention later on. For some children, giving more effective attention to early signs of difficulties can prevent the development of SEN.
>
> (Section 1 : 5)

This heralded the development of 'multi-agency support for children with SEN [which] will be a priority in our new pilot programme for early excellence centres' (ibid.: Section 1 : 7) and services such as Sure Start. The Revised Special Educational Needs Code of Practice (DfES 2001) continued to emphasise the importance of preschool/early learning by incorporating a whole chapter on the identification, assessment and provision of special educational needs in the early years. It also moved from the five-stage to a graduated approach through Early Years Action, Early Years Action Plus, School Action, School Action Plus and a Request for a Statutory Assessment. There are some clear fundamental principles of the Revised SEN Code of Practice that relate to individual needs, mainstream placement/ inclusion, child and parent perspectives and entitlement to a broad and balanced curriculum. This Code of Practice also takes account of the SEN provisions of the Special Educational Needs and Disability Act 2001:

- a stronger right for children with SEN to be educated at a mainstream school;

- new duties on LEAs to arrange for parents of children with SEN to be provided with services offering advice and information and a means of resolving disputes;

- a new duty on schools and relevant nursery education providers to tell parents when they are making special educational provision for their child;

- a new right for schools and relevant nursery education providers to request a statutory assessment of a child.

(DfES 2001:iv,7)

Importantly for the discussion about inclusion and special educational needs, it also contains chapters on working in partnership with parents, pupil participation and working in partnership with other agencies (ibid.:iv,7). Chapter 4 (32–43), for example, emphasises consistently the expectancy of multi-professional and parental involvement in the identification, assessment and provision of early years special educational needs. Examples of this are:

1. Early Years Development and Childcare Partnerships (EYDCP) bring together private, voluntary and independent settings in a receipt of Government funding to provide early education, with LEAs, Social Services departments, health services and parent representatives in the planning and provision of services in the early education sector.

(ibid.:32, 4 : 1)

2. The triggers for intervention through Early Years Action could be the practitioner's or parent's concern about a child. . . .

(ibid.:35, 4:21)

3. As an important part of the Early Years Action the SENCO and colleagues should collect all known information about the child and seek additional new information from the parents. In some cases outside professionals from health, social services or the education psychology service may already be involved with the child. The SENCO should build on the existing knowledge of the child; multi-agency input is often very significant for young children.

(ibid.:35, 4:23)

The Special Educational Needs and Disability Act (2001) amended the Disability Discrimination Act 1995, Part 4, aiming to prevent the discrimination against disabled people in their access to education. The new duties of this Act, which specify the requirements on those providing school education, came into effect in September 2002. The guidance states:

The duties make it unlawful to discriminate, without justification, against disabled pupils and prospective pupils, in all aspects of school life. The principle behind this legislation is that wherever possible disabled people should have the same opportunities as non-disabled people in their access to education.

(Disability Rights Commission 2002 : 5)

Early years provision not provided for in a school is also included within this legislation (ibid.:98). It is interesting to reflect on how the preschool sector, particularly voluntary and private providers, have been drawn into nationally provided procedures and systems through the legislation in this field, which refers to them as much as it does to state provision. By accepting what is, in many instances, minimal funding, providers are now subject to more and more accountability through the new Ofsted inspections, which combine education and care and review closely procedures and practices for those who have special needs. Not all practitioners feel secure in identifying difficulties and working closely with parents in these sensitive situations, and moves towards increasing qualifications have not always taken this into account. Since 2002, government legislation and guidance have focused on moving the education and social inclusion agendas forward and have also concentrated on meeting the individual/personal needs of *every* child.

What is inclusion and inclusive education?

It was at the United Nations Education, Scientific and Cultural Organisation (UNESCO) world conference in Spain, in 1994, that governments were first asked '[to] adopt as a matter of law or policy the principle of inclusive education, enrolling all children in regular schools, unless there are compelling reasons for doing otherwise' (DfES 2001a). This was the Salamanca Agreement and it is from this date that the terms 'inclusion' and 'inclusive education' were introduced into our legislation and educational practice.

It must be remembered that it was less than twenty years prior to this date that children with special educational needs were educated in segregated settings (*biological determinism*) (see Figure 11.1) and their 'disabilities' focused on. Without doubt, this, in the majority of cases, meant that educators and society in general had lower educational expectations of these children and thus much potential was wasted. Recognising these factors the Warnock Report (1978) suggested that children with 'handicaps'/'special educational needs' should have the same rights as other children to be educated in a mainstream environment. This propelled integration into educational settings. Integration is a fixed state, however, and still focused on children's deficits, but unlike segregation it considered that children, if given enough support, could change/improve enough to fit in with the mainstream system (*social constructivism*) (see Figure 11.1). Thus with integration, children have to change to fit into an established system or otherwise remain segregated. In fact, as Soan (2004: 7) stated: 'the learner is provided with support to access the curriculum and the school environment already in place. This will not be changed to assist the learner.'

It was in this atmosphere of change, therefore, that educational inclusion emerged and is still developing 'as an active, not a passive process' (Corbett 2001: 55). *Poststructuralism* (see Figure 11.1) is the theoretical model that can be aligned to inclusion and inclusive practice, moving away from a medical to a social model. Originally, inclusion was very much aligned to 'access' for all to a mainstream provision, but very quickly academic thinking has developed further:

> Inclusion is not about the placement of individual children, but about creating an environment where all pupils can enjoy access and success in the curriculum and become full and valued members of the school and the local community.
>
> (Mittler 2000: 177)

Inclusion promotes the valuing of learners, of diversity, the celebration of difference and the encouragement of trans-agency working. It does not focus on the deficits of an individual, but on the agencies and educators to identify barriers to learning and on developing solutions to them for every individual pupil. It therefore:

signals a significant mind shift. Instead of expecting children to 'come up to standard' or otherwise be segregated, the emphasis is on schools and settings to adapt and be flexible enough to accommodate each and every child.

(Tassoni 2003 : 11)

In *Inclusive Schooling* (DfES 2001a:3), inclusion is said to be about:

engendering a sense of community and belonging and encouraging mainstream and special schools and others to come together to support each other and pupils with special educational needs. Inclusive schools and local education authorities have:

a. an inclusive ethos;
b. a broad and balanced curriculum for all pupils;
c. systems for early identification of barriers to learning and participation;
d. high expectations and suitable targets for all children.

In 1999 the National Curriculum also incorporated a statement on inclusion 'to ensure that all pupils have a chance to succeed, whatever their individual needs and potential barriers to their learning may be' (DfEE 1999 : 3), and set out three key principles that are 'essential to developing a more inclusive curriculum:

■ setting suitable learning challenges;

■ responding to pupils' diverse learning needs; and

■ overcoming potential barriers to learning and assessment for individuals and groups of pupils.' (DfEE 1999: 30).

Despite much discussion and change in practice the Audit Commission's report, *Special Educational Needs – A Mainstream Issue* (Audit Commission 2002) still found that some of the targets set by *Excellence for All Children – Meeting Special Educational Needs* (DfEE 1997), to be achieved by 2002, still needed addressing.

In 2003 the Green Paper *Every Child Matters* (DfES 2003 : 9) took the inclusion agenda further than ever before by stating that the government intended to merge the education, health and social services for children 'within a single organisational focus', 'to achieve better outcomes for children and young people' (ibid.: 69, 5.7). As Carpenter (2005: 177) says, 'It sets out a range of proposals to "reform children's services for the 21st century" and gives early childhood intervention a new urgency and a high priority across all children's services'. The Department for Education and Skills (DfES 2004) a year later published *Removing Barriers to Achievement – The Government's Strategy for SEN*, in which can be found the responses to the Green Paper and also to the Audit Commission's findings of 2002. This highlights the aim of the government to develop an inclusive education system where separate structures and processes for special educational needs are no longer required. The strategy aims to achieve this by '[personalising] learning for all children, to make education more innovative and responsive to the diverse needs of individual children' (DfES 2004: introduction).

Importantly for early years practitioners, it also emphasised the need for early intervention, for early years education, preventative work and integrated services, stating that 'early intervention is the cornerstone of our strategy' (ibid.: 9).

Finally, the White Paper, *Higher Standards, Better Schools for All* (DfES 2005) attempted to broaden the inclusion agenda further by focusing on other issues of inequity in society outside of special educational needs, to provide children with 'an excellent education – whatever their background and wherever they live' (ibid.:7) and 'an education system that is designed around the needs of the individual' (ibid.:7–8).

This section of the chapter has outlined the framework of educational change during the last 30 years and the legislation and thinking behind it. Policies and legislation have dramatically altered society's way of thinking and the provision for young children with special educational needs and disabilities. Inclusive practice and inclusion are still causing debate especially in relation to special needs.

Moving forward together, through action and effective communication

The following section explores and debates issues and strategies identified above in greater detail.

1. Is there currently a need for both inclusion and special educational needs structures and processes?

As mentioned previously, the Revised Special Educational Needs Code of Practice (DfES 2001) still has to have due regard paid to it, and *Inclusive Schooling – Children with Special Educational Needs* (DfES 2001a), which resulted from this, is actual statutory guidance enforceable by law. Therefore, the current framework for identifying, assessing and meeting children's special educational needs is clearly provided for within these documents and is required to be followed, alongside others such as the *Disability Rights Commission Code of Practice for Schools* (DRC 2002). Thus the structures established during the era of integration and the early development of inclusive practice are still being utilised as the most effective way of ensuring that children with special educational needs are actually given the provision and support they require. It is this point that is currently being debated.

For many professionals working in an evolving inclusive environment, this framework does not take into consideration practices currently adopted by practitioners either in training or in early years educational settings. These would include:

curriculum differentiation; use of a variety of learning and teaching styles; adaptation of the learning environment; and effective transdisciplinary working practices. 'Transdisciplinary working' is the term used when 'professionals work across disciplines to provide effective responses to a child's needs' (Soan 2004 : 18). Professionals would argue that with this approach every child will be offered an education to suit his/her individual needs and they highlight the policy initiatives that are already in place supporting the early years, such as Sure Start, Early Support, Early Bird and the National Service Framework, saying that with these there is no need for the procedures laid out in the SEN Code of Practice (DfES 2001) to be maintained.

For others, however, there are still concerns that although there is already much good practice in place and a policy framework for early childhood intervention, there still needs to be greater demographic equality so that intervention services for young children are not 'a postcode lottery' (Carpenter 2005: 181). They would also argue that there is no national provision, nor strategies, as yet in place to ensure the key goals of *Removing Barriers to Achievement* (DfES 2004) are currently either available or achievable everywhere for every child. The key goals are:

- better integration of services;
- improved information and support for parents;
- new ways of working for professionals.

Indeed only 30 percent of the country is presently supported by a children's centre and, although it is now a statutory duty for the local authorities to establish this service, the level of support provided is not determined nationally. Funding for such centres has now shifted from central government to local authorities and it will be crucial that this funding is maintained for children's centres if they are to be properly sustained. Additionally, within this framework the health authorities are not immediately involved. This is a vital point as the national evaluation of Sure Start has found that the inclusion of health authority professionals positively influences the success of these programmes (BERA 2005). Policy and training are also developing inclusive practices, as can be seen with the Common Assessment Framework (CAF) (DfES 2005a) which encourages interdisciplinary practices and a child-centred approach. Greater refinement of training programmes, however, is still required to meet the needs of the professionals in early years provision, such as the Common Core skills framework for working with children (DfES 2005b). Undoubtedly, new training courses will enable professionals to cross disciplinary boundaries, but it is clear that these need time to be developed and implemented. What is the availability, for example, of these skilled professionals who can work effectively and appropriately in this transdisciplinary role at the moment? The people agreeing with this line of argument would therefore say that it is too early to remove the framework that legally ensures young children with special needs can seek the support and intervention they require. Clearly, parents may also be very nervous about relying on a service that may not have the qualified professionals, the resources or the structures to ensure that their child receives the help and support necessary for him/her to access, engage with and participate in an educational setting of their choice. By removing these structures and processes too soon would, if you agree with this thinking, not ensure that *all* children would be given a service that encapsulates inclusive education by:

- respecting;
- reflecting;
- responding

to their and the families' needs in a co-ordinated and coherent approach.

As the report *Improving the Life Chances of Disabled People* (Prime Minister's Strategy Unit 2005 : 85) states:

> The early years are a critical period for disabled children. Child development and future life chances – as well as those of siblings – are critically affected by the support and services received by young disabled children and their families.

For many, therefore, it is not yet time to remove the structures that for a decade have enabled parents and professionals to provide for children with special educational needs within a legislative framework. Others would argue, however, that all the time such processes are still in force, inclusion will only ever remain an aspiration.

2. Is inclusion achievable in the short term?

The Alliance for Inclusive Education details the nine principles that inclusive education is based upon in the following way:

- A person's worth is independent of their abilities or achievements;
- Every human being is able to feel and think;
- Every human being has a right to communicate and be heard;
- All human beings need each other;
- Real education can only happen in the context of real relationships;
- All people need support and friendship from people of their own age;
- Progress for all learners is achieved by building on things people can do rather than what they cannot;
- Diversity brings strength to all living systems;
- Collaboration is more important than competition.

(Tassoni 2003 : 12)

Few would argue that the nine principles listed above are not 'right' and justified. As inclusion is an ever-changing process, however, is it ever going to be possible to achieve? Also, by its actual existence as a term, does it not suggest that there still must be 'exclusion' even when it is considered that inclusive practice is being achieved?

Government documentation has also appeared to have slightly altered its focus recently, concentrating on phrases such as 'individual needs' and 'personalised learning'. Does this suggest that the government also considers that there are additional foundations to establish and secure prior to reaching the goal of educational inclusion and an inclusive society? Has it been acknowledged that the complexities of society cannot be so drastically moved forward to inclusion within a few years? As Tassoni (ibid.:3) says, 'most of us have been brought up in a society that has not been able to value the uniqueness of the individual', and also 'The way we think about disability affects the care and education of people with disabilities. It is important to examine the stereotypes and attitudes that are common in society. We must consider each person as an individual' (ibid.:7). Within these statements can be seen the need for time and opportunities for experience to influence an individual's thoughts and ideas. It is important, therefore, to take a smaller-stepped approach to developing educational inclusion, one in which practitioners can move at a manageable pace, and where training, resources, experience and success can provide them with reassurance and confidence.

3. What is a language for all? The importance of words

How professionals use words is, without doubt, important. At present, transdisciplinary working is hindered not only by different working practices and responsibilities but also by differences of understanding about terms and language used. It is therefore important when working in a new environment or with new professionals to have an open discussion about terms to be used around early years settings, whether discussing health, family or educational issues.

Language is a very powerful tool reflecting individuals' attitudes and values (ibid.:5). Due to this, many people dislike terminology such as special educational needs and definitions of need like 'dyslexia', seeing them as creating a language that focuses on deficits. Jones (2005), like Tassoni, recognises that the language of special educational needs used is crucial when trying to develop inclusive practice and that without challenging the language people use the beliefs and attitudes within us will not change. This can be easily demonstrated by the following example:

A – There are three autistic children in my nursery at present.

B – There are three children with autism in my nursery at present.

What is the difference between A and B? In B the language used, firstly, centres on the fact that there are three children; only then does it tell us that they have a specific need. In A the need is written before the word 'children', emphasising their need as the important factor prior to recognising the children as valuable individuals. How many times do we hear professionals, practitioners and parents say comments such as 'dyslexic children', 'she is a bed wetter', 'those SEBD children'? This and similar language immediately make us think of the children's negative differences instead of how, as professionals, we can help them as individuals to fully access the curriculum and the environment within their educational setting.

Currently, funding and legal support is tightly linked to definitions of need for children with special educational needs and so will continue to influence thinking and progress.

> Definitions can create stereotypes, and many dislike the labelling that they generate, BUT without them policy makers argue it would be impossible to create any enforceable laws and policies.

> (Tassoni 2003 : 3)

I suggest that now, however, especially with all the young children with complex multiple disabilities being born and entering early years provision, there is a need for a language that does identify need. This language should be a common language used by all professionals and practitioners; it needs to be constructed in a way that while providing valuable information and direction to the professionals and practitioners involved does not exclude or label the individual children negatively. Thinking about how you construct a sentence may well determine if a child is positively or negatively accepted and included into a learning and social environment. As mentioned many times, it is the provision that needs to be creative, flexible and responsive to individual needs.

Case study

Joe's parents were contacted by their health visitor from the local children's centre, who suggested they should consider sending Joe to the centre's nursery provision. She felt that with some collaboration with the nursery staff Joe, who suffered from epilepsy, severe communication needs and cerebral palsy, would be able to participate in sessions. The health visitor telephoned the nursery and made an appointment for Joe and his parents, after they had decided they would like to see it. On meeting the family, the nursery teacher immediately opened the conversation by saying that they did not take severely disabled children; it was a health and safety issue and they did not have the expertise to deal with Joe's difficulties. Joe's attendance at the nursery could only be possible if he stayed only for specific activities and if one of his parents stayed with him.

Within this very brief case study there are a number of problems with the joint professional working systems currently in place. What possibilities for improving this situation can you identify to create really effective transdisciplinary practice? When considering these issues think about how the professionals approached the needs of the child and what terminology and language they used.

4. The development of a nationally cohesive programme of early childhood intervention – the key to effective early childhood intervention

The government's Green Paper, *Every Child Matters* (DfES 2003), highlighted early childhood intervention as vital across all the services, recognising that there is still great inequality of provision and support across the country and that, with changing family patterns, negative outcomes for children are frequently associated with poor parenting, unemployment and homelessness. As a consequence of this there has been a plethora of policies, initiatives and childhood interventions in the UK during the last few years. The need now is for these to be consolidated into a nationally cohesive programme. Carpenter (2005:181) supports this view saying that:

> The political climate in which to develop a nationally cohesive programme of early childhood intervention is ripe. Through the many policy initiatives mentioned – including Sure Start, Early Support, *Removing Barriers to Achievement*, and the National Service Framework – there is a major imperative to translate the articulated aspirations into reality.
>
> (Carpenter and Egerton 2005)

Importantly for children with special educational needs, *Together from the Start* (DoH/DfES 2003), the first-ever published guidance for professionals working with disabled children (from birth to 3) was launched in 2003. This was produced by a multi-agency group who started with the premise that:

> Effective early intervention and support can produce improvements in children's health, social and cognitive development and help tackle some of the many social and physical barriers families of disabled children face to full participation in society.

Other initiatives and policies followed including the *National Service Framework for Children, Young People and Maternity Services* (DoH 2004). From these have evolved the Early Support programmes, Sure Start children centres offering child and family health services, early education and childcare, and family support. Full participation of children with special needs is still therefore high on the agenda within these new services – the new 'fourth arm of the Welfare State' (BERA 2005) and one which could so ably move inclusive education forward.

Buildings, policies and physical resources funded by government are imperative, but it is the role of the professionals that will enable the children's centres and other early childhood provisions to succeed, producing effective services that enable children and their families to become full participating members of society. As mentioned earlier, it is vital that training and working practices mirror the principles of policy and that the difficulty of achieving this is not underestimated. True partnerships have to be worked at over a period of time, as does the development of skilled and experienced staff. The needs of the individuals with special educational needs are central to this new collaborative way of working. As Jones (2005:93) says:

In order to rise to the challenge of developing greater inclusive practice, we need to meet the professional training needs of all of the adults who work with the children, not just in the class but also in the school context. In this, training issues of attitude, belief school and classroom procedures, as well as teaching and learning strategies, must form a central focus.

Conclusion

Since 1978, society's values and practices have changed dramatically in the UK and early childhood provision and practices have attempted to respond positively to the changing demands and challenges, always trying to keep the needs of children at the centre of practice, respecting the rights of each individual child. Perhaps, then, it is not surprising that the government has prioritised early years intervention in its attempt to develop the participation and provision for children with special needs as an important part of its focus on meeting the needs of every individual child and an inclusive system through transdisciplinary working practices and provision. As an 'Early Support' information booklet says:

> Inclusion is about providing children with what they need to thrive in ordinary schools and about changing 'the mainstream', by removing some of the barriers that prevent children with special educational needs from participating. (DfES 2004a:4)

Within this chapter, lines of argument in favour of and against inclusion and the continuation of a special educational needs framework have also been introduced to stimulate further thought and study of the literature.

Questions for reflection

1. Is there a need for separate special educational needs structures and processes, or can inclusive practice take their place?

2. Revisit the first part of this chapter and follow the progression of change in thinking from segregation to integration and then to inclusion. Discuss your own personal views and attitudes towards the theories and values behind each with colleagues.

3. Reflect on your own practice and consider:

    (a) your strengths;

    (b) your areas of practice requiring additional professional development.

4. Do you think transdisciplinary professional practice is the future for effective early childhood interventions and strategies? If you agree, say why, and then discuss how you think it can be achieved. If you disagree, highlight the difficulties of such development for early childhood provision.

References

Audit Commission (2002) *Special Education Needs – A Mainstream Issue*. London: Audit Commission.

British Educational Research Association (BERA) (2005) *National Evaluation of Sure Start*. Special Interest Group. London: Institute of Education, 2 December.

Carpenter, B. (2005) 'Early childhood intervention: possibilities and prospects for professionals, families and children'. *British Journal of Special Education*, **32** (4), 176–83.

Carpenter, B. and Egerton, T. (2005) *Early Childhood Intervention: International Perspectives, National Initiatives and Regional Practice*. Stourbridge SEN Regional Partnership.

Corbett, J. (2001) 'Teaching approaches which support inclusive education: a connective pedagogy'. *British Journal of Special Education*, **28**(2), 55–9.

DES (1978) *The Report of the Committee of Enquiry into the Education of Handicapped Children and Young People* (The Warnock Report). London: HMSO.

DES (1988) The Education Reform Act. London: HMSO.

DfEE (1993) The Education Act 1993. London: HMSO.

DfEE (1994) *Code of Practice on the Identification and Assessment of Pupils with Special Educational Needs*. London: DfEE.

DfEE (1996) *The Nursery Education and Grant Maintained Schools Act*. London:DfEE.

DfEE (1997) *Excellence for All Children: Meeting Special Educational Needs*. London: DfEE.

DfEE (1999) *The National Curriculum: Handbook for Primary Teachers in England*. London: DfEE.

DfES (2001) *Special Educational Needs Code of Practice*. Annesley: DfES.

DfES (2001a) *Inclusive Schooling: Children with Special Educational Needs*. Annesley: DfES.

DfES (2003) *Every Child Matters*. London: The Stationery Office.

DfES (2004) *Removing Barriers to Achievement: The Special Educational Needs Strategy*. Annesley: DfES.

DfES (2004a) *Early Support Programme: Family Pack and Professional Guidance*. Annesley: DfES.

DfES (2005) *Higher Standards, Better Schools for All – More Choice for Parents and Pupils*. Annesley: DfES.

DfES (2005a) *Common Assessment Framework*. London: TSO.

DfES (2005b) *Common Core Skills and Knowledge for the Children's Workforce*. Annesley: DfES.

Disability Rights Commission (2002) Code of Practice for Schools: Disability Discrimination Act 1995, Pt. 4. London: DRC.

DoH (1991) The Children Act 1989: Guidance and Regulations 6. London: HMSO.

DoH (2004) *National Service Framework for Children, Young People and Maternity Services*. London: Department of Health.

DoH/DfES (2003) *Together from the Start: Practical Guidance for Professionals Working with Young Disabled Children (Birth to Third Birthday) and Their Families*. Annesley: DfES.

Gross, J. (2002) *Special Educational Needs in the Primary School: A Practical Guide*. Buckingham: Open University Press.

HMSO (1996) *Education Act 1996*. London: HMSO.

Jones, P. (2005) *Inclusion in the Early Years: Stories of Good Practice*. London: David Fulton Publishers.

Mittler, P. (2000) *Working Towards Inclusive Education: Social Contexts*. London: David Fulton Publishers.

Prime Minister's Strategy Unit (2005) *Improving the Life Chances of Disabled People*. London: Strategy Unit.

Soan, S. (2004) *Additional Educational Needs – Inclusive Approaches to Teaching*. London: David Fulton Publishers.

Tassoni, P. (2003) *Supporting Special Needs – Understanding Inclusion in the Early Years*. Oxford: Heinemann Educational.

UNESCO (1994) *World Conference on Special Needs Education: Access and Quality*. Paris: UNESCO.

Wall, K. (2003) *Special Needs and Early Years: A Practitioner's Guide*. London: Paul Chapman.

Wedell, K. (1990) 'Children with special educational needs: past, present and future', in Evans, P. and Varma, V. (eds) *Special Education: Past, Present and Future*. London: Falmer Press.

12

Leadership in the Early Years

Gill Bottle

THIS IS AN exciting and challenging time for early years practitioners, as the government has recently introduced the most significant changes in the delivery of children's services for a generation. These changes bring with them particular challenges for those with an existing leadership and/or management role and those who aspire to become a leader or manager. First, this chapter will outline and discuss some of the changes and their ramifications for leaders and managers in early years settings. Secondly, because education is one of the central tenets of the new developments, the chapter will go on to discuss the development of the curriculum in an early years setting.

Leadership of the new children's centres

A number of government schemes, which preceded the latest plan, had already begun the transformation of our early years provision, for example, the Early Excellence Centre Programme (1997), The Sure Start Programme (1999) and the Neighbourhood Nurseries Programme (2001). The latest initiative is the Children's Centres Programme (2003). This initiative builds on the others and is driven by the publication of *Every Child Matters: Change for Children* (2004), which sets out to integrate front-line delivery of all the existing children's services. This latest initiative will mean that many more early years managers will be needed to lead the organisation and development of the new centres.

There were two key influences in the development of *Every Child Matters* and the subsequent legislation. These were the Victoria Climbié Inquiry (DoH 2003) and the Joint Chief Inspectors' Report on Safeguarding Children (DoH CI 2002). The Children Act 2004 is the legislative spine for the reforms of children's services within which the government endeavours to introduce far-reaching changes to the whole system of children's services with the intention of improving children's lives. The Act supports partnership, accountability, a sharper focus on safeguarding children and inspection. In order to give children an early advantage the present government has committed 'additional funding for early years education and childcare of £669 million by 2007/8 compared to 2004/5' (HM Treasury 2004). This injection of additional funds by the government is clearly intended to improve practice and the level of qualifications in the early years sector. Much of the available funding to date has been directed at the development of children's services in deprived areas of the country. The Sure Start project was one such initiative, which aimed to bring together, for the first time, services in support for young children and their families. The success of the Sure Start projects has meant that government now plans to develop new children's centres so that the ways of collaborative working, which have been developed within Sure Start, can be rolled out gradually to encompass the whole of the early years sector. This is an extensive project as government is planning to have 2,500 centres in place by April 2008 and 3,000 by 2010.

Within the new initiative for change there are five elements that children and young people have identified as being key in their lives. These elements, which form the basis of the new reforms, are: to be healthy; to stay safe; to be able to enjoy and achieve; to make a positive contribution and to achieve economic well-being in life. It is envisaged that the approach to children's services will undergo a radical change of focus in line with these elements. The agencies that provide children services will need to transform from a service that tries to address the damaging effects when things go wrong in children's lives to one that concentrates on prevention. As well as providing inclusive and flexible education along with care for children that need it, the new children's centres are expected to be centres for research and development, provide a focus for voluntary work and community regeneration and to make available family support services including adult community education.

Changes to the ways of working for early years professionals will be evident in the extension of the year-round provision that is already provided in Sure Start centres to all children's centres. Families will be supported by the provision of extended hours, sometimes called wraparound care, which caters for children's needs before and after school by, for example, the provision of breakfast clubs and after-school clubs. Adult carers and parents will be able to access the support they need to engage in training, for example in IT, and/or to meet with other parents and carers who have babies or toddlers by provision of breastfeeding clinics and parent and toddler groups.

All children require access to first-class universal services provided by a range of agencies from the public, private, voluntary and community sectors. It is important for children in need to have access to effective educational provision and good primary care services that ensure their health needs are met. The new children's centres will bring together many early years professionals including teachers, nursery nurses, play workers, child psychologists, health visitors, social workers, midwives and voluntary services who will work either within the centres themselves or with children's centres. As well as emphasising the value of integration between early years professionals, this initiative also stresses the importance of building strong partnerships between professionals, parents and the wider community. As these centres are developed a new breed of manager will be needed to work with the local community and to lead and inspire the new workforce including the teams of professionals who will be assembled for the benefit of the children and their families.

The quality of provision for children in the early years is also to be raised by enhancing practice. This push towards improvement includes a move towards a higher level of education, training and support for early years practitioners. Early years degrees have been a feature in many universities over recent years. [Undergraduates reading Early Years are learning to engage in health, social care and education and may be able to provide a link between the different services.] Practitioners with this qualification will already have a good understanding of working in a multi-agency environment and may be the catalyst that will generate wider debate. Another example of changes in education for early years practitioners is the Sure Start foundation degree. This is a work-based programme that allows established practitioners to work towards a foundation degree in early childhood. Courses such as these look at both the education and care of children. They develop participants' ideas about child development, look at the importance of health and develop their understanding of social work. Many of the students on these courses are already managing nurseries and early years settings such as play groups. Once qualified, some of these people will have the potential to work towards becoming the managers and leaders of children's centres in the future.

While the development of children's centres is a new initiative, the practice of agencies working together is not a new one. The difference now is the increased emphasis that government is putting on inter-agency working.[Early years practitioners, particularly those with a leadership role, will be instrumental in developing and putting policy into practice as it evolves.]The integration of services is not as simple as it might at first seem as the early years professionals that make up an integrated early years team will be drawn from different professions, each with its own culture, professional language and priorities.[Building and developing an effective integrated team will mean developing traditional roles for the new challenges of integrated working, breaking down cultural barriers and managing change.]The children's centre leader will have a key role to play in shaping and structuring these individuals from diverse backgrounds into a team.

Last year I was lucky enough to visit a Sure Start centre that had been recently re-designated as a children's centre. This visit gave me a glimpse into the future, which was very impressive in its complexity. The new children's centre was in a purpose-built building. It had a large nursery built around a central kitchen area. There were a couple of smaller rooms leading from the large room that could be used for sleeping babies or as a calmer area for children who chose to be quieter at times.

There was a large enclosed outside play area designated to the nursery. There was also a purpose-built after-school club room with a separate outside play area. This outside area had a number of climbing frames, logs to clamber over and a tarmacked area with painted games such as hopscotch.

Parents in the local community were also catered for. There was a job club for unemployed parents and carers to use and courses were run to increase their occupation-related skills, such as computer literacy. There was a café where parents and carers could meet informally and low-cost, nutritious meals were provided every day. There were more formal meetings too, either in the café or the adjoining meeting-room, for example breastfeeding support, a baby clinic and advice on health and safety in the home. Parents and carers could also buy home safety equipment, such as stair gates, socket protectors and door jamb finger guards at a reduced price. There was a parent and toddler group that met regularly on site and an affiliated playgroup that was held away from the main children's centre premises in the local church hall.

Upstairs in the children's centre there was one huge office in which all professionals with an early years brief worked. There were desks in this big room for all the professional staff including the play leader, health visitor, teacher, midwife, educational psychologist and children's social worker. The Sure Start manager explained to me that she had made a conscious decision to put all of the team in one room so that they were 'obliged to talk to one another informally'. She felt that this was just one way that barriers could be overcome as the professionals would realise, from informal conversation, that their aim, which is ultimately to support young children, is the same. The manager had also worked extremely hard to gain the trust and respect of the local community so that they would have the motivation and confidence to use the centre for the support they needed for their own and their children's well-being.

This example highlights the fact that the success of the new children's centres will depend largely on the development of effective early years practitioners and centre leaders. Managers who are able to build and motivate a multidisciplinary team will be essential to ensure that the quality of the experiences provided for children from birth onwards are improved. The task of any potential leader of an early years centre, then, is a complex and difficult one. This unique situation will require a distinct and special type of leadership. He or she will need to have drive and enthusiasm committed to the development of centres of excellence for children's services and be passionately committed not only to the centre itself but also to developing and serving the local neighbourhood as a whole, for without the backing and partnership of the community the centre will not develop to its full potential.

The leader may come from any of the professions that are involved in children's centres and could be, for example, a previous head teacher, nursery manager, social worker or health visitor. The children's centre leader would not only need to understand his or her own particular viewpoint and professional practice but would also need to be empathetic to different viewpoints, however subtle. He or she would be able to understand and dovetail differences in expectation, style and approach to education and care within one establishment. The difficulties of this should not be under-estimated. There is currently a requirement, for example, that all centres have a qualified teacher involved: this could be potentially problematic as there are often profound differences between those trained as nursery nurses and those trained as qualified teachers, and although they both seem, to the outsider, to come from a common educational background there can be fundamental differences in beliefs, philosophies and even pay that can affect their response to each other. An effective leader will be able to turn professional differences to advantage by respecting and valuing the contribution and expertise that all his or her co-workers can bring.

A strong belief that all children have the right to high-quality education and care whatever their background will be a prerequisite for the leadership role in children's centres so that a centre where the children are central and valued and where their emotional as well as their academic lives are acknowledged and nurtured can be developed. The leader needs to understand his or her personal philosophical and ideological stance towards child education and care and have the vision to know how the children's cognitive, emotional and physical development can be encouraged.

The ethos of any setting will be modelled and developed by the leader. One of the important areas for consideration is the welcoming of parents to the setting. Valuing your parents' and carers' contribution and realising that they have a vital role to play in the education and welfare of their children is an essential underpinning to successful beginnings for young children.

The importance of parents in the education of the child needs to be respected and understood. Parents are their child's first educator and this should be acknowledged and parents should be encouraged and supported. There is a danger of thinking, however, that we can give advice and involve parents in their children's learning in a way that is imposed or prescribed by the practitioner. Children at home will learn differently than in a setting and the nature of parental interactions with their children will depend, as do practitioner interactions, on their beliefs and values. Trying to impose ways in which the parent should engage their children can be detrimental to the natural contextualised learning that can often be seen in the home. In a research project, I observed young children in their home setting. A nursery leader advised one parent that she should play mathematics games with her child. Because of this advice the parent abandoned the rich contextualised mathematical experiences that her child had previously enjoyed in favour of the board games suggested by the practitioner. The parent thought that the 'expert must know best' and consequently abandoned her previous approach. With this in mind I believe that it is much more important to understand better the experiences that a child may already be having at home and to use this information for the benefit of the children by providing suitable resources and support for both the child and his or her parents or carers.

Understanding that the quality of a child's life can be enhanced by improving the quality of life of their parents or carers is imperative, and helping parents to cope well with their own lives is important. A balance needs to be struck, however, between giving support to parents and carers when they need it and helping them to become independent and self-sufficient.

Whalley (2005) underpins many of these ideas of leadership pointing out in his briefing paper for the Education Minister that research evidence on effective leaders in the early years phase indicates that they must be concerned with improving standards in teaching and learning and committed to the belief that all children and their parents have the right to access high-quality early years services. They also said that leaders should be skilful social entrepreneurs working within a strong value base, well-informed thinkers who are able to engage in rigorous debate and reflexive practice; and committed to their own learning and the learning of the people they lead. Additionally, they need to be aware and articulate human developers concerned with the people in the organisation in which they work and able to recognise and support the emotional lives of their organisations (Whalley 2005).

Muijs *et al.* (2004), on the other hand, are much more tentative about the role of the early years leader. They identify a lack of literature and paucity of research on leadership in early childhood, despite the growing need for leadership in the field. They conclude that the need to identify the processes and outcomes of effective leadership within early years practice is clear and that theoretically based studies that allow different models and characteristics to be empirically tested are long overdue. They also consider that there is a serious lack of leadership training and, as a consequence of this, many early childhood managers could be significantly under-prepared for their role.

One of the new government-funded projects involves training practitioners to lead the new children's centres. A new qualification called the National Professional Qualification of Integrated Centre Leaders (NPQICL) has been created to help those in leadership roles to develop an understanding of the distinctive quality and extraordinary challenges of their work. This is a master's level qualification that is envisaged as being equivalent in status to the now well-established National Professional Qualification for Headteachers (NPQH), although at this point the new NPQICL will not be compulsory, as is the NPQH. The content of the NPQICL qualification has been co-constructed by those involved in services for children such as staff from primary schools and early years settings and staff and students at the Penn Green Leadership Centre, as well as the National Colleges for School Leadership, Health Leadership and the Social Care Institute of Excellence. The stated intention for the NPQICL is to build a dynamic and supportive learning community where the challenges and complexities of leadership can be examined and shared in a climate of trust, and to examine the literature and discuss and write reflectively about the implications for their own leadership experiences in practice. It remains to be seen whether this qualification will develop the quality leadership that will be needed for the unique development of children's centres in terms of both quality and quantity. It is to be hoped that there will be evaluation of and research into the leadership education and training process and outcomes. Evaluations will be needed to inform the management training so that the most effective leaders for this immensely important role can be developed.

Curriculum development

One aspect that is important for an early years leader is to ensure that a curriculum suitable for the children in their care is developed. All early years leaders, whether they are head of a children's centre, manager of a preschool playgroup, in charge of a nursery, an early years co-ordinator or teacher in the Foundation Stage, will need to develop a curriculum that creates a stable and supportive environment that encourages the children's cognitive, emotional and physical development.

The curriculum, for the purposes of this chapter, is defined as a course of action carried out for reasons that best serve the desired outcome of providing the children with what they need in terms of their education and, in the case of the Early Years, their care (May *et al.* 2006). Curriculum in any early years setting, however, involves much more than formal guidelines provided by an externally imposed curriculum document such as *Curriculum Guidance for the Foundation Stage*. Interpretation and implementation of the curriculum will be influenced by the philosophies and beliefs, as well as social and cultural values, of the nursery or setting manager and other adults who work in the setting. So a child engaged in any activity will not merely be learning the processes and skills and knowledge involved in the activity itself but will also be learning about the attitude of the adults in the setting towards the activity. In settings, for example, where the practitioners work only with groups of children on adult-directed tasks and never engage in child-initiated play, the children will learn that the adult-led activities are more important.

In England, the expected outcomes in terms of knowledge, skills and concepts of children's early education are set out in the *Curriculum Guidance for the Foundation Stage* (QCA 2000). This document gives us the content to be learned that matches the knowledge, skills and understandings that are given high status within our society, such as being able to count and to read. This written curriculum is interpreted and transformed into what actually goes on by practitioners and leaders according to the beliefs and values of individuals within the setting. Because of this inevitable trans-formation of the curriculum, it is essential that any early years manager or leader has a sound understanding of the rationale for the curriculum presented, or which he or she intends to present, within the setting so that the children's cognitive, emotional and physical development is supported. Examination of personal beliefs about children's learning, your own cultural values and your individual attitudes to the purposes of education will give you valuable insight into the 'hidden curriculum' that any programme contains.

The extent to which there is variation in implementation of the Foundation Stage guidance in preschool settings was exemplified for me recently when I had the opportunity to make two visits to each of two settings. These settings were close to each other geographically but worlds apart in their interpretation of the *Curriculum Guidance for the Foundation Stage*. I try here to give a description of the two settings that I shall call, for the purposes of this chapter, Woodlands and Riverside. You can make up your own mind about the efficacy of the different interpretations that had been put on the same basic curriculum. It is the diversity of approach and differences in philosophical stance of the two practitioners that are interesting and, I think, worth exploring.

Inside Woodlands there were two rooms, and practitioners could be seen talking to children or observing. At the beginning of each session, time was allocated for child-initiated play. All of the children were encouraged to choose and engage in their own focus for play in one (or more) of the areas that had been previously set up. They chose activities such as dressing-up, painting, playing in the water tray and sitting on cushions to read a book. Materials were provided, for activities such as role play and art, which children used in any way that they chose. The session was concluded with a story that was either read or told and children joined in songs and nursery rhymes.

Evidence that the children were developing their own play scenarios from adult-initiated stimulation was seen during one of my visits. I watched a boy and a girl playing together with characters and artefacts from a nativity scene. There was no practitioner present at the time. The dialogue was as follows:

Boy (holding the Joseph doll): 'I am Joseph and I will take you to Bethlehem'.
Girl (holding the Mary doll): 'OK'.

Both children move their dolls towards the door of the stable. They get to the door and stop.

Girl (turns the Mary doll to face the Joseph doll): 'It's OK now, Joseph. I am going into the stable to have a baby, I don't need you cos I can manage on my own. You wait here.'

The children had been told the Christmas story the day before and the nursery manager had had the foresight to put out props that the children might use to extend their experience and understanding.

There was also an outside area at Woodlands which had small climbing apparatus set out on a grassy bank, a concrete path and patio, a covered area and a small wooded area. One or more practitioners were allocated to the outside space and children could ask to go out if they wished. There were wellingtons and waterproof coats available in case of rain. While I was in the outside area the children found a dead hedgehog. This became the focus of interesting and sensitive discussion between themselves and the practitioner.

By coincidence both Woodlands and Riverside were working on ice and its properties at the time of my visits. Their approach to the topic, however, was very different. Woodlands had developed this topic in response to some very cold weather and used the cold and icy conditions to develop the children's understanding. The children went outside and stomped in icy puddles. They brought some ice inside to see what would happen and compared the ice inside with the ice left outside. The day before, practitioners had filled rubber gloves with water and helped the children to put some of them in the freezer. On the day I visited, the children played with the gloves and felt the difference between those still filled with water and those now filled with ice. They snapped the fingers of the ice gloves and tried to break larger pieces of ice. They chose to put some ice in the water tray and some in the sand to see what would happen. A practitioner had also frozen some small toys in ice and asked the children how they might get them out. On the day that snow fell the children played in it. The next day the children were given the opportunity to play with shaving foam. They made 'snow drifts', 'snowmen' and pushed cars through the snow.

The Woodlands manager had recently abandoned the idea of planning through the stepping stones in the Foundation Stage *Curriculum Guidance*, which she had used to structure her planning previously, because they were too restrictive and did not fit in with her beliefs about children's learning and development. Instead, she said, she was relying on her 20 years' experience to make sure the children were given the opportunity to reach the Early Learning Goals.

The manager set up appropriate and interesting resources each day, either based on previously identified interests of the children or by introducing suitable stimuli, such as a story. The practitioners at Woodlands routinely met at the end of each day to review the children's learning, to evaluate the day's work and to decide what activities would be provided in the next session. In this way their planning was based on evaluation and assessment.

In transforming and implementing the curriculum in this setting the manager of Woodlands had clearly been influenced by her beliefs that the child is central to his or her own learning and the need for play is at the heart of the development of knowledge, understanding, concepts, skills and attitudes. Children were encouraged to pursue their own interests and take control of their own learning. Children's opinions and ideas were seen as important and their creativity was supported and valued. The manager of this setting also appears to believe that children learn and develop understanding from communication and mediated social practice, as well as from exploration and discovery (Bruner 1983), and that children learn effectively within shared problem-solving, where both the learner and the more experienced other participate in 'culturally organised activity' (Rogoff 1990).

She realises, too, that children need the support of others if they are to learn (Vygotsky) and that understanding develops most effectively in contexts that they can understand, which allow them to connect the unknown to the known. Practitioners in this setting, while confident in their provision, were not completely satisfied with it. They were open to new ideas and were eager to discuss their practice with an outsider.

Riverside, in contrast, emphasised a combination of whole-class interaction and playful activity. At the beginning of each session the children were taught as a class group. The setting had one big room that had a number of tables and a computer workstation. The role-play area was set up as an ice palace in line with the current setting theme of the Antarctic. There was an outside space leading directly off the classroom that had a concreted, covered area, grass and some small climbing apparatus. This outside space contained the water tray and the sand tray.

Sessions began with all children together on the carpet and involved some direct teaching and discussion. In the first session the practitioner talked to the children about the cyclical nature of day and night and helped the children to identify the sequence of a day with the aid of some pictures. Each picture had a small amount of text with it such as 'get up' and 'go to school'. Individuals were asked to come to the front to put the pictures in the right order. Some of the children were then put into groups and given a variety of related activities to do. Some children worked with a practitioner on colouring, cutting out and sticking some small pictures in the right order, and others were given sequencing-related activities to work on alone such as puzzles and threading beads. The remainder of the class stayed with the lead practitioner and worked on the recognition of numerals using number fans. The practitioner introduced an element of playfulness by giving the numbers names, such as Freddie Four and Tommy Two, as she held them up. The children looked for the number that matched the practitioner's number and held it up. These children were then sent off in groups to engage in activities supervised by a practitioner such as colouring numbers and writing numbers. Some children played on a number-based computer game.

The children at Riverside, like those at Woodlands, were also working on ice and its properties and the second session I observed included this work. The session, as before, began with all the children and one practitioner in discussion. This time they talked about the Antarctic. They found the Antarctic on a world map and children were asked to identify what might be found there. The children suggested animals that might be found such as penguins, seals and polar bears and the practitioner showed them pictures of the animals you would find and told them which animals you would not find. They also talked about the presence of snow, ice and icebergs.

After the discussion some children were sent to play in the 'ice palace' role-play area and some helped a practitioner decorate a previously prepared picture with tissue paper and cotton wool.

One group of six children went with a practitioner to the freezer to see what had happened to the water, in various containers, that they had put in the freezer the day before. They found that the water had frozen and become ice. The children took the ice to the water tray, outside their classroom, and looked at how the ice floated. They noticed that part of it was submerged, 'like an iceberg' and watched it melt. They realised that the smaller pieces of ice melted before the larger. Practitioner questioning kept the children focused on the activity.

The manager in this setting had long-term plans for the whole year that outlined the topics and themes that would be covered in the year. Medium-term plans documented the stepping stones that would be addressed each term. There was a weekly timetable and planning for sessions that included intended learning outcomes. The manager planned for the whole group and passed her plans to the other practitioners to carry out. The practitioners knew the purpose of each activity as they had clear objectives for the work they were doing with the children. They knew exactly what each child was being taught and the work was differentiated to suit the ages and abilities of the children. This way of working allowed the practitioners to assess the children's knowledge and understanding against the objectives set. The manager of Riverside indicated that she was secure in her approach to the curriculum. She was happy with all aspects of her planning and was confident that the children were progressing well.

In transforming and implementing the curriculum the manager in this setting was working systematically towards the early learning goals. She used the stepping stones to help her planning. Her beliefs seemed to be that children learn through a variety of means such as the transmission of knowledge and playful activity. It was evident that she thought that children needed to engage in some more open-ended play as she had provided play opportunities in the role-play area and sand and water in the outside area. This play, though, was seen as separate from and probably secondary to work. She felt that children need guidance in their learning and staff were assigned to support the children in well-planned, objective-led activity. The manager here thought that communication and skilful questioning by the practitioner were important and believed that children need to be scaffolded in their learning. She felt in control of the children's learning.

It is clear from these accounts that although both settings were working from the same curriculum document the actual curriculum that is presented to the children was diverse in its implementation. While sessions were similar in some of the content they were very different in process.

Different styles of teaching and learning mean that the attitudes and dispositions to learning the children will develop will be different. Children, for example, who have learned about ice by jumping in icy puddles and melting it in the classroom will develop a different understanding on this phenomenon and its relationship to their everyday life than children who have learned about it in the context of the freezer and floating it in water. The skills, concepts and different understandings that children develop, therefore, will depend not only on the knowledge content of what is being taught but also on the 'invisible pedagogy' being used within their setting.

Conclusion

This chapter has looked at two aspects of management in the early years. The latest government initiative is for the development of children's centres country-wide. The intention is that children attending these centres will have the opportunity to access high-quality education and care where they are central and valued. Inclusive and flexible education and care, research and development, family support services and a focus for voluntary work and community regeneration will be key features of the new children's centres. For this new initiative to be successful a new type of early years leader will be needed who can work with the local community and lead and inspire a multi-agency early years team for the benefit of the children and their families.

Within any early years setting, whether that is a children's centre or a playgroup, it is important that the leader is aware not only of the content of the curriculum that is presented but also the context within which it is presented. The curriculum interpretation that you think is the most appropriate for your setting will depend upon your own beliefs about how children learn, your own cultural values and what you consider are the purposes of education.

Questions for reflection

1. What do leadership and management involve? Are the two terms different? If so, how would you define each?

2. What personal qualities do you consider are necessary in an early years professional who aims to lead, for example, a children's centre?

3. Part of the role of an effective leader is to have 'vision'. What does this mean? Can you explore and debate this concept and decide whether, in your experience, you have worked with an early years professional who demonstrates this characteristic?

4. What are your beliefs about 'curriculum' in an early years context? Consider the two examples outlined and consider which one you endorse. Why? Explore each option carefully and link it to what you know about child development.

References

Bottle, G. (2003) 'Children's mathematical experiences in the home'. Unpublished PhD thesis, University of Kent.

Bruner, J. (1983) *Child's Talk: Learning the Language*. New York: Norton.

DfES (2004) *Every Child Matters: Change for Children*. London: DfES.

DoH (2003) *The Victoria Climbié Inquiry: Report of an Inquiry by Lord Laming*. Available at: http://www.victoria-climbie-inquiry.org.uk/finreport/finreport.htm [Accessed 16/06/06].

DoH CI (2002) '15: Safeguarding children: a Joint Chief Inspectors' report on arrangements to safeguard children'. Available at: http://www.dh.gov.uk/PublicationsAndStatistics/LettersAndCirculars/ChiefInspectorLetters/ChiefInspectorLettersArticle/fs/en?CONTENT_ID=4004286&chk=PZKIDJ [Accessed 16/06/06].

HM Treasury (2004) 'Childcare'. Available at: http://www.hm-treasury.gov.uk./media/426/F1/pbr04childcare_480upd050105.pdf [Accessed 16/06/06].

May, P., Ashford, E. and Bottle, G. (2006) *Sound Beginnings: Learning and Development in the Early Years*. London: David Fulton Publishers.

Muijs, D., Aubrey, C., Harris, A. and Briggs, M. (2004) 'How do they manage? A review of the research on leadership in early childhood'. *Journal of Early Childhood Research*, **2**, 157–69.

QCA (2000) *Curriculum Guidance for the Foundation Stage*. London: QCA.

Rogoff, B. (1990) *Apprenticeship in Thinking*. New York: Oxford University Press.

Whalley, M. (2005) *Developing Leadership Approaches for Early Years Settings*. Workshop presentation to the NCSL conference 'Leading Together', 21–22 April, NCSL Nottingham. (www.ncsl.org.uk/media/F58/76/communityleadership-together-im-whalley.ppt).

13

Research in the Early Years

Gill Bottle

RESEARCH MEANS 'FINDING out about things' (MacNaughton *et al.* 2001). It is 'a combination of both experience and reasoning and must be regarded as the most successful approach to the discovery of truth' (Cohen and Manion 1994). But research is only really useful if we can use it to develop early years practice to benefit the children.

Early years research brings with it its own distinct features and problems and we need to be cautious when we research into the lives of young children. There has to be a serious respect for the child's world and we need to be aware that children may well see their childhoods in a different way from the adults who are watching them. The interpretation that we put on children's behaviours will depend on our purpose for the research, the time and effort we are able to put into interpretation and the situation in which the children are engaged, for example, whether they are involved in something that engages them (Pramling-Samuelsson 2003).

Early years research brings with it its own distinct features and problems such as the complexity of culture and contexts that children in their early childhood inhabit, the ethical position of the researcher and the range of possible research methods available, such as case study, survey, action research, documentary analysis and ethnography. Within this chapter there is not room to discuss all of these important aspects of research; what are examined here are the aspects of research that have influenced and continue to impact on our practice.

Early years research and education

Traditionally, much of our educational practice has been based on the work of educational psychologists whose research tended to be conducted in experimental conditions. In more recent years, though, educational researchers have realised that in order to build on our basic understanding of child development and to gain a better insight into the development of children's understanding about the world they inhabit, they need to observe the children more naturally in their own environment. In endeavouring to interpret the puzzling realities of early childhood, it seems important, therefore, that we look deeply into the social life and behaviours of the children and how they occur. This means that rather than relying on the laboratory-style psychological research of the past for interpretation of childhoods, the current trend is to look at socially situated practice, developing each research strategy to suit the situation as it is revealed (Bottle 2003). This, in turn, leads to further, more informed, exploration of the circumstances that prevail.

In the continuing search for meaning about how the child's social world functions, the relationships between disciplines are also being explored and the links between sociological, anthropological, historical, neuroscientific and educational research are being investigated. These more recent associations come from a realisation that childhoods can be diverse and the environment and culture of the family or early years setting in which children find themselves will inevitably give rise to a myriad different contexts within which children live their lives. There is now acknowledge-ment that children are involved in the co-construction of their own childhood through participation in their own family life and in the community in which they live and that children have their own perspectives that may not be in line with those of the researchers who are watching them.

Early years research is, of course, somewhat meaningless unless it is used to support the welfare and development of young children. The DfES recognise this and identify the usefulness of early years research as being a basis for providing children with an excellent start in education so that they have a better foundation for future learning, finding out what makes a difference by understanding the longer-term impact of different types of preschool experience on children and their development and finding out which types of intervention in Early Years work best in preventing social exclusion (DfES 2004). Employed wisely, the findings from research can be used to provide children with the best possible start in life. The potential role of the early years research being carried out today is extensive; with the coming together of all aspects and disciplines it can be used to inform the development of advantageous levels of well-being and desirable health benefits as well as the traditional role of informing the education of young children.

In early years education in the UK there is a strong leaning towards a child-centred approach that draws on the Piagetian idea that children construct their understandings by actively engaging with concrete materials and that children learn by doing. Furthermore, Vygotskian ideas of social constructivism mean that there is a tendency to see early learning as grounded in children's activities, socially constructed and context driven. The importance of appropriate support from more knowledgeable others, and the suggestion that the acquisition of knowledge and understanding stems not only from exploration but also from mediated social practice (Bruner 1983; Rogoff 1990) and communication are integral to his theories.

Such understanding underpins the work of many early years practitioners in England. For many practitioners there is a sense that:

> Each child comes to a preschool setting with unique experiences from family, home and community; that childhood should be a time of spontaneity and of exploration according to individual interests; and that didactic, teacher planned instruction has no part in an early years teacher's repertoire – is in fact a waste of time – because children learn best through 'hands on' self chosen play experiences.
>
> (David 2001: 55)

Beliefs that place the child as central to his or her own learning have not just come about by *ad hoc* experiences or anecdotal reporting; indeed, the weight of research in the field of educational psychology suggests that children develop their knowledge most effectively in contexts they can understand.

Despite these theoretical underpinnings to early years practice in this country, I have become increasingly aware, over a number of years, that all is not well in some of our early years settings. Many early years practitioners whom I have spoken to do not feel secure and confident in their own practice and seem to be searching for a way to improve. Many express a strong philosophical base but are unable to synthesise this into practice, and some are very keen to justify their own practice in terms of other well-respected philosophies and even link and/or express their own practice using models from abroad.

Practice in this country and research from abroad

One area of research that practitioners often draw upon in the UK are the studies and products of thinking from abroad. There are many lessons that can be learned from looking at practice abroad and many ideas that come out of practice in other countries can be helpful as a stimulus for discussion about our own. We can consider how others' practice compares with ours and how knowing about other ways of approaching early childhood may illuminate our own. It can help us to study our own values, develop new understandings about our own views and opinions, develop our own philosophy and constructs of early childhood and examine them in the light of alternative philosophies, perspectives and theories. It can inspire us to develop our own pedagogical practice.

What we should not be looking to do is to take a model or programme from another country and somehow try to reproduce it either in its entirety or in part. Using someone else's knowledge, or trying to copy practice from other countries for our own use, will not be effective as their practice, as ours, is bound up in their cultural values, social context, political and economic circumstances. But in this country we seem to have the problem that practitioners (and sometimes policy-makers) appear to believe that we can 'consume a model or programme [for our own use], and by doing so be reproducers of someone else's knowledge' (Moss 2001: 132).

There have been a number of approaches from abroad that have been adopted in the early years in a variety of forms over the past 10 or 15 years. Although the evidence that I have gathered over the years is anecdotal in nature it seems to me that the examples I report exemplify some of the ways in which settings have tried, not always successfully, to implement approaches from abroad.

Perhaps the first one of these imported ideas that I noticed being implemented in early years settings was High Scope. I have often heard practitioners say that they were going to 'do High Scope' this morning or this afternoon. What they meant was that the children were going to engage in a 'plan-do-review' session, which is just one aspect of the High Scope Programme. During these sessions each child would choose and plan an activity, collect the necessary resources to carry it out and perhaps negotiate with peers, if it is an activity that involves other children. They would report back to practitioners and the other children at the end of the session. The social demands of planning and negotiating and taking responsibility, along with the problem-solving skills needed to plan, recall and sequence their own activities, was attractive to practitioners as a way of developing children's cognitive abilities. The full adoption of the programme was often not possible because the planning and review stage requires a high proportion of adult participation. The tendency, therefore, in some settings has been to limit the children's participation in the programme to one or two sessions a week. This is not in the spirit of the High Scope approach, which is reliant on a consistent routine.

The High Scope approach was designed and developed by David Weikart during the 1960s to help children make the most of their later educational experiences. It is an educational approach with a strong philosophy, based on 30 years of educational research and practice. Its aims are to develop a 'can do' culture where the expectations of practitioners are raised and children are seen as active learners who are given a sense of control over their learning. Children are encouraged to solve problems and make their own decisions, and because of this the children's self-confidence is raised. It is true to say that in High Scope settings children will be actively involved in hands-on experiences supported by adults who aid the children's cognitive development and help them to develop the language they need to express their ideas. But children will also, in their daily routine, have a great deal of time dedicated to their own open-ended exploration of materials, be involved in small-group time to help them develop closer relationships with their teacher, and engage in playing games, singing and movement activities during circle times. In settings where some limited ideas from High Scope have been implemented, it is the process of the practice that has been adopted rather than the ideological and philosophical underpinnings that are so important to the success of any programme.

More recently, I have relocated to a different part of the country, and because of this I have had the opportunity to visit a number of Foundation Stage settings that are new to me and this has given me a refreshed insight into what is going on. What I have seen may, of course, be limited to this area of the country only, but I doubt it. The approach that practitioners are attempting to import and implement at this time and within many of the settings that I have visited recently is what has been described to me on a number of occasions as the 'Reggio approach'. I have tried to unpick what this term means to the practitioners. The practitioners that I have spoken to recently seem to believe that this approach means that you don't plan in advance of the children's learning but that you plan 'retrospectively' (their term not mine). Retrospective planning, they believe, is part of the 'Reggio approach', and it requires the practitioner to observe the children and write down what they have done (this is then recorded as the planning). One setting, although using the term 'retrospective planning', actually used the information from observations in a meeting each day to decide what they would provide for the children on the next day or in the next session. Although this was quite clearly forward planning, they did not view it as such because it was recorded in note form and not written down in any formal way.

Some of the practitioners I talked to told me that free-flow play and creativity were important in the 'Reggio approach' and that these elements were being included in their own practice. One explained that she had set up her room so that the children could choose their own activities but she 'had decided against the mirrors and light boxes' as she could not really see the purpose. Another remarked that they did not have an artist but the children were allowed to paint what they wished. A third practitioner said, 'We haven't gone in for the cream walls but otherwise we are using a Reggio approach'. These practitioners, it seemed, had knowledge of some of the more obvious, outwardly visible, signs of the practice that can be found in the early years centres in Reggio Emilia, but they seemed to be lacking in a good understanding of the importance of the underlying philosophy that has developed over the last 30 years. What they had failed to grasp was the fundamental idea that this approach is about the importance of 'seeing oneself and constructing one's own identity' (Nutbrown and Abbott 2001: 2). The idea that the child is central and rich in potential, strong, competent and powerful and that the connections between the children and the adults in their life are paramount (Malaguzzi 1997) also seems to have passed them by.

From discussions, then, it was apparent that the practitioners in question had only tried to implement those parts of the approach that suited them. Furthermore, it was also clear from my observations that even the ideas that they claimed to have implemented were not necessarily evident in practice. On entering one early years setting it was obvious that the children were occupied on a variety of activities. Some of the children were working at the painting table, they had only brown paint on the table and they were painting paper plates with previously cut holes for eyes and pre-cut antlers. The practitioner was stapling the antlers on to the plates to make reindeer masks (this activity lacked the free choice and creativity claimed for it by the practitioner, not least because all children were expected to complete a mask). Some of the other children were listening to a story, others were in the home corner and some were playing with floor puzzles. There were a number of identical child-constructed Christmas cards on the wall along with a number of silver 'puddle' shapes with sequins and sequin holes, and silver scrap fabric stuck on.

In another setting there was an outside area for 'free-flow play' (practitioner's description). I was surprised to hear it described as such because the area did not appear particularly safe as it was open to a car park on one side and an out-of-sight adventure playground area on the other. Because of lack of enclosure I felt it would not really be possible to leave the door open to allow children to move in and out at will. All of the children were inside on the day I visited and the practitioner explained that the children were not outside as the water and sand needed changing. There was a shed that, I was told, housed wheeled toys, but these were not visible or used within the session. They were awaiting a bigger shed, the practitioner explained, so that they could get the toys out more easily. These observations of some early years practitioners' interpretation of the Reggio approach demonstrate, as do the reported response to the High Scope programme, the way in which practitioners in this country sometimes pick up on seemingly good ideas because they think they fit with their own beliefs about early education. They then try to apply parts of a programme or method to a situation that is not necessarily conducive to the overarching philosophical underpinning of that approach.

These experiences of practitioners modelling their work on research and practice from abroad have led me to speculate why, when practitioners may believe that early learning is grounded in children's activities, socially constructed and context driven, they sometimes do not trust in their own philosophy enough to develop their practice directly from it? In practice, the curriculum is often interpreted simplistically, and some practitioners, while they understand the importance of developing important skills such as problem-solving and encouraging positive dispositions and attitudes towards learning, are overly concerned with the knowledge content of the given curriculum. Most practitioners believe that children learn best within a context they understand and are interested in and yet, in some settings, adults never engage in child-initiated activity and children are only involved in practitioner-led activities. Perhaps practitioners are insecure in their own philosophy and/or ideology. Maybe they do not know how to develop their own beliefs into practice; or perhaps their perceived philosophy seems to them to fit more closely with a model from abroad than the models that are offered from home. There may be many more reasons, but what is clear is that we seem to be in a situation where although some practitioners are able to carry their philosophy and beliefs through into practice, others, while they may be able to state their preferred style of teaching and learning, are unable for one reason or another to carry them through.

In this country practitioners seem less sure about the efficacy of their own practice than are our early years colleagues from other countries. The main difference I have noticed in countries such as Sweden, Finland, Norway and the Netherlands is that they have not only a strong philosophical consensus built up over many years but they also know what works in practice and are confident in what they are doing.

The situation in which practitioners find themselves in the UK may not help them to be confident in the development of their own practice as there are a number of contradictory pressures on them. These pressures are many and varied but some of them are:

- the initial pages of the Foundation Stage *Curriculum Guidance* (2002) set out laudable principles for play, and the child as central, but later pages encourage an objective-led approach by giving lists of subject-led attainments;

- the Primary Strategy produces booklets for reception and nursery that interpret the play element of the Foundation Stage curriculum as playful, but adult-led, activity;

- the Primary National Curriculum (2000) is objective-led and primary teachers, who often become early years teachers and advisers, are taught to plan from an objective- and target-led model;

- practitioners are often worried about Ofsted reaction to their practice and feel that either a fairly formal curriculum is required or that they can justify their practice by citing a recognised model;

- practitioners, rightly or wrongly, believe that they need concrete, paper-based evidence that children are working towards the early learning goals;

- practitioners find it easier to keep track of, and provide evidence for, coverage of the curriculum in objective-led planning; and

- there is ongoing pressure from government (such as the proposed fast and first introduction to synthetic phonics), from parents who are anxious about their children's education and from the media.

It is not surprising, given these mixed messages, that practitioners sometimes lack confidence and the courage of their own convictions. Those of us in advisory positions and higher education must, I believe, also take some of the blame for practitioners' confusion. As we praise practice from abroad and try to demonstrate the ways in which years of research, strong philosophical underpinnings and beliefs can enhance children's learning, we probably undermine the practice that happens here to some extent. Practitioners sometimes pick up the wrong message; they take the practical application and the 'good ideas' that come out of anecdotal examples and, because they believe it might help their children to have a better experience and learn more effectively, they try them in their setting.

But as already discussed, we cannot take a model and simply transpose it. Copying processes from other countries or even other settings within this country will not have the desired effect of consolidating and improving practice. It is the philosophy behind the practice that will affect the outcome rather than the activities themselves. One way in which we may be able to develop our own practice in the UK is by encouraging practitioners to reflect on their own current practice and to develop their confidence in their own philosophy and ability to apply it. In order to develop this reflectivity, practitioners should be encouraged to engage in their own research within their own setting. Classrooms need to be places for reflection and sharing ideas and the teacher has to be competent in listening to, supporting and challenging the child (Siraj-Blatchford 1999). Practitioner research can give insight into the children's learning, their attitudes and dispositions towards learning, their social skills and their emotional development. Furthermore, it can help practitioners to examine their own learning, practice and attitudes and to develop practical applications from research that are led by their own philosophy.

Using research from home to develop your own practice

Research into the experiences that children have at home could be useful to practitioners in helping them to develop their practice. One way we could develop a model of pedagogical practice for our own country that suits our own cultural values and social context is to understand better what goes on in the home.

Most early years practitioners recognise that children arrive at the preschool setting having had a variety of experiences. In order to plan suitable learning experiences for the development of each child it is important that practitioners have a sense of what has gone before. Knowing what children do at home could help practitioners to develop a curriculum for the children that is based on their previous experiences.

We know from research that the types of activities that children engage in at home will vary from family to family. The variety, complexity and diversity of activity will differ from household to household but may include helping with domestic tasks, such as supermarket shopping and baking, or may be grounded in child-initiated activity such as playing with small toys, including construction kits, dolls, miniature cars, dolls' houses, garages and farms, as well as bigger toys such as bikes, scooters and dolls' prams. Some children will also have had experience of card or board games (Tizzard and Hughes 1984), some will also have access to books and, increasingly, computer games. What is the same about the learning in any home is that it is culturally and socially constructed with parents, children and siblings interacting together.

Children usually learn at home in a holistic way and different areas of learning, such as language and mathematics, are learned together along with important skills such as manipulation and problem-solving. In addition, children often have a personal interest in the activities they do because they have chosen to engage in them.

Personal interest allows children to engage in an activity more effectively, and their concentration span usually increases. Tim (aged 20 months) and his mother were playing together at home. He was trying to build a bridge for his toy car to go under but found that his car was too tall to go through it:

Tim   (*Builds a bridge with one piece of Duplo for each leg and a long piece of Duplo for the horizontal span. Tries to put his toy car under the bridge.*)

Mum   'It won't go through it'. (*picks up bridge and adds bricks to legs*)

Tim   (*tries to help*)

Mum   'That's it, like this'. (*shows Tim how to put the bricks together and builds a taller bridge*) 'Mum is going to make a toy bridge for your car' (*puts the bridge down on carpet*) 'Ready, ready . . .' (*pushes the car through the bridge*)

Tim   (*picks up the bridge and removes one leg*)

Mum   'Mummy's poor bridge'!

(Bottle 2003: 280)

Even within this short extract you can see that Tim had a personal interest in the activity. He was learning in a holistic way and many areas of learning were involved. He was developing his understanding of mathematics, particularly an appreciation of the space needed under the bridge for the car to go through, and learning about measuring by deciding how many bricks were needed to make the bridge high enough. He was also developing his language skills from the model given to him by his mother, his manipulative skills in putting the bricks together and taking them apart, and his problem-solving skills by testing out his ideas.

According to Donaldson (1978), young children learn most effectively in contextualised situations. Many children are able to engage in activities at home that are firmly embedded in everyday contexts. Tim (now aged $4\frac{1}{2}$) was involved in self-initiated, pseudo-household domestic activity. He was making pretend tea:

Mum   'Mummy could do with a cup of tea please'.

Tim   'Do you want any sugar?'

Mum   'Two please'.

Tim   'OK, but I've only got three'.

Mum   'OH well, three will be fine'.

Tim   (*pretends to put in three spoons of sugar*) 'One, two, three. It only had three but that's all right because I put three in yours'.

(ibid.: 284)

This activity gave Tim a practical context in which to practise his counting. This was one of many situations in which Tim's counting was put to practical use as he also counted trains, pictures in a book and pieces of paper chain. Children at home who have experiences that are rich in contextual versatility may develop a better understanding of the relationship between other areas of learning than a child who has not had this type of experience at home. If a practitioner understands better the nature of interaction that a child has experienced at home, he or she will be better able to plan opportunities suitable for all children.

Many of the contextualised, holistic activities that children experience at home, as shown above, are *ad hoc* and informal. Not all activities will be of this nature and not all children will experience such rich versatility of context. Some activities that happen at home are more formal in nature and are introduced by the parent with the probable intention of teaching the child a skill or concept – for example board games. Such activities, while they may have concrete experiences associated with them, such as moving counters along a board, are more narrow in context. They do not allow for as much integration of areas of learning as the more informal experiences and tend to be mainly confined to the practice of the concept area that was intended by the activity, such as counting.

Not only can the scope and context of shared activity in the home vary depending on the task, but it is also the case that the amount of interactions between parent and child at home can vary too. At one extreme there may be little or no participation or intervention from the parents and they can take a completely passive role towards the child's play, and at the other extreme there may be a great deal of participation or intervention.

By the time children reach the preschool setting they will have already built up dispositions to learning from their home experiences and will bring these learned dispositions to the preschool setting with them. Some children will be confident and have had a wide experience. They will be able to apply what they know to novel situations because they have experienced a rich variety of contexts in which to practise and test their skills and knowledge. Others will have been taught more formally by the parent, which may mean that they may be anxious or unsure about how they might use their acquired knowledge in unfamiliar contexts.

The home influence on child preferences for learning is strong and children's choice of activity in the preschool setting will reflect the type of activity they enjoy engaging in at home. Some children will inevitably have the advantage of their preschool setting experiences and home experiences being compatible and some will not. In order to minimise this effect it is really important to give them a wide choice of opportunities so that they can choose something that suits their own learning preference.

Knowing some of the variations that can occur in children's home experiences and understanding how these different experiences might affect their ability to apply their knowledge and their learning preferences as well as their dispositions and attitudes, will help you to understand the cultural and social aspects of children's learning in this country. Knowledge of the variety and scope of children's preschool experiences will also help you to consider the types of activity that might be provided in order to give all children the opportunity of access. More importantly, knowledge of some likely home practices will give a basis for discussion with parents that will help you to tease out the needs of each child in your setting so that you can tailor your own practice to the cultural and social values, not only to suit children in this country but also, more particularly, to children in your own locality. In this way knowing about children's home experiences can help you to develop your own practice to suit the needs of the setting within which you work.

Conclusion

Educational researchers are now interested in observing children in their natural environment. They feel that it is important to develop research strategies that allow them to examine socially situated practice and the behaviours of the children and how they occur. Relationships between educational research and research from other disciplines, such as anthropology, history and sociology, are being explored to try to understand better the relationships between children's learning, the environment, culture and the contexts in which children co-construct their own childhood.

The way in which we practise in early education in this country has been influenced by research. In particular, the work of educational psychologists such as Piaget, Vygotsky and Bruner has led practitioners to see the child as central to his or her own learning, which is grounded in socially constructed and context-driven activity. More recently, research from abroad has had some influence and is certainly useful in developing pedagogical practice in this country by stimulating discussion about our own values, understanding, views and opinions, in the light of alternative perspectives, theories, beliefs and philosophies. Sometimes, though, attempts are made to adopt a model from abroad. This is not helpful as it is not possible to transpose piecemeal an approach from a different social, cultural, political and economic background successfully. An aspect of research that could be helpful in developing your own practice is research carried out by you within your own setting. This can give valuable insight into the learning, attitudes and dispositions of the children and the practitioners, which can help you to develop practical applications that are led by your own philosophy.

Research into what happens in the home environment can also help you to develop practice that is tailored to the social and cultural backgrounds of the children who attend your setting. There are large variations in young children's experiences within their home environment, and by the time children enter preschool they will have already developed a preferred learning style. Some children will be outgoing and lively, some quieter and more sedentary. Some will be interested and motivated and some will appear to do very little to further their own understanding independently. The preschool curriculum offered, therefore, needs to take into account not only the knowledge that they have before they enter preschool but also their attitudes and dispositions towards learning.

Questions for reflection

1. Why is it so important to research into the early years? What can research tell us that will inform our early years practice?

2. What are the major studies into early childhood that we should know well as early years professionals? Why do you consider these so important and influential in our work with young children?

3. How can the knowledge gained from research into the early years help us to develop our own philosophies and practice?

4. What kinds of research can we undertake within our roles as early years professionals that will help us to understand and develop our work?

References

Bottle, G. (2003) 'Children's mathematical experiences in the home'. Unpublished PhD thesis, University of Kent.

Bruner, J. (1983) *Child's Talk: Learning the Language*. New York: Norton.

Cohen, L. and Manion, L. (1994) *Research Methods in Education*. London: Routledge and Kegan Paul.

David, T. (2001) 'Curriculum in the early years', in G. Pugh (ed.) *Contemporary Issues in the Early Years* (3rd edn). London: PCP.

DfES (2004) Research Strategy. Available at: http://www.dfes.gov.uk/research/prospectus/index.cfm [Accessed 16/06/06].

Donaldson, M. (1978) *Children's Minds*. London: Fontana.

MacNaughton, G., Rolfe, S.A. and Siraj-Blatchford, I. (2001) *Doing Early Childhood Research: Theory and Practice*. Buckingham: Open University Press.

Malaguzzi, L. (1997) 'No way, the hundred is there', in Filipini, T. and Vecchi, V. (eds) *The Hundred Languages of Children: Narrative of the Possible* (2nd edn). Reggio Emilia: Reggio Children.

Moss, P. (2001) 'The otherness of Reggio', in L. Abbott and C. Nutbrown (eds) *Experiencing Reggio Emilia*. Buckinham: Open University Press.

Nutbrown, C. and Abbott, L. (2001) *Experiencing Reggio Emilia*. Buckingham: Open University Press.

Pramling-Samuelsson, I. (2003) 'How do children tell us about their childhoods?' Paper presented at the EECERA conference, Glasgow, September.

QCA (1999) *The National Curriculum*. London: QCA.

QCA (2000) *Curriculum Guidance for the Foundation Stage*. London: QCA.

Rogoff, B. (1990) *Apprenticeship in Thinking*. New York: Oxford University Press.

Siraj-Blatchford, I. (1999) *Supporting Science, Design and Technology in the Early Years*. Buckingham: Open University Press.

Tizzard, B. and Hughes, M. (1984) *Young Children Learning: Talking and Thinking at Home*. London: Fontana.

14

International perspectives

Angela D. Nurse

THIS BOOK CONCLUDES with a reflection on the global context in which we now find ourselves and why this is important. Britons have always explored the world and lived and worked in far-flung places. Knowledge of the wider world not only expands our own context but also, as early years professionals, helps us to respond empathetically to the children and families for whom we have a responsibility, wherever their origins within the world. Many people have mixed responses about those who do not originate from similar cultural backgrounds. In this sphere, above all others, honesty and introspection about personal feelings and prejudices are crucial, so that children and families can be treated with respect and understanding. The United Nations Convention on the Rights of the Child 1989 states in Article 2:

1. States Parties shall respect and ensure the rights set forth in the present Convention to each child within their jurisdiction without discrimination of any kind, irrespective of the child's or his or her parent's or legal guardian's race, colour, sex, language, religion, political or other opinion, national, ethnic or social origin, property, disability, birth or other status.
2. States Parties shall take all appropriate measures to ensure that the child is protected against all forms of discrimination or punishment on the basis of the status, activities, expressed opinions, or beliefs of the child's parents, legal guardians, or family members.

Whatever the current discussions about the UNCRC, these two sections should encapsulate the basic respect we offer to children who are present in the UK. We have not always done so, particularly with regard to the children of asylum seekers or refugees. Visiting a group of children at the Medical Foundation for the Care of Victims of Torture in London early in 2006, the Children's Commissioner for England, Professor Al Aynsley-Green, commented:

There seems to be a complete absence of respect in the way the authorities deal with these young people. They are not being treated as children, they are not being listened to or believed. No one has sat down and told them what they are entitled to and what their rights are. No one has told them what is likely to happen to them.

(Internet 1)

The study of children as citizens is a relatively new one; though a number of years ago the French published books aimed at school aged children, drawing attention to their rights under the UNCRC. Alongside these, books for younger children were available which described what it met to be citizens of he European Community, written from the perspective of children in each of the member countries. More recently the Mayor of London has published a website for young Londoners (Internet 2) with links to the Unicef Youth Voice website (Internet 3).These sites draw the attention of children living in London to their rights under the UNCRC and invite them to have their say. Such a move is not always popular in the UK, where the viewpoint that 'children should be seen and not heard' often prevails, The difficulty lies in establishing agreement on the meaning and implications of being a 'citizen', looking which implies some form of 'participation' in the state to which you belong. A conference paper by Ruth Lister (2005) on Children and Citizenship explored this issue, looking at participation as opposed to protection and exploring the idea of responsibility as another way for the very young to claim acceptance as citizens, rather than waiting passively for citizenship to 'be bestowed on them by others' (p. 1). Age, however, is a difficult dimension as children mature to their responsibilities at different times. We have explored the position of young carers in a previous chapter and Lister raises it again in the context of 'citizenship'. The whole concept of citizenship in the UK needs further thinking and research, but young children should not be denied its protection solely because they are viewed as 'citizens in waiting'.

In constructing this chapter, two aspects have been included. Firstly there is an attempt to place British experiences in a global and historical context and, through relating these to current concerns and notions, raise questions which should be debated whenever we work with children and adults who originate from other areas of the world. In understanding their histories and comparing them with ours, our responses need to be more sensitive and comprehending. Second, there are a number of countries where particular educational philosophies have been developed which have informed and changed the way we regard our own idiosyncratic early years approach.

Resources

A number of resources are available to us that can provide starting points in expanding our knowledge and understanding of children's lives in different places in the world. Among these are materials produced by leading children's charities and non-governmental organisations, such as UNICEF, Save the Children, NCH, ActionAid, SOS Children and Oxfam, but there are also smaller charities which focus on particular aspects of childhood experience globally, such as 'street' children and those with particular disabilities. Medecins sans Frontières works in some of the most devastated and desperate areas of the world. Promotional literature circulated in 2006 includes case studies that highlight the scenarios in which they work. A comment from a British midwife working in Liberia vividly reflects the situation: 'On average, a Liberian woman will have 14 pregnancies but just five or six of these infants will survive' (p. 4). Other sources of information include The European Children's Network (EURONET), the United Nations Educational, Scientific and Cultural Organisation (UNESCO), the United Nations Children's Fund (UNICEF) and the Organisation for Economic Co-operation and Development (OECD). Each of these organisations has a substantial website which sets out its remit and describes its activities. UNESCO's website, for example, has a section dedicated to Early Childhood, which sets out the history of the organisation's growing involvement in this field in the last half of the twentieth century and its current mission statement. UNICEF produces an annual report entitled *The State of the World's Children*. These are not easy reading. The 2006 version, subtitled 'Excluded and Invisible'; opens with the statement:

> Millions of children make their way through life impoverished, abandoned, uneducated, malnourished, discriminated against, neglected and vulnerable. For them, life is a daily struggle to survive. . . . For these children, childhood as a time to grow, learn, play and feel safe is, in effect, meaningless.

(UNICEF 2006 : 1)

Sometimes the organisations work in co-operation. For example, between 1998 and 2004, the OECD undertook thematic reviews of twenty different countries, mainly European but with some from further field, including the USA. UNESCO is now working with the OECD to extend this project. In 2004–05 the two organisations initiated the worldwide Early Childhood Policy Review Project and have so far reviewed four countries worldwide (Internet 2). Of particular interest to readers in the context of this book will be the policy briefs written by Professor Peter Moss. In the first of these reviews 'The Early Childhood Workforce in "Developed" Countries' (2004a), Moss raises the issue of the 'core profession' in these countries, recognising that 'the professional role is becoming more complex' as services consider integration. He poses three challenges for the restructuring workforces, including 'overcoming the view that workers with young children are substitute mothers', then considering the status and cost of more highly qualified staff. His second review focuses on 'Continuing Education and Professional Development' (2004b). In this paper he reviews several examples from across the world, including Reggio Emilia, Hungary and Africa, where the Early Childhood Development Virtual University uses web-based materials.

Global communication

Another factor in extending the awareness of the wider world to the general population has been the growth of media coverage, especially on television. The expansion in TV ownership in the UK at the start of the 1950s (to coincide with the coronation of Elizabeth II) brought pictures from across the world into people's homes, often with a powerful impact that was not always positive but could attract sympathy and donations in the face of trauma and tragedy. The world has decreased in size (that is to say, distances are covered much more quickly) as it has increased in complexity. Communication is so much easier today and does not depend on the written or spoken word, with news received sometimes years after the event. In the past fifty years, photography, cinema, radio, television, telephone and computer have progressively given us immediate access to most areas of the world in 'real-time'. We can now view events as they unfold, as well as hear commentaries on them. The tsunami that hit the countries of the Indian Ocean on Boxing Day in 2004 was revealed to the world almost immediately. With this greater visual and auditory knowledge, however, comes the responsibility to analyse and interpret what we are seeing. Even if we are present at an event, we extract from it those aspects that are important to us, based on our previous experience and expectations. Memory can also alter and interfere with our recollections and no two people will view an event in exactly the same way. An event viewed via the media has already been subject to a process of selection and editing which is not under our control. Who chose to tell us that particular story of a baby pulled alive from a collapsed building days after an earthquake or whose decision was it to broadcast that picture of an injured child on world television? Often these heartrending images are broadcast on humanitarian grounds in order to strengthen appeals for aid. Sometimes they are to illustrate a political point. Sometimes visual images are altered, just as histories are rewritten, to put forward a version of an event that suits those in power at the time. It is well known that President Roosevelt, who had suffered from polio in the 1930s and used a wheelchair, went to great lengths with the collusion of the press to prevent the American people and the outside world from knowing that he had a disability because he feared it would detract from his ability to carry out his duties.

Powerful images or stories stay with us long after the event and colour our response to children and families we meet from other places across the world and with other cultural backgrounds. Not all Germans approved of the fascist regime; not all white South Africans believed in the apartheid system; very few Muslims are religious fanatics; very few asylum-seekers come to Britain primarily to take advantage of our welfare system. We must be wary of blanket statements which do not recognise the complexities of contemporary life and lead us to value judgements not based on fair evidence. It could be argued that some depictions have compounded certain concepts and prejudices about people from other global contexts. Images of starving children, families devastated by HIV infection or civil wars in economically poorer parts of the world tend to desensitise us to the individual human tragedies of children, families and communities. Often these images are received into our homes long before local populations are fully aware of what has happened. Growth in satellite communication, both on a national and global scale, and our personal ability to connect personally to anywhere in the world via computers and mobile phones, brings events instantly and directly to us. These snapshots, however, are rarely viewed in context nor are we always able to enter into a full debate on their meaning and impact.

A peculiarly British perspective?

In reflecting on the geography of the lives of ordinary people born in Britain in the first half of the last century, their experience was generally limited to their locality. There were, however, some notable exceptions affecting children and families at the end of the nineteenth century and during the twentieth, such as the experience of evacuation during the Second World War. Few owned cars until well after the Second World War and air travel for the majority did not become a possibility until the late sixties. Buses, trams and trains were the means of transport for those who had to travel. The first motorway was opened in the UK until 1959 and by 1969 1,000 miles of motorway had been completed. The journeys many people undertake every day now to get to work were then only attempted for the annual summer holiday. Sea travel for recreation was limited to the rich. A source of great excitement in our family in the early 1950s was a daytrip to France on the 'Golden Daffodil', an old paddle steamer. Restrictions left over from the war meant we could not land there, but much (adult) drinking and smoking was apparently enjoyed on board. Just three years old, I have strong memories of the voyage because of acute seasickness. Otherwise, as a child, my community rarely extended much beyond the boundaries of my home. During the first five years of my life, I moved only a couple of miles from where I was born. Much curiosity was aroused when two children moved into my primary class, one from the midlands (her accent was different!) and another from as far away as Scotland. She became my best friend possibly because I had Scottish ancestors on my father's side of the family. I was devastated when her family moved on again to Canada.

For some, the experience of 'empire', however, had offered opportunities to travel further afield. The Grand Tour had become fashionable in the eighteenth century, enabling normally more affluent men to complete their education by visiting the marvels of the world, firstly those to be found in Europe though later in Africa and Asia when transport and travel plans became more ambitious. Perhaps this was an early equivalent of a 'gap year' but undertaken in rather more style? The impact of these tours for Britain, particularly in a growing knowledge of politics and history, of different languages and impacts on fashion and architecture, was considerable.

Within the world of universities opportunities now exist for students and staff to spend time in institutions abroad, learning alongside other students or teaching alongside other tutors. This happens in Europe through programmes such as

Erasmus and Socrates; though well funded take up each year never exhausts the funds available and take up in the UK is paarticularly low. Other opportunities open to practitioners are available, so that a variety of staff can take part in visits and exchanges that enable different working practices to be viewed and assessed. This cross-cultural fertilisation allows for a sometimes deep reflection on our own systems and practices in the UK.

Where do we come from?

Although we live on an island, there are distinct cultures within our community. It is hard to identify an 'English' culture, though not so difficult to discern Welsh, Scottish or Irish traditions with their distinct characteristics. Our diversity has multiplied over the centuries as other groups have arrived and added to the richness of British cultural life. In order to break down some barriers and elicit an understanding of different cultural backgrounds, for a number of years we have explored family background with groups of sixteen-year-olds during university summer schools. These groups have often included young people from a range of different ethnic and cultural backgrounds. We ask them to think about their parents' and grandparents' origins and the languages that are spoken within their families. This has led to the recognition that many families, who now consider themselves truly 'British', have origins in the old empire and from European countries where ancestors were perhaps persecuted for political or religious beliefs. The young people are often astounded when they realise what has happened in their own families and then how quickly. One group contained a young girl who had been stereotyped by everyone, including the tutor, as born and bred in England. She was fair and blue-eyed, with a strong London accent. Her history, however, revealed that she was a Bosnian Muslim who had only arrived in England less than four years before, escaping the fighting which had devastated her country. The importance of these experiences where students have to confront stereotypical views about people from other parts of the world cannot be exaggerated, if we are to work with people from all over the world in our professional role.

Migration

Staying close to the place in which I was born had much to do with being a child in the 1950s but, although this pattern also reflected my parents' experiences, it did not necessarily mirror those of my grandparents and great grandparents. They were drawn to London from the four corners of Great Britain to escape poverty or to secure a better standard of living. Added to these are the families who had set sail for decades to colonise North America and increasingly New Zealand, Australia and South Africa. Some were banished as a punishment or emigrated through a spirit of adventure but generally these people went because they were seeking a better life for themselves and their families, either escaping poor economic conditions or political or religious persecution. They did not intend nor have the means to return to share their experiences and much of what we know comes from the few records that were kept in early days or stories recorded by those who could write. In the nineteenth and early part of the twentieth century, when 'Empire' was at its height, people from a variety of social backgrounds, but predominantly the wealthier, went to maintain British power and prestige in India, Africa or China, though most of these returned to Britain to retire.

Alexandra Fuller's (2002) account of her childhood in Rhodesia during the fight for independence from British rule (now Zimbabwe) is honest and revealing. She attends an all-white boarding school and recalls when these were integrated and multi-racial. Her fears before this occurs are honestly disclosed (p. 149): ' Tomorrow, children who have never been to school, never used a flush toilet, never eaten with a knife and fork, will arrive. They will be smelling of wood smoke from their hut fires'.

Unfortunately some people within our community still reflect these stereotypes in their thinking, including those who work with children and families. Fuller's preconceptions were quickly overturned: 'Instead the first black child is brought to the school. We watch in amazement as he is helped out of a car – a proper car like Europeans drive – by his mother, who is more beautifully dressed than my mother ever is . . .'

She goes on to describe other, less materialistic, events where her prejudices are further confronted and she learns to think in other ways, appreciating similarities rather than differences.

Nevertheless, for most ordinary families, including my own, experience of life beyond our shores was limited and viewed from a peculiarly British standpoint that recalled empire and power. As very small children at school, my generation celebrated 'Commonwealth Day' when we were made aware that Great Britain's place then was at the top of an hierarchy of nations which gave us a lot of power but should also have alerted us to our responsibilities. Growing up in southeast London in the fifties, I was fascinated by the people who had arrived from all over the world to work alongside my father within the National Health Service and Social Services. Their stories appear in factual books, such as *Windrush: The Irresistible Rise of Multi-Racial Britain* (1998) and in fictional works such as Andrea Levy's (2000) *Small Island* where the experiences of those who migrated, on invitation, from West Africa and the Caribbean to try to find a better life are related. The impact of 'empire' still can still be seen when young professional people come to the UK to work in the health service and to teach in our schools. It is likely that as practitioners working with young children, particularly in inner city areas, we will meet and work alongside many who have come here willingly and, occasionally, under duress. They have interesting stories to tell which not only help us to review our attitudes towards people from diverse places, cultures and ethnic groups but because it helps us to understand the experience of moving across the world from our own space into a society which sometimes seems very similar on the surface but can be deeply different.

In thinking about the rights of children, colonisation has a particular resonance for those studying childhood because of a strategy devised by the British and other European governments to send orphaned children to the colonies. Again, it is a policy that must have appeared benevolent to those who originally thought it up, expecting that the children who were taken to the colonial outposts would have a better quality of life and brighter futures. It was not until relatively recently that the true stories of what had happened began to unravel. In 1986 Margaret Humphreys (Humphreys 1995), a social worker in Nottingham, started to hear from people who had been taken to Australia as young children and who were attempting to find remaining members of their families. As she started to research, she uncovered thousands of stories where children, who were not necessarily 'orphans' without families, who had been placed with families or in other orphanages far from home. She estimates that 150,000 children from the age of three and four (with an average age of eight) were sent. The last children were sent in 1967. Margaret Humphreys has since set up the Child Migrants Trust to support those who were involved in this policy. Why did this happen? We know so much more about the holistic development of the child, emotional development, attachment theory, family dynamics, and so on now that is difficult to comprehend why these decisions were made. In the light of the political, economic and social contexts at the beginning and middle of the twentieth century, some in government probably truly believed that this would benefit the children, although in reality many became cheap labour, either for the families or the communities, including religious ones, which took them in. Many were abused. Others in government would have seen it as an acceptable policy to keep the colonies 'British', perceiving threats from outside as Britain began to lose its power in the world to other industrial giants such as Germany or to those within the colonies who wanted independence. Others saw it as a way to lessen the burden, costs, of looking after children without good family support. In this, we can see the dichotomy between state and family in owning up to a responsibility for children. It was also a decision which was at it roots 'classist' where children who were not middle or upper class were distanced from our society. In retrospect, it has to be said that the enforced transportation of children to the colonies showed little recognition of the needs of the children. It could be said that through this policy children, some as young as four, actually became responsible for their own financial support and survival. This is echoed in the situations of those unaccompanied children who come to the UK now.

It is interesting to compare this event with evacuation of city children to the countryside at the start of the Second World War or the rescue of Jewish children from Nazi Germany (see below). Here, there has been much more research and debate and the events are well documented. Jessica Mann (2005) has brought together the reminiscences of those affected by evacuation and raises questions about the wisdom of this policy, with the benefit of hindsight, because of the lasting effects on many of the children who, as adults and parents, could not contemplate doing the same. Yet it is hard to place ourselves now in the situation of those parents who agreed to this at the time. My mother, although just sixteen at the time, was sent briefly London to Wales by her father because of the fear of mass bombing and gassing as the war loomed. My grandfather had been gassed as a soldier in the First World War and this was probably the cause of his anxieties. Unlike the mass child migration, perhaps it is because these latter two events add to our sense of national pride in the hardships people were enduring and so have spoken of and not hidden?

Mass migrations from the British Isles have decreased in recent years though people still continue to leave to seek better lives elsewhere; the drive to do so mirrors the attempts today of many from poorer parts of the world to escape persecution and improve their life chances, especially for the children. Some parents are so desperate to ensure their children survive and prosper that children are sent to the UK unaccompanied. This is not a new phenomenon. In the 1930s, before the Second World War, groups of Basque children were sent here to escape the Spanish Civil War. Most returned (Bell 1996) but some stayed (Internet 4). More poignantly, Jewish children were evacuated without their parents from Germany by the Kindertransport programme to rescue them from the Nazis. Some never saw their parents or families who stayed behind again and became integrated into the societies that accepted them. Harris and Oppenheimer (2000) have gathered together personal accounts from those children, now adults, who were involved in this. Their introduction (p. 19) states 'it shows that racial discrimination and ideologies which lead to mass murder do not draw the line at the persecution of innocent children'. We have witnessed many further examples of this in more recent years in Africa and the Balkans, much nearer to home.

Other models of childcare and provision

At the beginning of this final chapter, one of its intentions was stated to be an exploration of different models of early childhood provision worldwide. This is not intended to provide a full description of each of the approaches, rather to consider their impact and explore their relevance to the UK. Pam May and Gill Bottle have referred to other systems, particularly Reggio Emilia, in earlier chapters. For those readers new to an investigation of other models, Devereux *et al.* (2003, ch. 11) provide a clear introduction. The OECD (2004) (Internet 5) offers a detailed overview of these five different approaches:

- Belgium   Experiential Education (Ferre Laevers)
- Italy   The Reggio Emilia Approach

- New Zealand   Te Whāriki
- Sweden   The Swedish Curriculum
- USA   The High Scope Curriculum

The UK is not the only nation to have focused on young children now and in the past and much of what we see has been borrowed and reconstructed from the experiences and models of others. Carlina Rinaldi who has been instrumental in the creation of the Reggio Emilia preschool system in northern Italy at the beginning of a study tour there gave thanks to the other models worldwide which had influenced their own practice and philosophy. These included traditional British nursery education, as well as Steiner, Montessori and HighScope. David Weikart established High Scope as one of the Headstart programmes for very young disadvantaged children in the USA in the 1960s and led the follow-up research into those who took part. He also always paid tribute to his British mentor and our nursery tradition. Rinaldi, however, was also very clear that you cannot pick up one country's system and transport it wholly into another's. Provision should reflect and therefore be part of the culture and context in which it has developed. The integrity of a particular system's philosophy stems from the understanding of those from its own community. This is not to say that *aspects* from other philosophies cannot be extracted and used to debate our own views and perhaps move practice on. This has happened in the case of High Scope when nurseries have reviewed their accommodation and resources and restructured settings to allow children access at all times to the resources they need to complete their work. We are still absorbing all the implications of the Reggio Emilia philosophy where children are in control of the majority of decisions which concern their learning, in comparison to the adult-led situation which has developed here with a curriculum which, if not intended to be prescriptive, has certainly been interpreted in that way by many early years settings. Some of the most questionable early years practice stems from partial understanding and appreciation of other systems. Settings perhaps adopt the 'plan, do, review' aspect of High Scope or use the Montessori materials but not the full rationale for each of these approaches. The latest 'horror story' reported to me by a colleague was of a setting where 'they do Reggio Emilia every Tuesday morning'. From this, it seems, that the 'art and craft' aspects (rather than 'creative') have been emphasised, with limited understanding of the full implications of Reggio Emilia where adults step aside and allow children to take control. The OECD (2004) writes:

> Within the Reggio Emilia schools there are no planned goals or standards indicating what is to be learned as 'these would push our schools towards teaching without learning' (Malaguzzi, in Edwards *et al.*, 1993). The children are encouraged, in collaboration with teachers and one another to construct their own personalities and to determine the course of their own investigations and learning.
>
> (OECD 2004: 13)

What this model advocates is a respect for children and a belief in their strengths and capacity to decide for themselves. This is echoed by others but it requires national resolve to lessen the control that adults like to have over children.

In the context of this chapter, where we have explored Britain's place in the world and a professional's responsibility to understand other people's histories and concerns, Te Whāriki from New Zealand offers us an approach which interweaves the perspectives of two different cultures, Maori and English. In deciding the programme for each early years centre, those responsible need to incorporate the following principles, as well as responding to local priorities:

- **Whakamana**: The curriculum will *empower* the child to learn and grow;

- **Kotahitanga:** The curriculum will reflect the holistic way children learn and grow:

- **Whanāu Tangata:** The wider world of the **family, Whanāu and community** is an integral part of the curriculum:

- **Ngā Hononga:** Young children learn through **responsive and reciprocal relationships** with people, places and things.

(OECD, 2004 p. 18)

These principles are accompanied by five strands which relate directly to children's experience: well-being, belonging, contribution, communication, exploration. These are echoed by the five outcomes for children and young people in the UK, expounded in *Every Child Matters* (DfES, 2003): being healthy, staying safe, enjoying and achieving, making a positive contribution, economic well-being. It is, however, important to recognise that these concepts come from two different societies. The danger in comparing, borrowing and implementing other people's philosophies is, as Gill Bottle highlighted, that we only recognise the superficial and do not understand the whole.

Conclusion

This final chapter has hopefully raised a number of issues which need to be considered seriously in the context of the world in which we live. As early years professionals our duty is to children, whatever their circumstances and wherever they come from. We can all remember instances from our own childhoods when our sense of self worth has been damaged through comments made by adults. The best we can offer children is never to do this. A student commented in an essay some years ago:

> Those privileged to touch the lives of children and youth should be constantly aware that their impact on a single child may affect a multitude of others a thousand years from now.

Questions for reflection

- What is your own family history? How does this inform who you are and what your attitudes towards others are?

- How can we extend our understanding of the experiences of children and families who come from other places, cultures and ethnic groups? Why is it important, in our role as early years practitioners, to do this?

- What can we, or should we, learn from the early years philosophies, provision and practice in other countries? What does the knowledge of other systems bring to our own practice?

References

Bell, A. (1996) *Only for Three Months*. Norwich: Mousehole Press.

Devereux, J., Miller, L., Paige-Smith, A. and Soler, J. (2003) 'Approaches to curricula in the early years', in Devereux, J. and Miller, L. (eds) *Working with Children in the Early Years*. London: David Fulton Publishers.

DfES (2003) *Every Child Matters*. London: TSO.

Fuller, A. (2002) *Don't Let's Go to the Dogs Tonight: An African Childhood*. London: Picador.

Harris, M. J. and Oppenheimer, D. (2000) *Into the Arms of Strangers: Stories of the Kindertransport*. London: Bloomsbury Publishing.

Humphreys, M. (1995) *Empty Cradles*. London: Corgi Books.

Levy, A. (2004) *Small Island*. London: Headline/Review.

Lister, R. (2005) *Children and Citizenship*. Paper presented at a Glasgow Centre for the Child and Society seminar, 3 November.

Mann, J. (2005) *Out of Harm's Way: The Wartime Evacuation of Children from Britain*. London: Headline.

Medecins sans Frontières (2006) *Effective Medical Care* (promotional literature). West Malling, Kent: MSF.

Moss, P. (2004a) *The Early Childhood Workforce in 'Developed' Countries: Basic structures and education*. UNESCO Policy Brief on Early Childhood No. 27, October. http:unesdoc.unesco.org/images/0013/001374/137402e.pdf

Moss, P. (2004b) *The Early Childhood Workforce in 'Developed' Countries: Continuing Education and Professional Development*. UNESCO Policy Brief on Early Childhood No. 28 November–December. http:unesdoc.unesco.org/images/0013/001377/13731e.pdf

Philips, M. and Philips, T. (1998) *Windrush: The Irresistible Rise of Multi-Racial Britain*. London: HarperCollins.

UNICEF (2005) *The State of the World's Children 2006: Excluded & Invisible*. New York: UNICEF.

Websites

Internet 1 – www.torturecare.org.uk/articles/news/737

Internet 2 – www.london.gov.uk/young-london

Internet 3 – www.unicef.org.uk

Internet 4 – http:www.mousehold-press.co.uk/detail_three_months.html

Internet 5 – http:www.oecd.org/dataoecd/23/36/31672150.pdf

Médecins sans Frontières – www.msf.org

Medical Foundation for the Victims of Torture – www.torturecare.org.uk

EURONET – www.europeanchildrensnetwork.org

OECD – www.oecd.org

UNESCO – www.unesco.org

Index

Routledge
Taylor & Francis Group

Health and Safety in the Early Years Series

Lynn Parker

It is essential that adults working in early years settings are well informed and aware of health and safety issues and procedures that they may face on a day-to-day basis. This series of practical books provides clear and concise information about health and safety, whilst also fully translating the legislative documentation that surrounds it to ensure Ofsted requirements are met and that children are kept safe.

Each book includes:

Step-by-step advice on how to carry out correct procedure and policy for various scenarios.

End of chapter summaries and best practice checklists

Templates for policies to reflect local guidance

Guidance on communication with parents and carers to meet the specific needs of the child

How to Keep Young Children Safe
2006 ISBN 9781843123010 £16.00

How to Avoid Illness and Infection
2006 9781843122999 £16.00

How to do a Health and Safety Audit
2006 ISBN 9781843123033 £16.00

Routledge
Taylor & Francis Group

Developing Early Years Practice

*Foundation Degree Texts Published in Association with
The Open University*

Linda Miller, Carrie Cable and Jane Devereux

2005
Paperback
ISBN 978-1-84312-317-0
£17.99

This book provides readers working in a diverse range of early years settings with the underpinning knowledge required to increase their effectiveness in working with young children. It explores a wide number of issues including:

The roles and responsibilities of practitioners

Developing reflective practice

How children learn and develop

The early years curriculum

Working with parents and professionals

Developing inclusive Environments

VISIT www.routledge.com/education